GANN MASTERS
TECHNICAL ANALYSIS COURSE

HALLIKER'S, INC.
Publisher of
Trader's World Magazine

(c) 1995 Halliker's, Inc., ALL RIGHTS RESERVED. No part of this publication may be reproduced, stored in a retrieval system, or transmitted, in any form or by any means, electronic, mechanical, photocopying, recording, or otherwise, without the prior written permission of the publisher.

This course was prepared from information believed to be reliable but not guaranteed by us without further verification and does not purport to be complete. Opinions expressed are subject to revision without notification. We are not offering to buy or sell securities or commodities discussed. Halliker's Inc. or one or more of it's officers, and or authors may have a position in the securities or commodities discussed herein. The names of the products and services presented in this course are used only in editorial fashion and to the benefit of the trademark owner with no intention of infringing on trademark rights. Products and services in this course are subject to availability and prices are subject to change without notice.

The charts in the publication are printed by permission of Omega Research. They are developed from SuperCharts and TradeStation. Spread sheet examples were developed by the Microsoft Excel Spreadsheet program and are printed with permission of Microsoft Corporation.

This course is dedicated to Stella Bittel who recently passed away. She had the endurance to fight diabetes for the last fifty years.

Printed in the United States of America

Halliker's, Inc.
2508 W. Grayrock Dr.
Springfield, MO 65810
Phone (417) 882-9697
Fax (417)886-5180

CONTENTS

Chapter 1	W.D. GANN A LEGEND	5
Chapter 2	STUDY AND BE PREPARED	15
Chapter 3	CAPITAL REQUIRED	21
Chapter 4	RIGHT KIND OF CHARTS	23
Chapter 5	KNOW THE TREND	31
Chapter 6	MATHEMATICS	36
Chapter 7	ELLIOTT WAVE THEORY	54
Chapter 8	THE TIME FACTOR	65
Chapter 9	SUPPORT AND RESISTANCE	72
Chapter 10	TIME AND PRICE OVERLAYS	77
Chapter 11	TABLE CHARTS	90
Chapter 12	TIME AND PRICE ANALYSIS	110
Chapter 13	FORECASTING TIME	121
Chapter 14	FORECASTING PRICE	136

Chapter 15	EXCEL SPREAD SHEET	145
Chapter 16	SWING CHARTS	147
Chapter 17	GAPS	150
Chapter 18	TOPS AND BOTTOMS	152
Chapter 19	VOLUME AND OPEN INTEREST	156
Chapter 20	GANN CHANNELS	160
Chapter 21	TYPES OF ORDERS	163
Chapter 22	MAKING IT WORK	165
Appendix A	TEST APPLICATION	168
Appendix B	CERTIFICATION	170
Appendix C	CATALOG SUPPLIES	172

CHAPTER 1

W.D. GANN A LEGEND

W.D. Gann grew up around cotton warehouse where cotton was king.

William Delbert Gann was born June 6, 1878, in Lufkin, Texas, to Sam H. and Susan R. Gann, immigrants to Texas from the British Isles. Lufkin is midway between Houston and Texarkana. This part of Texas is cotton country and Gann's parents lived on a Neches River bottom cotton ranch near Lufkin. He grew up around the cotton warehouses in Angelina County where cotton was king. W. D. Gann was raised in a very strict Methodist church family. His mother, a very religious person, encouraged him to read the Bible at a very early age, and in fact, wanted him to become a minister. Gann was not sure he wanted to become a minister, but studying the Bible was certainly easier than working in the cotton fields, as was his father's wish. He attended church every Sunday with his parents and as he listened to the sermons found his interpretation of the Bible scriptures to differ from the minister's. In the Bible he discovered time cycles, repetition of important numbers, and references to the wise men following the stars. Also, that it was written in veiled language that made interpreting the real meaning difficult. Since Gann had a photographic memory, by age 21 he had nearly memorized the Bible.

During his school years Gann excelled in mathematics and was generally called as a gifted mathematician. His tremendous appetite for knowledge and his open-minded attitude led him into many different fields of study that eventually resulted in discoveries in the markets that would otherwise have been overlooked. He completed high school in a time when most children were only able to attend school through the third or fourth grade.

As a teenager, Gann liked to be called W. D., and he used these initials the rest of his life. W. D. pestered his parents until they relented and signed a minor release form that he needed to obtain a job. His first job was that of a News Butcher on the passenger train between Texarkana and Tyler, Texas. This job required him to be quick-witted, aggressive, and able to deal with all kinds of people. During his teen years, he worked in the cotton warehouses in Lufkin and Texarkana, Texas. While working in the cotton warehouse, he was introduced to commodity trading.

In 1902, at age 24, W. D. Gann made his first commodity trade in cotton, the market he knew best. The small profit from that trade marked the beginning of what was to become one of the most remarkable and legendary careers the speculative markets have ever known. Over the next 53 years, Gann took over $50,000,000 from the markets. It has been reported by a man who worked for Gann the last eight years of Gann's life, that approximately 1/3 of the money he made was for himself and the other 2/3 was for the accounts he supervised for clients. From that very first trade, it is believed Gann was using principles and techniques he continued using throughout his trading career. The notations on some of his early charts substantiated this belief. As time progressed, his trading methods were refined.

In 1906 W. D. went to Oklahoma City. He worked as a broker for a brokerage firm, trading for himself while handling large accounts for clients. He studied the cause of success and failure in the speculation of other traders. He found that over 90% of traders who enter the markets without knowledge and study usually lose in the end. Gann also lost a significant amount of money and admitted his trading was based on hope, greed, and fear. Later on, in his books and courses, he cautioned all traders about these emotions.

Early on, Gann began to note the periodical recurrence of rise and fall in stocks and commodities. This led him to conclude that natural law was the basis of market movements. He then devoted ten years to the study of natural law as applicable to the speculative markets. During that time he traveled to England, Egypt, and India to gain knowledge in ancient mathematics and astrology. In the British Museum in England he conducted extensive research on market cycles. In an Egyptian temple it is believed he found the basic construction of what was to become known as his Square of 9 Chart. After exhaustive research and investigation of the known sciences, he discovered the Law of Vibration enabled him to accurately determine the exact prices to which stocks or commodities would trade within a given time, and that each stock or commodity had its own rate of vibration.

At age 27, Gann was a well-known name in the Southwest. His views on the analysis of cotton prices were so well respected that a Texarkana newspaper, The Daily Texarkanian, ran a story on Gann's cotton predictions.

In 1908, at age 30, Gann moved to New York and opened his own brokerage office at 18 Broadway. He began testing his theories and techniques in the market. On August 8, 1908, he made one of his greatest mathematical discoveries for predicting the trend of stocks and commodities. This was "The Master Time Factor." Within a year, it became clear to others that his success was based on more than just luck. No one researched time cycles as extensively as Gann. His charts show the cycles with which he worked, went back to history's beginning, and bore no resemblance to other researcher's time cycle studies.

In October 1909, Richard D. Wyckoff, Owner and Editor of The Ticker and Investment Digest asked Gann for an interview to document his trading ability for one month. The interview was granted, and Gann's trades were monitored for 25 market days during the month of October in the presence of a Ticker representative. At that time the markets also traded on Saturday. Gann made 286 trades in various stocks, both long and short. There were 264 trades that resulted in profits and 22 in losses. 92.3% of the trades were profitable. The capital used doubled ten times resulting in 1000% gain on his original investment during those 25 trading days. What makes this even more phenomenal is that Gann did this with an average time between each trade of about twenty minutes. In one day Gann made 16 trades in the same stock, 8 of which were in either the top eighth or the bottom eighth of that particular swing. Such a performance is unparalleled in the history of Wall Street. As stated by James R. Keene, the famous speculator of that era, "The man who is right 6 times out of 10 will make his fortune."

It seems a foregone conclusion that Gann was picking tops and bottoms with a high degree of accuracy. At this point of time, in 1909, he was only 31 years of age, so whatever methods he was using had already been discovered.

This biographer believes that after his sensational performance Gann regretted having granted the interview, as it was stated in the printed article that he did not know the results were to be published. When the article was printed in The Ticker Investment Digest, Gann was besieged with people asking how he was able to pick tops and bottoms as he had demonstrated. His only answer to them was he used The Law of Vibration to make all his calculations. At this conjuncture there were only two choices: l) to give away his secret discoveries and risk destroying the markets, or 2) to detract from his method of picking tops and bottoms by writing books and courses about mechanical trading systems, the use of geometrical anges, the use of Time and Price Charts, such as the Octagon Chart (Square of 9), Master 12 Chart (Square of 144), Hexagon Chart (the cube), Square of 90, Square of 52, 360 Degree Circle Chart, and many other trading techniques.

If Gann had continued trading using only his method of picking tops and bottoms, without a doubt he would have become one of the wealthiest men in the world, and in so doing would have attracted too much attention. He would have been asked too many questions by traders and would have been compelled to explain. However, at certain times, he probably used his method to advantage. Gann had a profound understanding of natural law, so rather than place himself in an embarrassing situation, he chose to trade using his mechanical systems and other techniques he had developed. Also, having more capital than was required for a good living was not important to him, as he was more interested in the knowledge possessed by ancient civilizations and the occult sciences. Gann understood how the Laws of Nature controlled human beings and, therefore, he understood the markets, because the markets are nothing more than an expression of the actions of human beings.

The two previous paragraphs are my belief. You may agree or disagree, but before you arrive at a conclusion, carefully study Gann's 1909 trading demonstration. He made 286 trades in 25 days, which is 11 trades per day. To do this, you must pick the tops and bottoms on a short intraday time period.

If what I believe is true, it is very sad to think that a genius individual such as W. D. Gann, had to disguise the truth throughout his life, with a smoke screen of many trading methods and techniques.

In 1918 his office address in New York was 81 New Street and in the early 1920's was at 49 Broadway. Over the years, Gann maintained several offices in New York all located on Wall Street with the address numbers of 78, 80, 82, 88, 91, 93 and 99.

At the height of Gann's career, he employed 35 individuals who made charts of all kinds, did analytical research at his direction, and performed many duties involved with his various publications and services. The name of one of his businesses was W. D. Gann Scientific Service, Inc., and the other, initiated in 1919, was W. D. Gann Research, Inc. The firms published the following Supply and Demand Letters: Daily Stock Letter, Tri-Weekly Stock Letter, Weekly Stock Letter, Daily Commodity Letter, Tri-Weekly Commodity Letter, and Weekly Commodity Letter. Telegraph Service was all offered as follows: Daily Telegraph Service on Stocks, Daily Telegraph Service on Cotton, Daily Telegraph Service on Grain, and Telegrams on important Changes Only, on Stocks or Commodities. Published under Annual Forecasts were: Annual Stock Forecast, Annual Cotton Forecast, Annual Grain Forecast, Annual Rubber Forecast, Annual Coffee, Sugar and Cocoa Forecast. Supplements to all Forecasts were issued and mailed on the first of each month. Special Forecasts on stocks or other commodities were made on request. Also offered were daily, weekly, monthly, quarterly, and swing charts on stocks and commodities. Gann taught advanced courses of instruction entitled Master Forecasting Method, at a cost of $2,500, and New Mechanical Method and Trend Indicator, at a cost of $5,000, to those who want it for their own use and will not publish, sell, or teach it to others. It is too valuable to be spread broadcasted. The cost of these courses and personal instruction in today's economics would be $25,000 to $50,000, or more.

As early as 1923, Gann offered a service entitled "The Busy-Man's Service." This was a service for professional and businessmen where Gann supervised their trading accounts by advising them what and when to buy and sell. In later years the name of this service was changed to "Personal Service." The cost of this service was on a 1 month, 3 months, 6 months, or annual basis, or on a Part-of-Profit Plan where the monthly fee was smaller and Gann received 5% of the net profits. Under the Part-of-Profit Plan it was required that a minimum of 100 shares be traded. The clients were advised by telegram or letter.

An article in The Evening Telegram dated New York, Monday, March 5, 1923, used the words "prophet" and "mathematical seer" to describe Gann. It also stated his followers declared he was 85% correct in his forecasts. He predicted the election of Wilson and Harding using fortunate numbers and fortunate letters combined with cycles. He predicted the abdication of the Kaiser and the end of the war to the exact date six months in advance. His predictions were based on mathematics. He stated if he had the data he would use algebra and geometry to tell exactly by the theory of cycles when a certain thing is going to occur again. He further stated that there is no chance in nature, because mathematical principles of the highest order lie at the foundation of all things. The article pointed out that Gann received calls every day from prominent persons asking him to cast their horoscope. It also said he told politicians whether or not they would be elected and solved problems for clergymen, bankers, and statesmen.

In another article in the Morning Telegraph, dated Sunday, December 17, 1922, the Financial Editor, Arthur Angy, stated that "W. D. Gann had scored another astounding hit in his 1922 stock forecast issued in December, 1921, I found his 1921 forecast so remarkable that I secured a copy of his 1922 stock forecast to prove his claims for myself. And now, at the closing of the current year of 1922, it is but justice to say I am more than amazed by the result of Mr. Gann's remarkable predictions based on pure science and mathematical calculations."

W. D. and his wife, Sadie H. Gann, had one son and three daughters born to their marriage. Their son, John L. Gann, was in partnership with his father for several years in the late 1930's and early 1940's, operating under the firm name of W. D. Gann & Son, Inc. Apparently, the two personalities were not always compatible, as their association was ended in the mid 1940's. This writer has been told one of their main differences concerned astrology, as John did not believe astrology had any effect on market movements, or human behavior. This probably upset W. D. as he knew well the effect of planetary motion on the markets and the individual. Following the association with his father, John served as a broker for many years for the firm Sulzbacher, Granger & Co. in New York City. It is believed that John passed away in 1984.

For many years Gann maintained a home in Scarsdale, New York, which was, at the time, the estate bedroom community for New York City. In an article that appeared in the May 26, 1933 New York Daily Investment News, it was reported that Gann left New York in the first 1933 model Stinson Reliant airplane, piloted by Flinor Smith, a woman aviator, to conduct an extensive tour of the country analyzing cotton, wheat, and tobacco crops, and business conditions. The airplane was equipped with navigation instruments, radio receiving equipment and extra-large fuel tanks that gave a flying range of 750 miles. It was powered with a Lycoming engine and cruised at 135 miles per hour. Gann was the first Wall Street advisor to use an airplane for studying market conditions so he could advise clients much faster of changing market conditions. During his trip he was a speaker to members of Kiwanis, Rotary, Chamber of Commerce, and other business organizations in various larger cities throughout the United States.

In 1935, Gann made an airplane trip to South America for studying crop conditions, and to gather information on the increase and production of cotton in Peru, Chili, Argentina, and Brazil. He logged 18,000 miles by air and another 1,000 miles by automobile.

In July of 1936 Gann purchased a specially built all metal airplane, which he named "The Silver Star," and used in making crop surveys. In July of 1939 he purchased a new Fairchild airplane for the same purpose.

Gann was a member of the Commodity Exchange, Inc. of New York, the New Orleans Cotton Exchange, the Rubber Exchange of New York, the Royal Economic Society of London, the American Economic Society, the Masonic Lodge, the Shrine, the Chicago Board of Trade, and was a devout Christian in the Methodist Church.

Gann had a winter home in Miami, Florida, and in the 1940's moved there on a full-time basis. His office was at 820 S. W. 26th Road in Miami. While in Florida, he continued his advisory services as well as teaching his commodity and stock market courses, either in person or by mail. By the late 1940's he had a recommended list of Books For Sale that included the subjects of numerology, astrology, scientific, and miscellaneous. He was involved in real estate holdings, and enjoyed large automobiles, especially Lincolns, which he purchased new yearly. In 1954, after making several successful coffee and soybean trades, Gann purchased a fast express cruising boat that he named "The Coffee Bean." It was reported that Gann wore the same type of suit throughout his life, and that his home was filled with items collected in his world travels. He vacationed often in South America. But, in the opinion of his peers, he did not live beyond his means.

W. D. Gann wrote some of the best books ever written on the stock and commodity markets. The following is a list of the books written by him and the year they were published:

Speculation a Profitable Profession
The Truth of the Stock Tape
The Tunnel Thru the Air
Wall Street Stock Selector
Stock Trend Detector Scientific Stock Forecasting

How to Make Profits Trading in Puts and Calls
Face Facts America. Looking Ahead to 1950
How to Make Profits Trading in Commodities
45 Years in Wall Street
The Magic Word
How to Make Profits Trading in Commodities

Gann was a prolific writer. His style of writing was unique. Readers of his books considered him to be a poor writer with a limited use of the English language. Not so! Upon methodic study of his work, the reader will discover in time the Gann method of teaching. He will inspire the reader to research everything from the origin of numbers to the musical scale and vibrations.

W. D. Gann, in my estimation, was a genius. He was born a Gemini with a high intellectual capacity, and a dual personality that caused him to be both genial and obstinate. He was a gifted mathematician, an expert chart reader, and had an extraordinary memory for figures. Take away his science and he would beat the market on chart reading alone. One of Gann's most important technical tools was his charts and no one kept up as many as he did. Gann's charts encompassed 55 years, from 1900 to 1955. During this time thousands of daily, weekly, monthly, quarterly, yearly, and other various charts, were made with great care, each a work of art. He believed charting was an art and if you understood everything the chart was showing, it would aid in forecasting the next day, week, or month's, price movements. Gann was a workaholic, at times working 17 hours per day, 6 days per week. He was very demanding of those who worked with and for him, and expected the same effort from them that he himself put forth. He expected to issue instructions only once and did not feel it should be necessary to repeat them.

Gann was deeply analytical and studied price actions of various stocks and commodities back through the years. He spent nine months in the British Museum working day and night researching stock and commodity prices and dates from 1820, and wheat prices and dates from 1200. He also spent long hours and long days in the Astor Library in New York City researching stock and commodity markets. He was a student of numbers, number theory, progressions, and the progression of numbers. His trading system was based on natural law and mathematics. Since time progresses as the earth rotates on its axis and in its order, and time is measured by numbers and progression of numbers, and prices in their movement upward and downward are also measured in numbers, it is understandable why Gann had an intense interest in numbers, number theory, and mathematics. A keen understanding of natural laws and their effect on mankind have a direct effect on the markets. The markets are only extensions or reflections of man's actions.

In Gann's time there were no calculators. He used a slide rule and the various master charts he developed, such as the Square of 9, for his calculator. He kept an open mind to any trading ideas to achieve perfection. When making his forecasts, he used many methods to arrive at the time for a trend change, and all of them to confirmed he was correct. In his early trading he made thousands of dollars. But, by listening to false rumors and other people's ideas, he also lost thousands of dollars. In 1913 and again in 1919, he lost small fortunes when the brokerage firms he was trading with went bankrupt. One of these firms was Murray Mitchell and Company. In those days the client's funds were not protected by exchange regulations in case of a failure, as they are today.

During this time he was also involved in two bank failures. Regardless of these losses and misfortunes, he was always able to rely upon mathematical science to aid him in making a financial comeback. This is why Gann states that knowledge of the market is more important than money.

Today, people believe "times are different," but Gann's time saw its bull markets and panics in the stock market, bull markets and panics, in the commodity market, wars, inflationary periods, depressions, bank closings, etc. In 1921 the rate of inflation was 100%. Strikes were rampant, jobs impossible to find, and productivity at very low levels. The Great Depression of 1929 to 1932 and the outright confiscation of the citizen's gold that was exchanged for printed money, left deep scars on the country and it's citizens. W. D. Gann was avidly against the New Deal and Roosevelt's creeping socialism. Therefore, to learn from other people's past experiences, people today should understand Gann's famous quotation, "The future is but a repetition of the past, or as the Bible says, the thing that hath been, it is that which shall be; and that which is done, is that which shall be done; and there is no new thing under the Sun." Gann said, "The average man's memory is too short. He only remembers what he wants to remember or what suits his hopes and fears. He depends too much on others and does not think for himself. Therefore, he should keep a record, graph, or picture of past market movements to remind him what has happened in the past can, and will, happen in the future. Panics will come and bull markets will follow just as long as the world stands and they are just as sure as the ebb and flow of the tides, because it is the nature of man to overdo everything. He goes to the extreme when he gets hopeful and optimistic. When fear takes hold of him, he goes to the extreme in the other direction."

The following is taken from 45 Years in Wall Street and is very good advice and very true in today's world. "Every man takes out of life just exactly according to what he puts in. We reap just what we sow. A man who pays with time and money for knowledge and continues to study and never gets to the point where he thinks he knows all there is to know, but realizes that he can still learn, is the man who will make a success in speculation or in investments. I am trying to tell you the truth and give you the benefit of over 45 years of operating in stocks and commodity markets and point out to you the weak points that will prevent you from meeting with disaster. Speculation can be made a profitable profession. Wall Street can be beaten and there is money operating in commodities and the stock market if you follow the rules and always realize that the unexpected can happen and be prepared for it."

In How to Make Profits in Commodities -- Gann made the following comments regarding knowledge as he believed knowledge is power. All who read this should heed and always remember his advice. "The difference between success and failure in trading in commodities is the difference between one man knowing and following fixed rules and the other man guessing. The man who guesses usually loses. Therefore, if you want to make a success and make profits, your object must be to know more; study all the time; never think that you know it all. I have been studying stocks and commodities for forty years, and I do not know it all yet. I expect to continue to learn something every year as long as I live. Observations, and keen comparisons of past market movements, will reveal what commodities are going to do in the future, because the future is but a repetition of the past. Time spent in gaining knowledge is money in the bank. You can lose all the money you may accumulate or that you may inherit - that is if you have no knowledge of how to take care of it - but with knowledge you can take a small amount of money and make more after time spent in gaining knowledge. A study of commodities will return rich rewards."

Sometime in 1947, Gann sold W. D. Gann Research, Inc. to C. C. Loosli, a San Francisco attorney. He became disenchanted with the business and on February 14, 1948, W. D. Gann Research, Inc. was transferred to Mr. Joseph L. Lederer of St. Louis, Missouri. The office for W. D. Gann Research, Inc. was maintained at 82 Wall Street in New York until 1952. Then it was moved to Scarsdale, New York, and in 1956 relocated to St. Louis, Missouri, where its only business was that of investment adviser.

In 1950 in Miami, Florida, Gann and a partner, Ed Lambert, founded Lambert-Gann Publishing Co. Ed Lambert was an architect who designed the Inter-State Highway System in the greater Miami area Lambert Gann Publishing Co. published all Gann's books and courses.

W. D. Gann passed away in the Methodist Hospital in Brooklyn, New York, on June 14, 1955, at the age of 77. He was survived by his wife, Sadie, three daughters, and a son. That day the world truly lost a market legend.

After Mr. Gann's death in 1955, Ed Lambert continued to operate the business that included a chart service of updated Gann style charts. He was not as active in promoting Gann's writings as when Gann was alive, so for the following twenty years Gann's work became quite obscure. In 1976 Bill and Nikki Jones of Pomeroy, Washington, purchased Lambert-Gann Publishing

Co. and the Gann copyrights. In the purchase were all of his personal research including thousands of his charts, papers, books, and writings he had collected through fifty years of trading and research. There were also tables and miscellaneous office furniture used by Gann. The largest Mayflower moving van available was required to transport this purchase to Pomeroy, Washington. Following Billy Jones' death in September 1989, Nikki Jones continues to operate Lambert Gann Publishing Co., carrying on the Gann tradition with the sale of his books and courses. In this biographer's opinion, W. D. Gann was the greatest market researcher of all time. His trading career spanned more than a half century. During that time he devoted his total life to market research and trading. He researched every possible aspect of natural laws in conjunction with variables of price and time in market movements. This study became an obsession to find the cause and effect of market fluctuations, which he did. The trading techniques Gann developed work the same today as they did when he used them. His library contained volumes of books and manuscripts on harmonic waves, proportion, growth, gravity, electricity, nature, and natural phenomena. However, there were no books on open interest, volume, stocks, or commodities.

The only books and courses on commodities and stocks were his own. He was a humble man who stated, at age 75, that he had not learned all there was to know, and yet, he knew more about the markets than any trader who ever lived. There is an important lesson to be learned from the study of his life and his work. For those of you who have diligently studied his writings, you will understand my statements. Hopefully, for those of you who are not familiar with Gann, this writing will inspire you to begin.

This introduction of W.D. Gann was written by Les Clemens

CHAPTER 2

STUDY AND BE PREPARED

"Many times the reading of a book has made the fortune of a man and has changed his way in life."

If when you are trading, you find yourself feeling inadequate and unable to face making decisions with enthusiasm and confidence, then this course is for you. Are you finding yourself making trades that lose money. You can change and force yourself to become more confident and successful in trading and awaken a new trader within you with Gann Masters. It doesn't matter who you are or what type of person you are, you can find self-confidence in trading.

If you look around at your friends and business associates that you know trade or invest in the markets, you will find that very few of these people are successful in the markets. Most of them lack the confidence and conviction in trading. The majority have surrendered to losses. Statistics say that 90% of people lose in the commodity markets. People blame their brokers, floor traders, outside circumstances or other conditions for their failure to trade profitably. Eventually, most people think that their trading is so much controlled by outside events that they give up trying to improve their results and eventually quit.

W.D. Gann, the greatest trader of all time wrote, "Speculation or investment is the best business in the world if you make a business of it. But in order to make a success of it you must study and be prepared and not guess, follow inside information, or depend on hope or fear. If you do, you will fail. Your success depends on knowing the right kind of rules and following them." He said that lawyers, doctors, engineers and professional men who make a success spend anywhere from two to five years time studying and preparing to practice their profession before making any money. Yet people enter into speculation in Wall Street without any preparation. They have made no study of it at all. They try to deal in something they know nothing about. Is it any wonder then that they lose? Speculators and investors who simply guess, follow tips, rumors, newspaper talk and so called "inside information" have no chance of ever making a success. Unless they follow some well-defined plan based on science and supply and demand, they are sure to lose".

Gann Masters is in a unique position to give you the rules of successful Gann trading. The years of study and experience by the writers of this course will give you the necessary rules and instructions that will lead to your success in the markets. You must be willing to study and learn the chapters in this course. It will take you long hours of study and practice, but you cannot get something for nothing. It will cost you time and money, but it will be worth it in the end.

You must change your inner aspect of what kind of a trader you are. You must believe that you are different from most all other traders and that you are going to be as successful as W.D. Gann was in the markets. You are not what other people think you are, but what you think you are.

Don't concentrate on your limitations or your failures of past trading. You have been conditioned since you started trading by people with false ideas and values. This has limited your full potential. You have the power to change your trading. You must realize your worth as a strong person and a very successful trader.

We can't change the trading of everyone, but we can help you to change your own trading. You as an individual trader must take it on yourself to improve your trading. This course will give you all the information you need to do this. There is a lot of information contained in this course. One sentence or statement may contain the necessary missing link in your trading. That link may be what makes you a successful trader. You must study every part of this course and not ignore anything. The time has come for you to stop your bad habits of trading and start putting in the time and money to become a very successful Gann trader.

It has been determined that it takes approximately three weeks to learn a new idea. It will take you that long to fully understand what is in a chapter. Don't misunderstand me, you may understand what was written, but it will take three weeks of review before it is imbedded into your mind and it is a habit. Put all things aside while you are studying a chapter. The hours you spend will be a small investment compared to the return that you will receive.

To get the best results from these chapters, read the entire chapter through once. Then return to the chapters that will help you understand the current one. If necessary reread the current chapter to pick up anything you missed. Emerson once said: "Many times the reading of a book has made the fortune of a man and has changed his way in life. To use books rightly is to go to them for help; to appeal to them when our knowledge and power fail; to be led by them into wider sight and clear conception of our own." Now, if you are ready, let's begin.

You must now assume that the truths you now hold to be true may in fact be false and those truths may hold you back from your full potential as a successful Gann trader. Don't believe that you can become a very successful trader just with will power alone. Negative ideas in your imagination can defeat you. No matter how hard you try, it will be of no use.

You must open your mind freely to all new ideas and forget all false truths you believe to be true. There is no limit to what you can do if you use your full imagination to work to becoming a successful trader. Once you believe that you are a trader as good or better than W. D. Gann, then you will act as though it were true. You have been unknowingly limiting your full potential through your "mistaken certainties" in your mind. If you can eliminate these "mistaken certainties", your potential for successful trading will go well beyond anything you know.

You must now awake to the truth and limitations that you have imposed on yourself. You must now assume that many truths you now hold are in fact false and that these truths are keeping you back from fully using your potential. You are primarily a product of what you have been taught up to now. If you want to change and become a successful trader, you must learn to understand everything that is taught to you and not believe it to be true, until you have proved it to yourself. You will be given many Gann trading techniques, but do not accept them as truth, until you have proved them out to yourself.

You must be self-reliant. This will be a deterrent to the idea that other traders are smarter, wiser or more intelligent than you are. And, so, you look to them for support for trading ideas that may be unprofitable. It is impossible to become a very successful trader if you are thinking other traders are smarter than you are.

When you become self-reliant you also will have the courage to listen to your inner feeling for hints or signs that you are on the right track. You will be taking a cue from the successful trader you are, not listening to someone outside of your inner thoughts. When you learn to follow the signs correctly and your inner promptings for hints on how to trade a particular situation, you will be a successful trader.

Dependency on the ideas of another trader is slavery by your own consent. It's very degrading for you to be dependent on the trading ideas of another person. One sure sign of dependency is that you will look up to the other trader as superior.

Advice from others in the trading arena is everywhere. Most of it is free and not worth anything. You can have at any one time a dozen unpaid advisors who want to give you their opinion. Most of these advisors are, in fact, not qualified to give advice, but merely have the title that shows that they must know what they are talking about. Most of these advisors can't trade their own accounts successfully, so how can they advise you to trade successfully. Overcoming your dependency on other traders is difficult to do. You have been trained since childhood to depend on other people. It did play an important role in your growing up and education, but it was never meant to take over your individual identity or thinking.

Remember this important saying, "No one can ever let you down if you haven't been leaning on them." No one can make you lose money in the markets, if you are not dependent on them for your trading ideas. Once you have developed your self-reliance, you do not have to procrastinate or evade making a decision to make a trade, because you will be confident to meet the situation with total self-assurance.

You must accept yourself as a successful and intelligent trader. You can never be better than your own self-acceptance as a successful trader. Almost all of your problems in making trades are directly a result of how you feel about yourself as a successful trader. You can never be a better trader than how good of one you feel you are. You must have positive self-esteem about your own trading talents and abilities.

Many traders seem to have a high self-esteem about their own trading talents and abilities on the surface. However, underneath, they are victims of their own low self-esteem. This low self-esteem gets worse the longer they trade, until they go broke or completely give up. If you hope to be a successful trader, you must develop a high self-esteem of your own trading abilities.

You must love studying and applying the techniques of Gann to the markets. Learn to love studying and applying the trading techniques to the markets. There is not one successful Gann trader who does not fully love what he is doing. You will have to spend many hours studying, learning and researching mathematical trading techniques, but it will be enjoyable and financially rewarding. How much you love what you're doing, whether it be your current job or studying the techniques of W. D. Gann, will determine how successful you are.

Everything you need for successful trading lies within you. Your mind is your most usable asset to succeed in learning and trading the techniques of W.D. Gann. If you knew the powers in your mind, it would stagger your imagination. You must make full use of this very powerful resource to succeed in trading. You need to go way beyond what you think your mind can do. Don't let it be limited by what you think it can do. Don't look elsewhere for help, because you have in your mind all the great power to understand and fully use Gann techniques to trade and succeed with.

Successful trading requires that you devote yourself to fulfilling specific financial goal. If you do not fully commit yourself to this goal, you will be like a ship without a chart to follow and will eventually end up shipwrecked on a lost shore. Studies have shown that individuals that have a definite plan are more likely to succeed and be happy in life. At this time in beginning your studies of Gann, you need to make a plan that will use all your talents and abilities. You must take the time right now to figure out how much you want to study and what you want to do with this knowledge of trading, otherwise, you will end up like a shipwrecked captain.

If you are to achieve your maximum potential as a trader you must give yourself a physical and mental rest and relaxation period with inner communication through meditation. The meditation will establish a contact with the inner source of power within you. It will cleanse your mind and open it up to be receptive to the techniques of Gann. When you have trouble understanding a part of Gann, it will guide you back to the right path again and help you to achieve your full potential. It will also help you feel totally a peace with yourself.

Eliminate fear of failing. Fear has been around in trading the markets since they began. It has been the major cause of all market crashes. Fear is your enemy and a destructive emotion which will destroy your self-confidence in trading. If you are afraid, it is impossible to become very successful at trading. To remove any fear in yourself, you must have a positive mental attitude about yourself. Use the power within you to gain success at trading the markets and eliminate fear. Live a day at a time. Make positive statements to yourself continually during the day to help your mental attitude.

You must study the markets and know and understand them fully. You must prove all rules and techniques you have in your tool box. When you see the rules and techniques work over and over again, your confidence will overtake the fear you once had in trading the markets. As you cultivate a positive mental attitude about trading with the techniques of W.D. Gann, a new successful you will occur to trade the markets. You will be a trader with power and direction. Once you have fully committed yourself, you will never be the same again.

CHAPTER 3

CAPITAL REQUIRED

You must make a plan of capital preservation to be successful in the markets.

It is very important that you understand the amount of capital required to trade the markets. You want to have the ability to continue to trade the markets for the next year to twenty years without being wiped out. Most traders have no capital trading plan, use fear and greed to trade by, and over trade. It's no wonder that 90% of commodity traders lose. Those 10 % that do make money, of course, are the ones that have learned how to trade. They make all the money that the others lose. If you make a plan of capital preservation, you will always have the necessary capital to trade with, even if you have the expected losses in the markets. If you put all your capital at risk in the markets on a couple trades, like so many traders do, then you will surely lose it all and be out of the game. "Preservation of capital" is your first rule to apply with all your trades.

On the Chicago Board of Trade, the grains trade in units of 5000 bushels. When wheat is trading where it is now at $3.50 - $3.75 per bushel, you need 20% of the value of the total contract to safely trade the market, though the exchanges charge only 5% margin. If you fully leverage your position on the 5% margin, you will be scared out of the markets with fear and greed and will surely lose, so use the 20% margin rule to safeguard your capital. If wheat is selling at $3.75, you would multiply this amount times 5000 bushels to get $18,750 as the total value of the contract. 20% of the contract value is $3750. Therefore to trade a 5000 bushel contract of wheat at $3.75, you should have $3750 of capital. The exchange margin on a contract of wheat at that level is about $1000 or 5%. You therefore have an excess of $2750 over the initial margin required. Divide the $2750 by 10 giving you a potential of 10 trades possible with a maximum loss of $275 each before you're out of the game. Your average risk, should never be more than 10% of the excess capital above the initial margin rate of the contract. You should have enough money to trade the market 10 times, and have ten straight losses, before you would be wiped out. This should never happen, if you have a trading plan and trade according to the rules of successful trading, which you will learn in this course. It's very rare that you would even have three consecutive losses, and even if you did, then the next trade could make you 10% on your money giving you a large gain over your small losses. Your capital for trading commodity markets should be at least 20% of the total contract value. You should never risk more than 10% of your excess margin money on any one trade, so you can trade at least 10 times before you are out of the game. If the market is in a major uptrend, as the market gets higher, you will need more capital to trade. If wheat rises to $4.50 per bushel, you will need $4500 to trade each contract and you would never risk more than 10% of your excess margin capital on each trade, so you could have 10 losing trades before you were out of the market.

In the stock market, the capital requirement rules are different. If you buy stocks, you have two choices, either put up the full purchase price of the stock or put the stock on margin and put up 50% of the value of the stock and pay interest on the other 50% usually at 1% above broker call rate. In either case, you still must follow the rules of capital preservation. Never risk more than 10% of your trading capital above the initial margin required on any one trade. If you purchase 100 shares of a stock at $50.00 per share the total amount of the transaction is $5000. I am not taking into account commission for this example, but for your own trading you also need to take into account commission costs. If you purchase this on margin, you would have to put up 50% or $2500. You should have at least 50% of the total value of the stock above the initial margin. Divide this 50% into 10 equal parts to figure out what amount each stop should be. You can vary this percent, but it must be based on how active the stock is. If you use the same rule that is used in commodities, you would not risk more than 10% of the excess margin on any one trade. Therefore in this case, 50% of the total value of the stock is $2500 and that divided into 10 equal parts is $250 maximum loss per trade to stay in the game.

Margin for trading a contract of wheat
3.75 per bushel
X 5000 bushels
_____

$1850
X 20%
_____

= $3750 necessary capital
- $1000 initial capital
_____

= $2750 excess capital
divided by 10
_____

= $275 the amount of stop for each trade

which means there is a maximum of 10 losing trades with this stop

EXHIBIT 3.1 Capitial Preservation

CHAPTER 4

RIGHT KIND OF CHARTS

To start trading according to the rules of W.D. Gann you must have the right kind of charts.

It's very important to have the right kind of charts to follow stocks or commodities. The major problem with most traders is, they do not have the right kind of charts to study the market correctly. If you talk to a carpenter or a surgeon or any professional person, they will tell you the importance of having the necessary tools to get the job done right. Can you imagine a surgeon operating on a patient with a dull scaple or a carpenter using a dull saw? We'll that's precisely what a trader is doing when he trades with most of today's published chart services. Traders risk thousands of dollars trading with ineffective tools. If you are going to build a house, it is very important to build it on a strong foundation. To start trading according to the rules of W. D. Gann you must have the right foundation, and that's proper and correct charts.

BAR CHARTS
Bar charts are the type of charts that you should set up. They should be set up correctly according to price and time. They must be set up either on a high, low, close basis or on an open, high, low close basis. It is necessary that you have enough update space so you can project out future points of time and price. The update space should be labeled out in the future with the year, month and day's date. This is another thing that is very wrong with most chart services, they don't put enough update space out to the right of the chart so you can the proper projecting of prices. On a daily chart you should have at least 1 year of update space, a weekly chart should have 2-3 years and a monthly chart should have 3-5 years of update space.

HOLIDAYS
A holiday on a daily chart must be omitted (do no leave a space for it). When you are projecting out into the future you must be aware of when the holidays occur so you can adjust your charts for them. Usually toward the end of the prior year, around November to December most brokerage firms and some financial magazines will publish the dates that the exchanges are closed on.

There has been much discussion regarding the type of charts to keep. Should you keep a regular Gann type chart which omits weekends and holidays? This type of chart plots only market days. Or, should you keep up a calendar day bar chart. This type of chart leaves blank spaces for both holidays and weekends when the market did not trade. The answer to this important question is that it takes too much time to keep both types of charts up. You should only keep up Gann style charts and use the Excel spreadsheet for calendar day time counts. You do need to be aware of both calendar and market day timing. When a market makes a high it will bottom out a set number of market trading days and calendar days out in the future. Time counts will be discussed in a later chapter.

MARKET REPORTS

It's very important to mark on the update space on your charts the market reports that directly effect your commodity or stock. For example, if you are trading cattle, you would mark on the update space the dates of all the cattle-on-feed reports. You also need to mark the quarterly pig reports on the chart as they affect cattle prices. The grain reports have some influence on cattle prices, so they should also be marked on the charts also. Often important projected highs or lows will occur on the day after a market report. If you have several important cycles hitting near a major report day, then probably the day after the report day will be the timing or reversal day. Most important reports come after the market closes. That's why we say the day after the report will be the timing day. If the report is during the trading hours of the commodity or stock, then that day will probably be the timing day.

MOON AND SUN CYCLES

It's also very important to mark on the update space on your charts the days that full or new moons and Sun Ellipses occur. Many major pivot points in the markets occur during these cycle times of the sun and moon.

IMPORTANT FUTURE MONTHS

A good set of charts should include the key months of future contracts of the year in commodity future contracts. For example, in most commodities the 12th and 6th positions of the cycle (December and June) are the most important and the 3rd and 9th positions (March and October) are the second most important. You should keep charts on all four of the important months, if you are trading actively.

PROPER SCALE

The proper scale is very important. The correct scale can be determined from how plastic overlays fit the charts. You will learn about overlays in a later chapter. The master time and price overlays were one of the most significant discoveries W.D. Gann ever made. He said that himself before he died. To determine if your overlays are working properly, the 1 x 1 angle on the overlays should usually hit the 50% reaction of prices and bounce off at least the first time. Once you see this on many charts you will understand the principal. The scaling is also very important. The rule in commodities is to use the following order in scaling. See Exhibit 4.1 in this chapter for more exact details on what to use on each individual commodity.

DECIMAL commodities	FRACTION commodities
.10	1 cents
.20	2 cents
.40	4 cents
.80	8 cents
1.00	10 cents

TIME FORMAT

The charts you use should be correctly formatted into the right time format to be effective for trading. We recommend using charts going back 20 - 100 years in the following time formats:

>Daily
>Weekly
>Monthly
>Yearly

For intraday charts you should use the following time formats:

>60 Minute
>30 Minute
>15 Minute
>5 Minute
>2 Minute

SCROLLS

Since the charts you use will be Gann style, they will be very long and it will be necessary for them to be in scrolls. This is a much better method than laying them on top of each other, because they can be more easily and compared to each other. Comparison of this years chart patterns with prior harmonic years is very important. W.D. Gann did a lot of pattern matching of past markets with current ones. Your charts are very important. They are the life blood of your trading. Some traders use a cardboard mail box of slots that they can slide their scroll charts into. This cardboard mail box can be purchased at most office supply stores. It keeps them safe and dry.

LINKING CONTRACTS TOGETHER
In using Gann Style charts it is necessary to link the contracts together correctly. The procedure for linking contracts together is very simple and is necessary for the proper continuation of the time series of prices.

DAILY
For the current contract, for example, December 1990 corn, plot all the prices to the end of the contract including the last trading day. Then start with the next contract, 1991 corn and start plotting those prices in sequence till the end of the 1991 contract then start with the 1992 contract. Always use the same month of contracts linking them together, for example Dec. 1989, Dec. 1990, Dec. 1991 and so on.

WEEKLY
For weekly charts plot all the daily prices inside the weekly to the end of the contract. For example if the trading on a commodity like Dec. 1990 corn stopped in the middle of the week, stop there and continue the daily prices on the Dec. 1991 contract in that same weekly price bar.

MONTHLY
For monthly charts plot all the daily prices inside the monthly to the end of the contract. For example if the trading on a commodity like Dec. 1990 corn stopped in the middle of the month, stop there and continue the daily prices on the Dec. 1991 contract in that same monthly price bar.

YEARLY
For yearly charts plot all the daily prices inside the yearly to the end of the contract. For example, if the trading on a commodity like Dec. 1990 corn stopped in the middle of the year, stop there and continue the daily prices on the Dec. 1991 contract in that same yearly price bar.

CONTINUOUS
Many people use a type of chart called a continuous contract chart. These are the type of weekly charts that are in almost of the chart services. In this type of contract all the nearby months of a commodity are linked together, for example, Dec. 1990 corn, Mar. 1990 corn, Jun. 1990 corn and so on. It's OK to use this type of chart to find rough cycles with using an Ehrlich Cycle Finder, but they are not very good for projecting accurate price and cycle projections according to the rules of W.D. Gann.

TIME AND PRICE LABELS
The time and price labels at the bottom of the chart are very important. The

date bar should be correctly labeled at the bottom of the chart showing year, month and day. The prices should be correctly labeled on the side with price divisions in circle numbers if possible. Circle numbers will be explained in another chapter.

CHART SERVICES
The availability of good charts is hard to come by. Most chart services do not give you daily prices that go back far enough. They usually give you only about 6-7 months of daily data. That is not enough to do long term research necessary for Gann trading. You should have at least 3 years of daily data linked together according to the methods of W.D. Gann. The weekly and monthly charts they put out are nearby continuous charts that cannot be used correctly due to incorrect highs and lows.

DOING CHARTS BY HAND
Making and keeping up charts by hand is very time consuming, but it does give you a special feel of the market that you would not otherwise get having prices updated automatically in a chart service or computer. If you feel that you have the necessary time for this activity, then the chart paper and printed data can be ordered from Gann Masters.

COMPUTER CHARTS
You can also buy a computer and obtain a charting software program which can do precision long term paper charts. There are two programs that can do this. One is the GannTrader by Peter Pich and the other is MAX:CHART by Infinity Data. You also need a source of long term data. There are many services available. CSI, Technical Tools, and Genesis are very popular. What ever data service you get, you must make sure that their data software has the ability to link the data into Gann continuous style format. If you are a serious Gann student, you will eventually want to go this way. MAX:CHART and GannTrader are available through Gann Masters. GannTrader lists for $1295 and MAX:CHART for $79.95. These programs are precision printer programs that can print Gann style charts. These programs give you the flexibility in setting up your charts. These programs produce large, beautiful, open, high, low close charts or high, low close charts. The charts can be up to 10 feet tall. The programs produce the charts in strips according to what size of Epson printer you have. The strips can be either 8 1/2" wide or 15" wide. You can select three grid sizes. 12x12, 10x10, or 8x8 lines per inch. Grids can be highlighted every 4th or 5th line. The programs require an IBM compatible computer with 640 RAM and an Epson or compatible printer. Both programs also have a screen technical analysis module that allows you to do much of the standard technical analysis that includes RSI, stochastics, moving aver-

ages, etc. GannTrader has the ability to draw planetary lines and the Gann squares directly on the screen. MAX:CHART does not have this ability.

NEW COMPUTER SCREEN PROGRAMS
In the last two years Omega Research has come out with SuperCharts and TradeStation, which are precision screen programs for MS Dos Windows. These programs are impressive. They can do many of the techniques necessary for Gann style trading. Most of the examples in this course are from these programs. The advantage they give you is the ability to do quick research on trading methods. Their disadvantages are they lack some of the essential timing tools and that they do not have update space to the right of the chart. Omega Research is working on these problems so the necessary tools will be available on a future program update. One of the most impressive features of these programs is their ability to display large amounts of data on the screen at one time in daily, weekly or monthly format. TradeStation can display data in any time format even including intraday. At this time, we feel that these two programs are the best screen programs available for the Gann Trader.

NUMBER NINE VIDEO CARD
Using a video card like Number Nine, you can view a much larger virtual chart on your computer screen which acts as a portal view on windows chart programs such as TradeStation or SuperCharts. The resolution of these video cards can go up to 1200 x 1600. The virtual screen can be up to 4 times your current screen size. This Number Nine video card used in combination with a 17" flat screen computer monitor is almost like trading on long term chart paper. We must warn you that trading on a computer just using a regular DOS chart program and regular VGA video card is not good and will sooner or later get you in trouble. Most of the 90% of traders that loose in the markets trade with this type of setup, using limited data and various oscillators. To be a successful Gann trader, you must know and trade the big picture with longer term charts.

GANN MASTERS BIG CHARTS
You can have Gann Masters make you the necessary charts to trade with. The charts sell for $3.50 each either in daily, weekly or monthly format and are shipped via 2-day U.S. Priority mail. The daily charts are printed back 3 years and have update space for 1 year. The weekly charts are printed back 10 years and have update space for 2 years. The monthly charts are printed back for up to 30 years and have update space for 7 years. The charts are up-to-date on the day they are shipped. The charts are printed on continuous heavyweight 15" wide computer paper and are available in several commodities.

SCALES FOR CHARTS

Commodity	Daily	Weekly	Monthls
Barley	.40	.80	2.00
British Pound	.20	.40	.40
Cattle	.20	.40	1.00
Cocoa	.10	.20	.40
Coffee	.40	.80	4.00
Copper	.20	.40	2.00
Corn	1	2	4
Cotton	.20	.40	1.00
Crude Oil	.40	.80	1.00
DMark	.0004	.0008	.0010
GNMA	4/32	8/32	32/32
Gold	2.00	4.00	8.00
Heating Oil	.20	.40	.40
Hogs	.20	.40	1.00
JYen	.0020	.0040	.0040
Unlead Gas	.20	.40	.40
Lumber	.40	1.00	2.00
NYSE	.20	.40	1.00
Oats	1	2	4
OJ	.40	.80	1.00
Platinum	2.00	4.00	8.00
Pork Bellies	.40	.80	1.00
Rapeseed	2	4	8
Silver	.10	.20	.40
Soybeans	4	4	10
Soymeal	.40	.80	1.00
Soyoil	.20	.40	1.00
S&P	.40	.80	1.00
Sugar	.10	.20	1.00
SFranc	.0020	.0040	.0040
TBills	.20	.20	.40
TBonds	4/32	8/32	32/32
Wheat	2	2	4

EXHIBIT 4.1 Scales to use for charts

CHAPTER 5

KNOW THE TREND

Trend is the most important thing you can know about the market.

The most important thing you can know about the market is its trend. The market can do three things:
1. Go up
2. Go down
3. Consolidate sideways

TYPES OF TRENDS
The market can have these three types of trends:
1. Short term
2. Intermediate term
3. Long term

ENTRY TECHNIQUE
Gann's entry technique for trading is as follows:

TO BUY
If the long term trend (monthly charts) is up, wait for the intermediate term trend (weekly charts) to break up out of a long running consolidation and then buy after the first short term (daily charts) drop turns up.

TO SELL
If the long term trend (monthly charts) of the market is down, wait for the intermediate term trend (weekly charts) of the market to break down out of a long running consolidation and then sell after the first short term (daily charts) rally turns down. To illustrate this technique look at Exhibit 5.1. The monthly lumber chart is in a long term uptrend since it had been making new yearly highs and lows since 1990. In Exhibit 5.2 you see a weekly lumber chart that had been in a downward consolidation since March of 1992. In September it made a new weekly high over the high it made in July of 1992 showing that the intermediate trend had broken up out of its consolidation range. In Exhibit 5.3 wait for the first daily short term trend to bottom out after its correction

and buy it which would have been on October 26, 1992. The move that then occurred was one of the largest moves that ever occurred in any commodity market.

LOW VOLATILITY ENTRY

In a situation like this you can put on your position with low volatility and close stops without too much risk. In this technique you are using Gann's rule of buying based upon the market making new highs on the monthly and weekly charts, but using the daily short term reactions to enter your positions. You'll never make consistent money in commodities unless you have the psychology to buy high and sell low. Don't be afraid do this because this technique produces some of the biggest profits from trends in the markets.

MARKET IN STRONGEST POSITION

The market is in the strongest direction when all three types of trends are in one direction as indicated:
1. Long term up
2. Immediate term up
3. Short term up with this technique, you will have all three trends in the same direction.

EXHIBIT 5.1 March 1993 Lumber monthly

WHAT CHARTS TO USE
To figure out the trend of the market, you should use:
1. Daily charts to tell short term
2. Weekly charts to tell intermediate term
3. Monthly and yearly charts to tell long term

MARKET ACTIVITY
The market will typically have low activity at the bottom and abnormally high activity at the top. Watch the average daily, weekly or monthly range to indicate if you're near a top or bottom. See Exhibits 5.1, 5.2, and 5.3 which clearly suggests this. The previous example was just a general technique and did not go into real detail regarding what makes a trend change. This will now be explained.

TIME FACTOR
The time factor is very important for showing a change in trend. When the trend of a market makes a change, the number of days of a reaction will increase over the last reaction. This is probably one of the first indications of a change of trend in a market. You need to keep an eye on the number of days reaction in both calendar and market trading days.

EXHIBIT 5.2 March 1993 Lumber weekly

CALENDAR DAYS

To count calendar days, you count all trading days plus weekends and holidays. It's very simple. It is much easier to use the Excel spread sheet for calendar time counts. This will be explained in a later chapter.

TRADING DAYS

To count trading days you must follow two very important rules: 1. Don't count inside days. Those are days in which the current trading day's high and low are inside the previous day's high and low . 2. If a market rallies stops and backs up over 50% of it's move, you start your count over. 3. To be a valid swing, the market must make a 2 day swing. That means that the market must have 2 days of consecutive newer highs or lows. 4. You must figure out the minimum amount of a move to count for a swing. In the case of TBonds, I determined the minimum was 1 full point. 5. The market will usually have approximately the same number of swings in its thrusts and reactions. There will be more on this in a later chapter. The market swings should be labelled for easy identification. In all uptrends mark all swing points. Mark all downswing points. There will be more in a later chapter concerning these swing numbers. It's best to buy or sell on number 3 tops and bottoms.

EXHIBIT 5.3 March 1993 Lumber daily

POINTS MOVE

In Exhibit 5.4, you will see that the points moved are closely related to the Fibonacci number series. In later lessons we will explain the points move in more detail.

1ST MOVE UP

In this example, TBonds bottomed on 6/23/92 and started to rally. They rallied 16 calendar days and 9 trading days for approximately a 3 point move.

2ND MOVE DOWN

The market topped on 7/10/92 and started its reaction. It declined 5 calendar days and 3 trading days. Notice that when a market only reacts 1- 3 market days, it is in strong position.

3RD MOVE UP

The market bottomed on 7/25/93 and rallied 32 calendar days and 19 market days, showing that the market was in still a very strong position. It exceeded the number of days of it's last rally.

EXHIBIT 5.4 June 1993 TBonds

4TH MOVE DOWN
The market topped on 8/13/93 and dropped 5 calendar days and only 1 market day. It still showed that the market was in a powerful uptrend.

5TH MOVE UP
The market bottomed on 8/17/92 and rallied 4 calendar days and 4 market days. In both cases this was less than the previous rally. This meant that the momentum was beginning to slow, a reason for caution.

6TH MOVE DOWN
The market made a top on 8/12/92 and fell 5 calendar days and 2 trading days. This reaction was slightly more than the previous reaction, still indicating that the momentum was declining.

7TH MOVE UP
The market bottomed on 8/26/92 and rallied 13 calendar days and 7 trading days.

8TH MOVE DOWN
The market topped on 9/8/92 and fell 14 calendar days and 8 trading days. This greatly exceeded the previous reaction indicating that the trend had changed due to an overbalancing of time. Now it's time to label the market for the downside. Change this 8th move down to the 1st move down in an intermediate downtrend. Get ready to sell short on the beginning of the 3rd down.

THE IMPORTANCE OF THE TIME FACTOR
The time counts of a market are very important. They tell you when a market is turning. Sometimes the turn is hard to detect. This is one way to determine a change in trend. There are other methods that you must use with this method to be more accurate. You will learn those later in other chapters.

TIME SHEETS
To know the accurate time count on a market is necessary. You should keep a written record on the market. See Exhibit 5.4 June 93 TBond chart in this chapter. Using the time sheet in Exhibit 5.5 you can keep a record of both calendar and trading units move of a market. This can be used on daily, weekly and monthly charts. This time sheet also has the ability to tract points move. Notice in this example how many of the calendar and trading days are Fibonacci numbers. It is quite amazing. Also notice on the points moves that very few moves exceeded 3 days. The 3 day figure is a natural Fiboancci timing number.

The Excel template that is available in this course has the ability to do calendar time counts. It will save you many hours of calculations. With the Excel spread sheet program, you can copy and make a time sheet on each individual commodity or stock that you are following. There are many other timing sheets that are available on this template.

TIME COUNT EXAMPLE

Description: June 93 TBonds   Start Date: 6/22/92   End Date: 9/8/92
Calendar Units: Trading Units: 53 Points Move: 8
Major Trend: Up Intermediate Trend: Up Minir Trend: Down

No.	Start Date	Calendar Units	Trade Units	Points
1	6/23/92	16	9	3
2	7/14/92	32	19	5
3	8/17/92	4	4	1 1/2
4	8/26/92	13	7	3 1/2
5	7/10/92	5	3	1
6	8/18/92	5	3	1
7	8/21/92	5	1	11/20
8	9/8/92	14	8	3
1	9/8/92	14	8	3
2	9/23/92	12	7	2 1/2

EXHIBIT 5.5 Time count example

CHAPTER 6

MATHEMATICS

Mathematics is the basis of all forecasting in the markets.

Using mathematics is an absolute necessity to trade the stock or commodity markets successfully. The traders who master the art of trading the markets with mathematics will be successful. Those who don't will fail. It's as simple as that. Traders who rely on tips and rumors will eventually lose. By taking this course you are showing the desire to succeed by going beyond the what the normal trader will do. You are showing your desire to study, understand and apply mathematics to the market. It will take a lot of study for you to succeed, but you are on the right course. Those traders who think they can use computer trading programs alone with simple oscillators will fail. Many of these traders spend hundreds of hours of their valuable study time trying to make some definite pattern or way to use oscillators. They won't be able to do it. You need mathematics to succeed in the markets.

It looks so easy to trade with oscillators when you look back on past charts. You just sell when the stochastics is at the top and buy when it's on the bottom. It works some of the time, but sometimes it sets you up for a blood bath. For example, sometimes when the stochastics gets to the top, in an apparent sell mode, the market will take off and explode, leaving you with big losses if you shorted the market. The same thing happens when the stochastics gets to the bottom. If you buy when the stochastics is at the bottom, sometimes the market will fall out of bed giving you huge losses. Traders who follow only oscillators don't know when the market is approaching major or minor geometric angles or timing cycles. They have no idea of where the market might be heading. They will short the market when the stochastics oscillator is at the top and not know that the market is resting on a major geometric angle or time cycle. The market will then explode giving them huge loses. Check around with traders that use oscillators. You will find that they generally loose money in the markets. The only traders who consistently make money in the markets are traders who use mathematical methods of trading. These are based on the true mathematics behind the market caused by the vibration of numbers. Prior highs and lows and their interactive harmony waves and geometric angles are the real cause behind market movements.

Oscillators can be used to successfully trade with, but only if they are used with other time and price trading techniques to support them. In this course we go over how displaced moving averages, stochastics and MACD can be used to trade the market mathematically. It is the only Gann way to use oscillators.

It's a puzzle why most traders don't use mathematics to buy and sell stocks and commodities and to forecast trends in the markets. It's very easy after you learn the mathematical trading techniques and it's 100% more reliable than using other techniques. It's also much more consistent. Mathematics is something that you can depend on. In this course, after you learn the principles of trading market mathematics you will never want to hear tips or rumors again. You will find that if someone offers their view of the market to you, you'll want to shut them out and not let them influence you. After you know the rules of mathematics behind the market you will find your sixth sense develops and many of the techniques you learned in this course will start relating to each other. Your mind will have a unique sense of where the market is headed.

In using mathematics for trading the markets, it is important to know that the market can go only two directions. It can go up or down or it can just move sideways. Prices can increase or decrease or just stay the same. They can do nothing else. We will use mathematics to figure out if the markets will go up or down. There are various methods to use to determine this. They involve the use of mathematical trend analysis and timing techniques developed by W.D. Gann.

THE CUBE

There are three measurements in a cube: length, width and height. We can use these measurements to figure out market movement. The market can be clocked in time in two different ways. One way is using trading days and the other is using calendar days. Many traders will use both as a check on each other. For example, a market might make a bottom and advance 90 market days to the next major top. That move would be 126 calendar days if you added the weekends. Most of the time the calendar day count will coincide with the market day count. The two together, will usually give you a time window. This window will contain 2 - 3 days where the market will top or bottom. In this example there are 90 trading days. Divide 90 trading days by 5 days to the week. You get 18 weeks. Weeks have two weekend days, so multiply 18 times 2 to get 36 weekend days. Add these 36 weekend days to 90 and you get 126 calendar days, which is very close to the 120 circle number. The ratio of trading days to calendar days is 1.4 which is close to the Gann Square of 144 or 10 times 1.44 is 144 a very important number.

Time measurements can be based on several techniques. One technique is using natural fixed numbers. These are the numbers that can be divided into the circle of 360 degrees. These are: 9, 18, 27, 36, 45, 72, 90, 120, 180, 270 and 360. Markets fall or rise by these exact numbers. The other technique is using variable numbers based on market highs, lows and ranges. If the market makes a high at 540 and a low of 410 the difference is 130. The markets often retrace one half of this or rise for 65 days.

The vertical or height movement of the market is price. Price calculations can use the same techniques as time measurements such as natural fixed numbers or variable numbers. For example, if the market makes a bottom at 90 it can rise 90 days and 90 points and square at that point and turn down.

A combination of height, width and length of a cube is volume of a cube. A market has to move up and down a certain number of vibrations to fill the volume of a cube before the market will change directions. Count the swings of a bull market and it should equal the swings of a prior bull market. See Exhibit 6.2. A bear market also should have the same number of swings as prior bear markets and they should be in proportion to prior bear markets and bull markets. A simple example is the Elliott wave counts of the market. Wave one is a count of 1, wave two down is 2, wave three up is 3, wave four down is 4, and wave five up is 5. Inside of these waves are smaller waves and the total wave count of one bull market should equal some prior bull market of the same commodity or stock.

A cube also has six sides. This means that the market will repeat itself every 6 intervals. That means you should check back every 6 days, 6 months, 6 years, or (6 X 10) 60 years and the market will repeat itself. Be careful as the market has inversions in those repeat time cycles. That means for example 6 months ago if the market made a low, today it might invert and make a high instead. You should be watching for price patterns so you don't get caught in an inversion.

In geometry there are 3 basic shapes: the square, the circle, and the triangle. See Exhibit 6.4. The square, of course, represents time and price. The horizontal is time and the vertical is price. From the square we determine everything, both timing and price projection. If we put the 360 degree circle inside of the square and the three sided triangle inside the circle and the square this will give us the means to determine time and price points for forecasting the markets. As you remember, the fixed time points are from the circle of 360 degrees. The triangle helps us divide the circle into the three points of 120 degrees. The 120 degree points are some of the most important points of the circle. The Gann wheel or the Square of 9 is constructed from the square, the circle and the triangle.

We can use three different basic angles to determine time and price within the markets: the vertical, the horizontal and the diagonal line. The vertical is price, the horizontal is time and the diagonal is a combination of the two which is change of time and price. The horizontal and vertical lines divide the circle into the important 90 degree points. The triangle can then be used to divide the 90 degree points into 45 degree points. From these three geometric shapes, we get all the calculations in mathematics for time and price projections in the markets. In combination with the angles, we can use the squares of both odd and even numbers to get the cause behind the market movements. These numbers are actually part of the square when they are laid out according the Gann Square of 9.

CONSTRUCTING CHARTS PROPERLY

For geometric angles to work properly on charts, it is necessary for the charts to be constructed properly. If the charts are not constructed properly, then one small error can throw off your measurement and give you a loss in the markets. A very small error at the beginning can lead to a huge loss later on.

Now here are the rules for constructing proper charts from which to trade with. Construct daily charts with a vertical bar showing the open, high, low and close for the day. Allow no spaces for holidays or weekends. This is not to say that weekends or holidays are not important in regard to time measurements. Time goes on even though the markets stop trading. However, you don't have to put the blank spaces on your charts. You can use Excel spreadsheet as time calculator to count calendar days. In plotting of the market days, do not allow any days to be missed or omitted as this will later on cause big errors in your calculations. Date the bars at the bottom of the charts for market trading days. When doing time counts in the markets, it is necessary to keep track of important turning points using both trading days and calendar days. It is very important to know how many days, weeks or months the market is away from important highs and lows.

For spacing of your charts, the best is, of course using a 1 x 1 scale. That is, 1 cent in the price of corn for every 1 vertical square. This worked very nicely when Gann was living, but it does not work today. You will have to condense the prices in the squares to get them to fit on a chart. One way to know if you have the right price per square is to use the best fit method. Make charts up using 1 cent, 2 cent, 4 cent per square. It's nice to have a program like MAX:CHART to do this for you. It saves a lot of your time. After you have the three charts draw the 1 X 1 angle on them and see how the prices react on it. You will notice immediately which chart has the right scale, as it will just fit better with the angles. You will have to do this with all your daily, weekly and monthly charts. Each chart will have it's own scale based on its level of price movement. The pricing per square should be set up on the basis of so many cents per square. Set it up on the basis of the following even numbers: 1, 2, 4, 8 or 10. Use only these numbers for pricing per square. The means for example, price corn as 1, 2, 4, 8 or 10 cents per square. On a daily chart, you can get away with 1 cent per square, but on a long monthly chart, you may have to use 2, 4, 8 or 10 cents per square. These numbers keep your Gann angles correct with time and price.

The 1 x 1 scale is important, because the market moves according to dollars. Gann traded mostly grains which are set up properly to use the 1 x 1 scale. In corn, for example, your charts (daily, weekly and monthly) should be set up so 1 square equals 2 cents per bushel. Every 1 cent equals $50 dollars. So 2 cents per square means that one square equals $100. So the market can move according to time in a 1 to 1 ratio. One day can equal $100 or one week can equal $100 or one month can equal $100. Most people set corn up so 1 square equals $50 dollars. This works out in most cases, because the 2 x 1 angle which is a very strong angle works instead of the 1 x 1 angle on this scale. On any chart you use, you must convert it to use $100 per square measurement. Gann angles will not work properly unless you do this. The best markets to use with the 1 x 1 angle are the grain and metal markets, because they are the easiest to convert to the $100 per day scale.

If you have a chart service and you don't have the MAX:CHART or the GannTrader program, you can always figure out the scale mathematically. That is figure on a calculator that if the market made a high three years ago on a monthly chart, you can deduct 36 months x $100 off the price of the commodity and figure where the 1 x 1 geometric angles should be.

It's important to use Gann style charts. Avoid nearby continuation style charts. Nearby continuation charts will not give you correct price projections, support, or resistance levels and will not give you good time projections points.

GEOMETRIC ANGLES
Geometric angles accurately measure time and price movements. There are 360 degrees in a circle and certain numbers in the circle are very important. In this course, you will learn which numbers are important. These numbers will indicate to you when important tops and bottoms are being formed. They will also indicate important support and resistance levels in regard to both time and price. You must study and practice with these numbers once you learn them to determine their importance.

Geometric angles are used to measure time and price movements because they are much easier than using addition, subtraction, multiplication or division in the markets, provided you use correct rules for drawing the angles correctly. Angles can correct mistakes in mathematics. For example, if you count across the bottom of your chart 90 squares across and 90 squares up and draw a 45 degree angle down from the left high point, the angle should intercept the 0 line at exactly 90 squares to the right. Thus angles, if drawn properly, will help you to correct mistakes in mathematics on your charts. Angles, will help you to know the position the market is in all the time. If you figure the market using mathematics such as addition, subtraction, multiplication or division and write these calculations down on paper, you will misplace and lose these calculations much of the time. Having the angles drawn on your chart allows you always to know the position the market is in all the time and you will always know when the market changes trend.

A mean-average can also be determined by taking the high and low of the day, week, month and dividing it by 2 to figure out the average price of the time period. This average price can be used alone and put into a moving average such as a 9, 18, 27, 36, 49, etc. day to determine the price trend. This mean average will give you an idea of how many dollars per day the market is moving in. Moving averages should be based on the number 9. This is the highest number in the system. All numbers repeat after the number 9. For example, look at the following number count:

```
         1 2 3 4 5 6 7 8 9
   add 9 to each of the above to get the next
      10 11 12 13 14 15 16 17 18 19
   add 9 to each of the above to get the next
      20 21 22 23 24 25 26 27 28 29
```

GEOMETRIC ANGLES PROPORTIONATE TIME AND PRICE

Geometric angles accurately measure and divide time and price into proportionate parts. If a stock or commodity makes a low on a certain price for example 34, it has three dimensions of time and price. It can move sideways for 34 time units, it can move up for 34 price units, and it can move diagonally 34 time and price points from which it began. Accurate measurements can be taken from previous highs, lows, and the ranges in between. There is always proportion between previous highs, lows, and swings of the market.

90 SQUARE CHART

The 90 square pattern chart is very important to use in trend analysis. See Exhibit 3.3. To construct the 90 square chart do the following. First, you must determine the chart paper you are going to use and its scale. Once this is determined, take a piece of this paper at least 100 x 100 squares. Tape it to a table and tape a piece of plastic overlay to the chart paper. Use a permanent pen marker which is capable of drawing on plastic. Follow the following instructions:

1. On the plastic overlay draw a square 90 points across and 90 points down.

2. Draw a diagonal from the upper left corner to the lower right corner and from the bottom left corner to the upper right corner. This separates the square into 4 triangles.

3. Now where the diagonals intersected at the center of the square draw a horizontal and a vertical line. These lines separate the square into 4 smaller squares.

4. Now draw all symmetrical angles in the square from the corners intersecting the top, middle, and bottom of the other side of the square. Now you can draw the division angles intersecting the 1/4 points and 1/3 points of the other side of the square from each corner. For even more division you can use 1/8, 1/6 and 1/16 points.

5. Now draw the inner square, which are the lines that diagonally intersect the 1/2 points of each side of the square. This is one of Gann's most important discoveries. Many Gann traders omit this inner square. This is a big mistake. You will learn how to use the inner square as time goes on.

The square of 90 will be the basic pattern of the squares that you will draw. You must fully understand this square and how it is constructed and it's full meaning as time goes on. The Square of 90 can be used to supplement and replace all other squares. In this chapter we have included a square of 90.

The 90 degree square also helps you to understand the principles of Gann's mathematics. First you divide the number by the odd or even numbers such as 4 or 3. Divide the sides of the square first by 4 and then by 3 giving you 1/4, 1/2, 3/4, 4/4, 1/3, 2/3, 3/3. Then if necessary divide the sides even further by going one step further such as 1/8, 1/4, 3/8, 1/2, 5/8, 3/4, 7/8, 8/8, 1/6, 1/3, 2/3, 5/6, 6/6. What you are doing is multiplying the 4 and the 3 by 2 to get the next divisions of 8 and 6. To go even further you multiply by 2 again to get 18 and 12. Keep going out further to find the more precision numbers.

1 X 1 ANGLE (45 DEGREE)

The Gann angles are very important to understand. See Exhibit 6.1. The most important angle to draw is the 45 degree. In Comex gold, for example, this means that the market will move up at $100 per day on a daily chart, $100 per week on a weekly chart and $100 per month on a monthly chart. The contract specifications on gold is 100 ounces. Therefore one dollar per ounce move equals $100. This angle divides time and price into 2 equal parts, on into 2 triangles. In an uptrending market, as long as price stays above this angle, it is considered in strong position. You can buy it and put a stop right below this angle.

Another important signal is if you draw a 45 degree angle down from the top and the market gets above it but later gaps down under this line then it is a sell signal. A stop can be placed above the trend angle.

The amount of the stop you use with this trendline should be based on the level of prices and the volatility of the prices which is usually the same thing. Gold selling at $350 per once will not need as much of a stop as gold selling at $500 per once. If the stops are broken, then the market will usually go temporarily lower and you can also play the market that way.

Gann geometric angles almost always will stop a market from advancing or declining the first time prices hit them. Many times the market will go through the angles, if the wave pattern is not complete. If you don't understand wave pattern, you will not be able to effectively use the Gann angles. In this couse we will explain using wave patterns in a later chapter.

2 X 1 ANGLE (63 3/4 DEGREE)

The 2 x 1 angle is the second most important angle. It divides the space between the 45 degree angle and 90 degree angle. When a market is above this uptrending angle, it is in very strong position. If the market breaks this angle, then it will fall to the 45 degree angle.

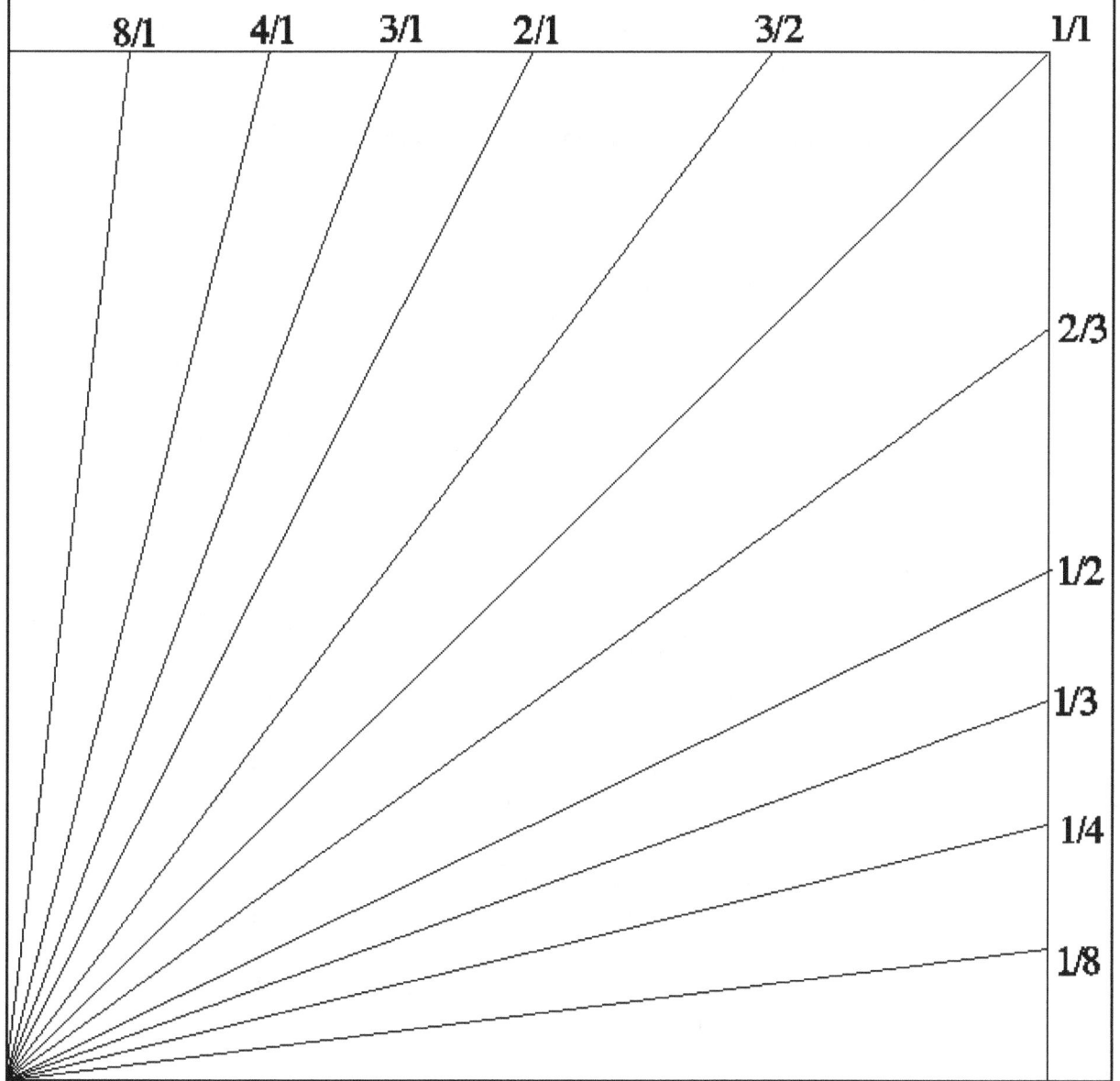

EXHIBIT 6.1 Geometric angles

4 X 1 ANGLE (75 DEGREE)
When the market is above this uptrend steep angle, it is the very strong. This is many times the angle that blows off on and which you can make tremendous amounts of money with. The move that starts off from these angles usually comes from important major time cycles that hit the market. When the market breaks below this angle, then it will go to the next lower angle.

8 X 1 ANGLE (82 1/2 DEGREE)
When the market is above this angle, it is in a very strong position. It rarely happens on the daily chart, but more likely on weekly or monthly charts. When the market breaks below this angle, then it will go the 4 x 1 angle.

16 X 1 ANGLE (86 1/4 DEGREE)
The very steep angle is usually apparent only on weekly or monthly charts. For example in corn the market must rise 16 cents per week on a weekly chart or 16 cents per month on a monthly chart. Of course, as we have said before when this angle is broken, it will decline to the next lower angle the 8 x 1.

3 X 1 ANGLE (71 1/4 DEGREE) AND THE 3 X 2 ANGLE (54 3/8 DEGREE)
These are important angles to use on long term weekly and monthly charts after a market has been in a uptrend for a very long period of time. After the trend has been in duration for a long period of time and breaks these angles, the long term trend should change.

Note: The above angles are the ones you use when the market is above the 45 degree angle. When the market drops below the 45 degree angle, you use the next set of angles.

WHEN TO DRAW DAILY ANGLES
When do you draw the angles on the chart? You draw them only after the market has been in a downtrend for at least 3 days and then the market has a three day rally making higher tops and bottoms. The first angle you draw is the 1 x 1. You next draw the 2 x 1 and then the 4 x 1. If the market stays above the 4 x 1, it will accelerate. If the market breaks the 1 x 1 then you should be begin using the bear angles below the 1 x 1.

WHEN TO DRAW WEEKLY AND MONTHLY ANGLES
On the weekly and monthly charts you draw the 1 x 1 and 2 x 1 angles after the market has been in a down trend for at least 3 weeks or months and makes higher highs and lows for at least 2 weeks or months. Also use the 1/3 and 2/3 on the longer term charts.

DRAWING BEAR ANGLES

After the market makes a top using some of the rules for tops, which you will learn in this course, and it breaks the 1 x 1 angle, you start using the next angles down which are the bear angles. The first angle down from the 1 x 1 is the 1 x 2 (26 1/2 degree). When prices drop to this angle the market will bounce off this angle and hold it for a while, however when the price eventually breaks it will go to the next angle down.

4 X 1 ANGLE (15 DEGREE)

The next angle down of support is the 4 x 1 (15 degree). When prices hit this angle they will again rally, but eventually when the angle is broken prices will drop to the next angle.

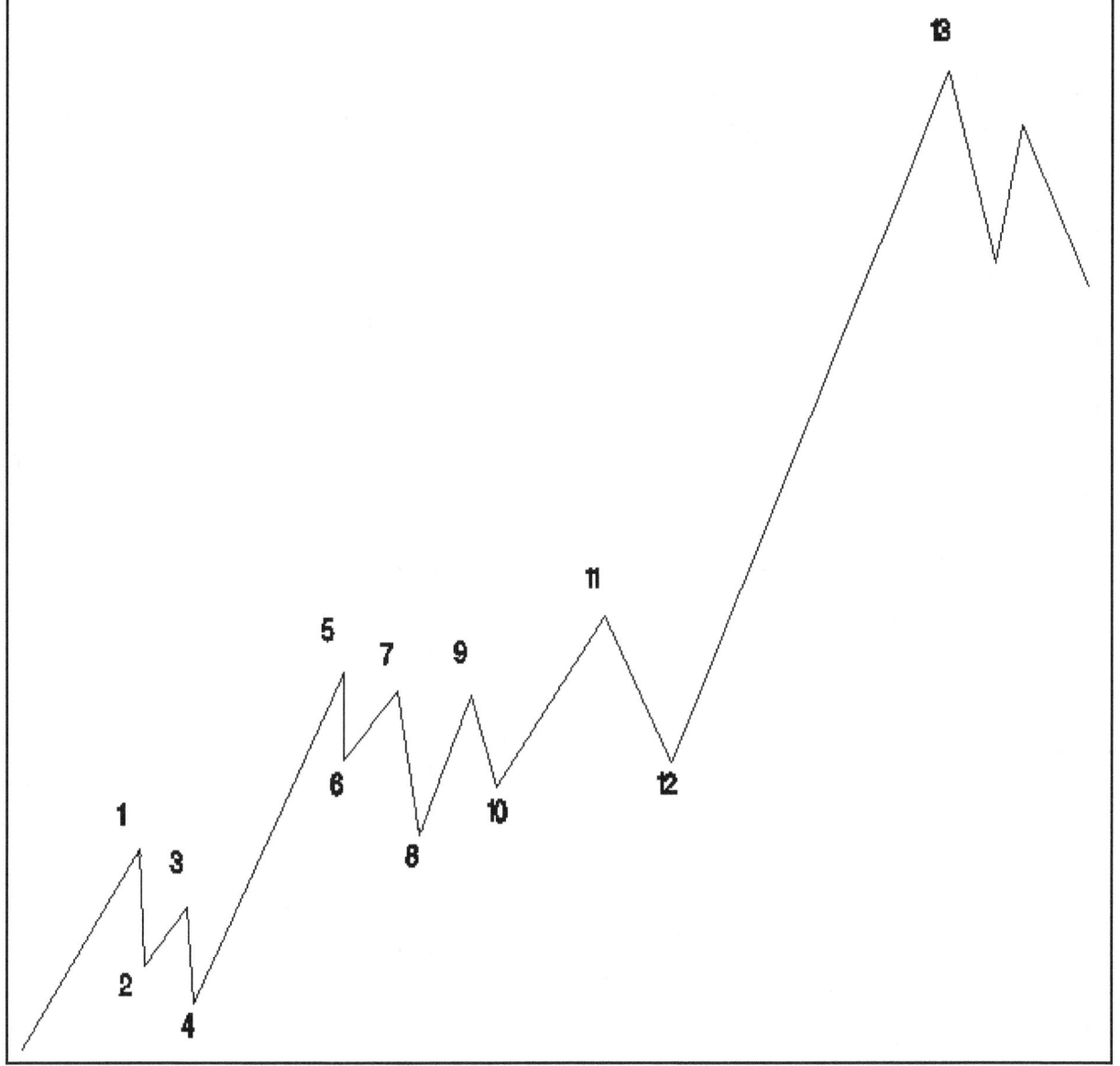

EXHIBIT 6.2 - Swings of a bull market

8 X 1 ANGLE (7 1/2 DEGREE)

Then next angle of support is the 8 x 1 (7 1/2). This is very often a very important angle of support. After a market has had a long term downtrend this angle is many times the angle that turns the market around back to an uptrend. This angle is very important to use with weekly and monthly charts.

1 X 16 ANGLE (3 3/4 DEGREE)

The next angle of importance is the 1 x 16 (3 3/4 degree). When this angle is hit there is usually a small bounce as the market is in a weak position.

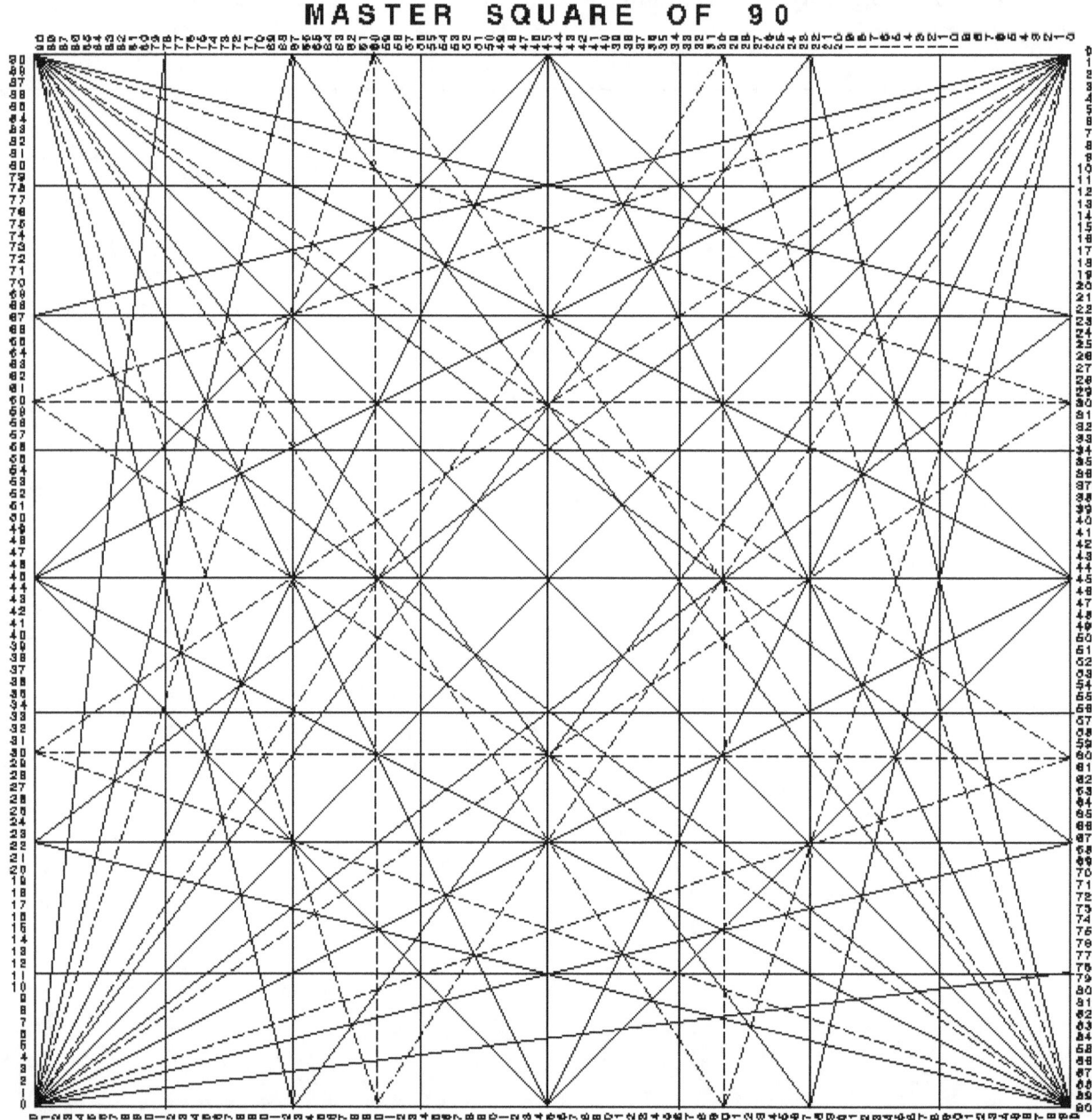

EXHIBIT 6.3 - The square of 90

3 X 1 ANGLE (18 3/4 DEGREE) AND 3 X 2 ANGLE (35 3/4 DEGREE)
The 3 x 1 (18 3/4) and the 3 x 2 (35 3/4 degree) angles are very important to use on long term charts such as weekly and monthly charts. When you begin using this angle on the long term charts you will see it's importance as a timing angle.

WHEN TO USE BEAR ANGLES
After the market has made a top using the rules of this course and has broken a previous bottom and has declined for 3 days, weeks or months, you can begin drawing the downtrend bear angles.

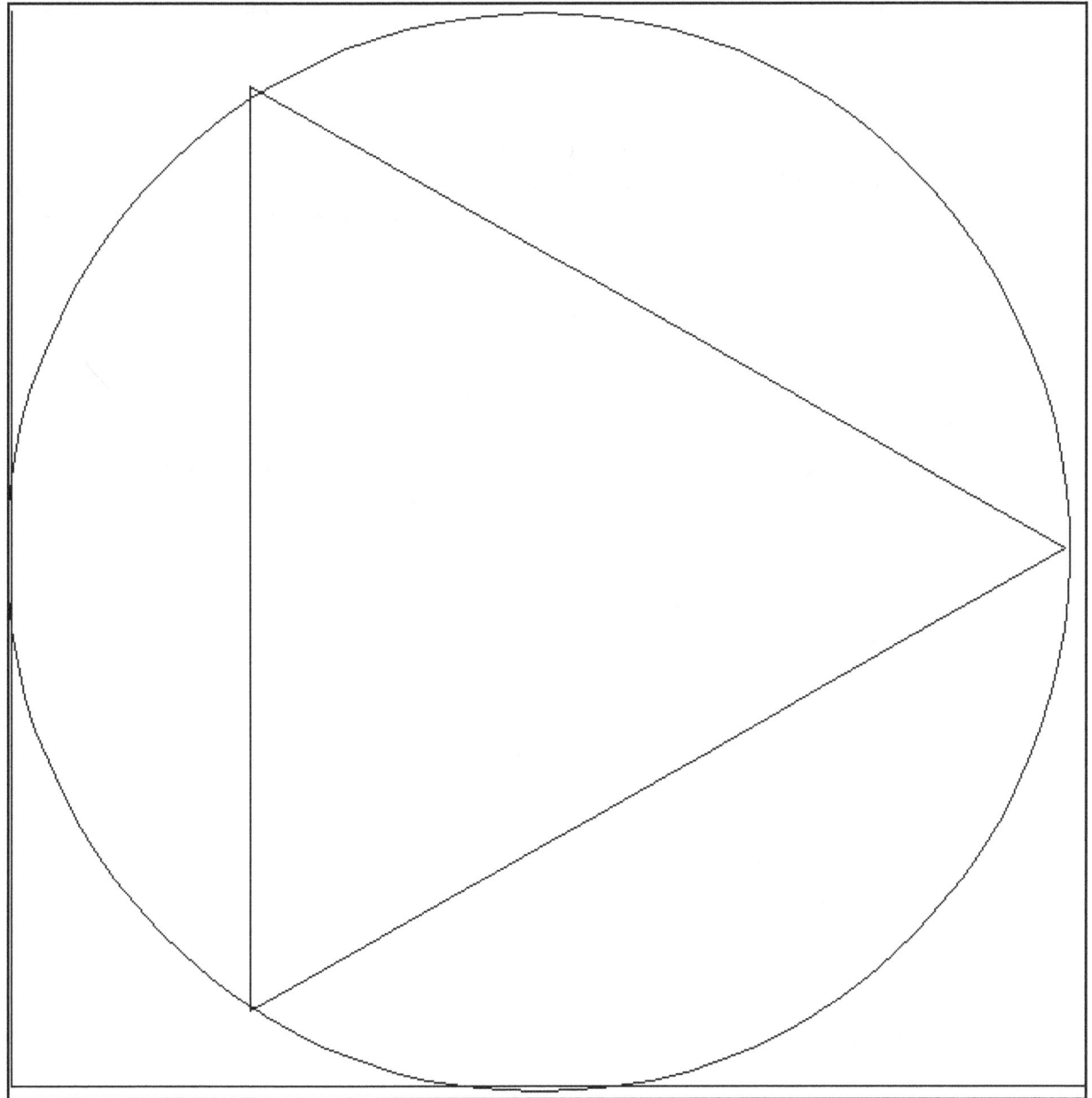

EXHIBIT 6.4 - Three basic shapes

START WITH 1 X 1
Start by drawing the 1 x 1 downtrend angle. When the market is below this angle, it is in a very weak position.

THEN USE OTHER BEAR ANGLES
When the market is below the 1 x 1 down trending angle you can use many of the other bear angles below the 1 x 1.

UNDER THE 2 X 1
The market is in the weak position when it is under the 2 x 1 angle. That means it loses $200 in gold per day, week or month. The next weakest position is when it is below the 4 x 1 angle and the next weakest position is when it is below the 8 x 1 angle.

GAPPING ABOVE THE 2 X 1 ANGLE
When the market is in a downtrend and crosses the 2 x 1 angle to the upside, especially by gapping, it indicates it is in a stronger position and it has a chance to rally. This, of course depends on how long of a downtrend the market has been in.

MOVING ABOVE THE 1 X 1 ANGLES
When the market has been in a long trend downtrend and finally crosses the 1 x 1 angle it indicates that the market has changed it's direction. When the market has rallied at least 3 days on a daily chart, 3 weeks on a weekly chart and 3 months on a monthly chart, you can begin drawing uptrending bull angles on the chart again. The market is beginning to change into a bull market.

APPROACHING THE 2 X 1 ANGLE
After the 1 x 1 angle has been crossed, the first downtrending angle to draw is the 2 x 1. Crossing this angle puts the market in a stronger position.

NEXT HIGH ANGLE IS THE 4 X 1
The next angle to draw is the 4 x 1.

NEXT ANGLE IS THE 8 X 1
The next angle to draw is the 8 x 1.

WHEN TO DRAW BULL ANGLES
When the market has crossed the 1 x 1 and rallied to the 2 x 1, it will run into selling and back off. When it gets up through the 4 x 1 and the 8 x 1 finally, it means the market is in very strong position once again. You should now draw the bull angles up from the bottom.

3 X 1 AND 3 X 2 ANGLES ON WEEKLY AND MONTHLY CHARTS

Keep in mind always to watch the 3 x 1 and the 3 x 2 angles on long term charts. When this angle is crossed many times the long term market direction has changed.

PRACTICE WITH ANGLES

Practice with all of these geometric angles over and over again. Knowing how to put these angles on your charts will tell you the position of the market at all times. The 1 x 1 angles should be put on all previous major highs and lows. The 1 x 1 should be drawn on all zero points. This means if the market either reaches a major low or a major high on a certain date a 1 x 1 angle should be drawn on 0 all the way up the chart. This angle can be calculated mathematically by figuring out where the angle will be coming up from so you don't have to have a chart going down to the point of 0. Also remember, for geometric angles to work effectively, you must know the wave position of the market. That is the secret as to when the market will stop on any one particular angle. To show you how important geometric angels are, we have constructed a Gann style monthly chart on December corn. That means we are taking December Corn from every year and linking them together. You cannot use the continuation charts put out by all the chart services. You must use charts created either by MAX:CHART or GannTrader for this to work. This chart is long term and started back in 1969. It is set up on the scale of 2 cents per grid, or $100 per grid. We also set the division point at 1.20. This means that we know a major division line rests on one of the important major circle numbers 1.20. You should determine what major circle number is close to the commodity or stock you are studying. This represents a major resistance and support line. Now lets look at the chart.

DRAW FIXED NUMBER LINES

The first thing to do is draw the major circle division horizontal lines on the chart. These again are the numbers that can be divided by the circle. In this case we used the numbers of (1) 1.20. Notice how these 120 numbers divide the chart range into 3 equal parts. See the divisions on the charts and how the corn market breaks on these important lines. You can also divide the chart up into 60 square intervals which would give us the additional numbers of (5) 1.80, (6) 2.40 and (7)3.60. I have drawn these lines with dashes to distinguish them from the 45 square lines. All of these lines are fixed numbers and are very important.

DRAW TOP AND BOTTOM OF RANGE LINES

You should also draw horizontal lines for both the top of the range 4.00 and the bottom of the range (9) 1.12. All major and minor angles will square when they intersect these lines.

DRAW ALL 1 X 1 ANGLES

The next thing to do is to draw all 1 x 1 angles from all major tops and bottoms. When the market makes a bottom or top, you can draw the following angles.

a) Draw the first 1 x 1 angle from the top or bottom on the exact price point.

b) If it is either a high or low you can draw a zero point 1 x 1 angle from the bottom. To do this you must calculate where the angle must come up at the base line. Therefore on the first low that based at 1.12, the zero 1 x 1 angle line comes up off the base line over to the right 112 spaces.

c) If it is a low you can draw a 1 x 1 angle from the top of the range down to the bottom of the range.

d) If it is a high you can draw a 1 x 1 angle from the bottom of the range up to the top of the range.

e) Draw 1 x 1 angle up and down from the midpoint under the high or low.

f) All angles can bounce off the top or the bottom of the total range.

When these angles hit either the top or bottom of the range, or midpoints of ranges, the midpoint of the entire range, or if they intersect each other, price and time will square and the market will reverse.

Now let's get into the real drawing of the 1 x 1 angles. Lets draw all the 1 x 1 angle types off of the following major highs and lows:

10) from the low of 1.12 of Mar. 1969.
11) from the low of 1.12 of Sept. 1971
12) from 3rd wave high of 3.33 on Aug 1973
13) from the 5th wave high of 4.00 on Oct. 1974
14) from the C wave bottom of 1.90 on Aug 1977
15) from the 3rd wave high of 3.29 Jul. 1979
16) from the 5th wave high of 3.96 on Apr 1981
17) from the C wave bottom of 2.14 on Oct 1982
18) from the C wave top of 3.76 on Aug 1983
19) from the 5th wave bottom of 1.51 on Dec 1987

DEC CORN EXAMPLE

Now lets explain what you see on this chart. Almost every time a major range low angle ran up to the top or the opposite a high range angle line ran down to the bottom, a major yearly cycle high or low occurred.

When ever two cycle lines intersected there was a major cycle change. Also where two cycle lines intersected became temporary support or resistance.

The high of the range of this market is 4.00 and the low of the range is 1.12. The total range of this market is 144 squares or $1440 dollars. Dividing the range by 2 gave the center of gravity of this market - 2.54. You can see how the market oscillated around this key line.

When an angle rose and price was above it, gave support to the market declines and when an angle fell and price was below it, gave resistance to the market rallies.

Geometric angles will hold only when the 5th, 3rd or C wave of a market is complete. If the wave pattern is not complete, then the angle will eventually break. This is why so many people lose money trading the Gann angles. They do not know what they are doing. If the market is falling and it lands on the 1 x 1 angle and it is only in its 3rd wave down of a 5th wave move, it may bounce off the 1 x 1, but on the next down it will penetrate the angle and go to the next angle until the market completes the fifth wave down. When the market does complete the 5th wave, then and only then can you look for the nearest Gann angle for support. This is one of Gann's secrets, which he failed to reveal in his courses. You must know not only the Gann angles, but also know where in the wave pattern you are. This tells you the direction of the market. The Gann methods only tell time and price support points.

The geometric angles from major highs and lows are very important as you can see on the monthly Corn chart in this chapter, Exhibit 3.5. Every timing low or high and all resistance levels are the result of these geometric angles. They are so important that you must super impose these important geometric angles on your weekly, daily and even hourly charts. These are the real angles that the market trades on, and you must know where they are on all of your charts. In the December corn chart the market moves $100 per month on a 1 x 1 angle or $1200 per year. On a weekly chart the same angle is moving at $1200/52 or $23.04 per week. On a daily chart the market is moving at $1200 / (52 weeks x 5 trading days - 8 holidays) or $4.76 per day.

Follow the chart from the beginning and you will see how time and price squares with the Gann geometric angles.

1) The first 1 x 1 angle from the low of 1.12 on Mar. 1969 squared with the top of the range exactly between the time of the major double top of 1980.

2) The second 1 x 1 angle from the double bottom of 1.12 of Sept. 1971 squared with the range top two months from the timing high of 1983.

3) The first 1 x 1 angle from the low of 1.12 hit the midpoint of the range at 2.54 and this was the timing low of 1975.

4) The second 1 x 1 angle from the low of 1.12 hit the midpoint of the range at 2.54 and this was the timing high of 1976.

5) The 1 x 1 angle off the 3rd wave high in 1973 came down from the top and hit the range low which was the exact timing low of 1982.

6) The fifth wave high of 1974 came down hit the range low which was the timing low of 1986.

If you continue to look at the angles, you will find that almost all major highs and lows were the result of either an angle hitting the range top or bottom or intersecting with another angle.

REPEAT CYCLES OF THE MARKET
As you learned in this chapter the market repeats every six years, months, weeks or days. In this case let's break it down into every three years. Lets look at the repetitions (Remember the market can invert some years - in other words the market makes make a major high instead of a low):

    20) Major low 1971
    21) Major high 1974
    22) Major low 1977

LENGTH OF THE MARKET
Now lets look at the length of the market:
    1) From 1969 we went into a 1, 2, 3, 4, 5 up to the top of 1974.
    2) From the low of 1974 we went into an a, b, c down to 1977.
    3) From 1977 we went into an a, b, c bear market rally into the top in 1980.
    4) From the top of 1980 we went into another a, b, c pattern down to 1982.
    5) From the low of 1982 we went into another a, b, c rally up to the top in 1983.
    6) From the top of 1983 we went down in a 1, 2, 3, 4, 5 down to the low of 1986.

Gann Masters 53

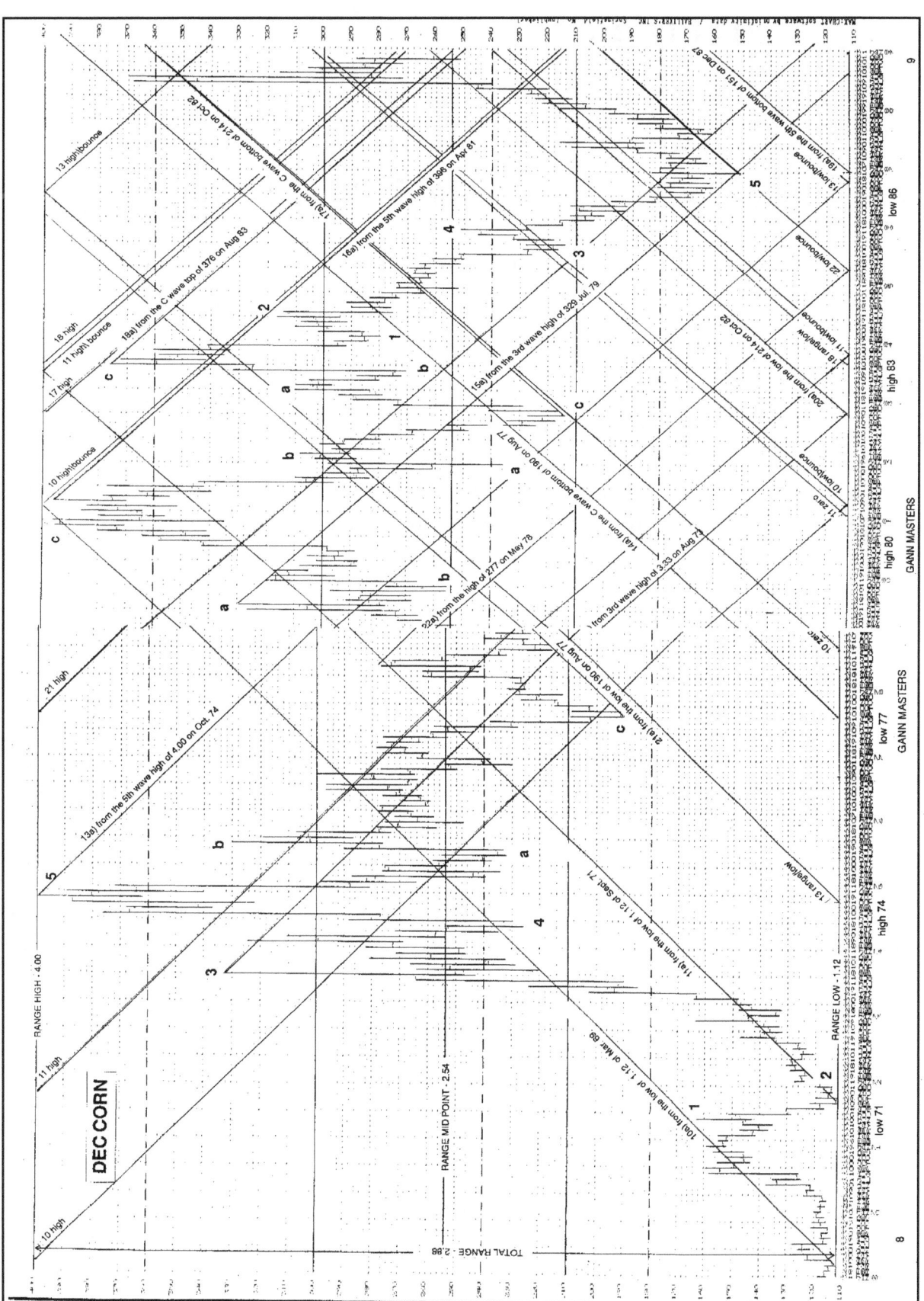

EXHIBIT 6.5 - Dec corn example

CHAPTER 7

ELLIOTT WAVE THEORY

••

Elliott waves should be a necessary part of your overall trading method.

The Elliott Wave Theory uses a very complicated set of rules that are subject to change anytime. You will find that very few Elliott wave traders can ever agree on what wave pattern they are in, until it's all over. Two Elliott wave technicians can look at a chart and both of them can see two different patterns. This is perhaps why Gann did not get into the complex reading of waves. He did, however, understand simple waves and how to read and use them with his time and price points. This chapter expalins a practical way to use the Elliott Wave Theory in conjunction with other Gann time and price points.

About 50% of the Elliott Wave techniques are simple and clear and the other 50% are complex, too difficult and subject to differing interpretation among Elliott wave technicians. For the Gann trader, the best approach is to use the 50% that are simple and clear. Elliott waves should be a necessary part of your overall trading method. Gann time and price points tell you where the market has been and were it is going. The Elliott Wave Theory tells you where you are on the road map. It can be used very nicely in conjunction with the other Gann time and price points. The Elliott Wave Theory used alone, will get traders into big trouble as they are constantly relabeling waves to fit the pattern that they currently see. The Elliott wave approach we recommend will work most of the time in conjunction with other Gann rules and help to put the whole puzzle together as to where you are in the overall trading structure of the market.

USING GANN RATIOS
There are actually two types of ratios that can be used with the waves. They can be Fibonacci or Gann ratios. You should check the market you are trading in to determine which of the two types of ratios the market is best working with. The following is a listing of the differences in the ratios. Gann ratios are determined by basically dividing full numbers into halves and thirds as far down as you need to. Here are the ratios used: Divide the number by 2 or 4 or 8 or 16 and divide by 3 or 6 or 12. By doing this we get the following as

compared to the Fibonacci ratios used by most Elliott wave traders:

BASIC RATIO DIFFERENCES
Gann .25 - .33 - .50 - .66 - .75 - 1.00 - 1.25 - 1.33 etc.
Fibonacci .382 - .618 - 1.00 - 1.382 - 1.50 - 1.618 etc.

As you can see the Gann ratios are very similar to the Fibonacci ratios used by Elliott wave traders.

TWO BASIC WAVES
Elliott waves can be classified into two basic parts (See Exhibit 7.1):

1) The impulse pattern that is in the main direction of the market that ends at a Gann time and price level

1) The corrective pattern that the market will retrace to some important Gann time and price point.

THE IMPULSE PATTERN
Impulse patterns consist of usually five waves in the main direction of the market. That main direction of the market can be either up or down.

1) The first wave of an impulse move is usually not very strong as traders are unsure of where they are in the market.

2) After the first wave runs up to the top of wave 1, it will pull back usually very quickly and violently and test the bottom and hold without making a new low. This is wave 2. Traders are still bearish and are short and thinking the market is still going lower. Some may even add to their shorts.

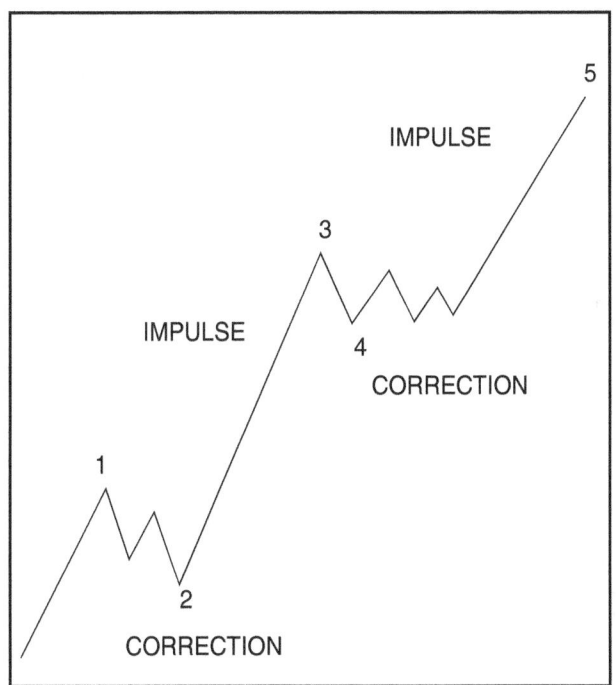

EXHIBIT 7.1 Impulse/Correction

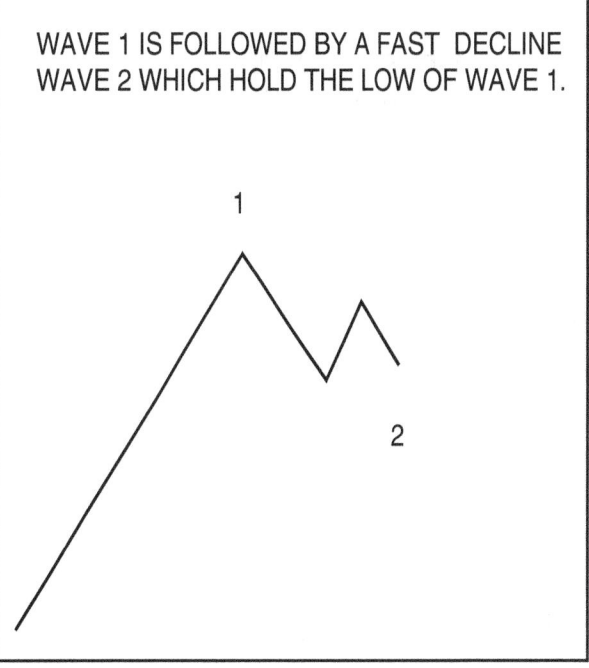

EXHIBIT 7.2 Wave 2

Most short traders will now have their stops above wave 1.

3) The beginning rally of wave 3 is usually very slow and will finally make it up to the top of wave 1. Traders are still bearish and many have added to their short positions. There are a large amount of stops above wave 1. The rally of wave 3 continues and pushes above wave 1 where there are a tremendous number of stops. When these stops are hit the market explodes and many times gaps up because of order imbalances. The gaps are a main indication that you are in wave 3. The volume increases and many other traders get on the bandwagon and start to buy. Traders that were long at the bottom start to add to positions. Traders that were short that got stopped out decide that market is also going higher and they take long positions. At this time, the majority of traders are now long and the market is in a main trend up. Wave 3 is always longer than at least one of the waves 1 or 2 and it can never be the shortest wave of the three.

4) Finally the buying of wave 3 starts to subside and profit taking starts to come in. Traders who were long at the bottom decide to take profits, or they might put in close stops to protect their profits. This causes a general orderly pull back which is wave 4. Notice the differences between the wave 2 pull back and wave 4 pull back. Wave 2 was fast and violent and wave 4 was orderly. Gann knew what wave the market was in, because of the wave's characteristics. Most traders are still bullish in wave 4 and many take this opportunity to add to their positions and many that missed the entire move, decide to enter the market in wave 4. Wave 4 should never come down under the peak of wave 1 in cash markets, but it can come down 10 - 20% under wave 1 in futures markets, because of car-

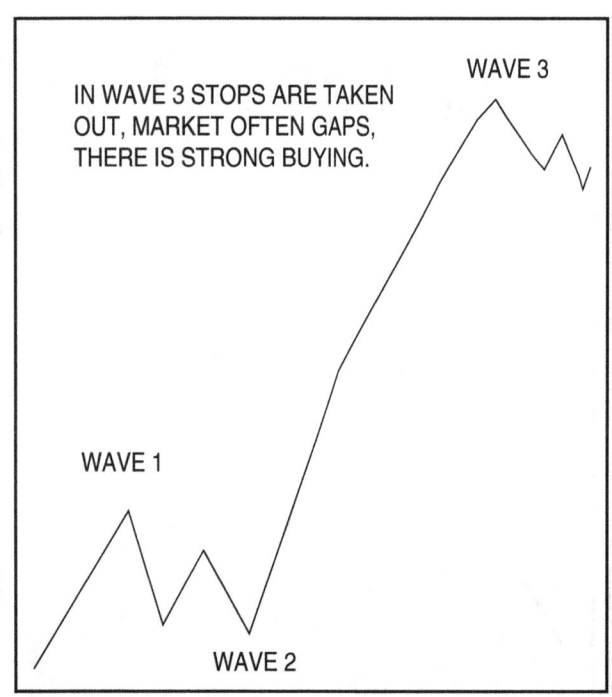

EXHIBIT 7.3 Wave 3

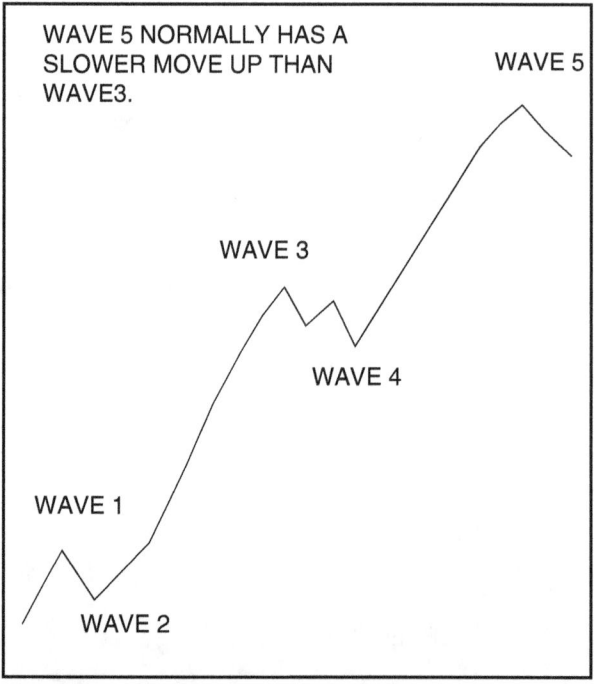

EXHIBIT 7.4 Wave 5

rying and storage charges.

5) The market now starts up in its wave 5. It does not have the power that wave 3 had because of the stop buying and new initial longs being taken. When the market hits the top of wave 3, it usually goes through, but not with a lot of enthusiasm. The rally is very lackluster. The prices make a new high and that is the top of wave 5 and the market tops out.

CORRECTION PATTERNS

Correction patterns usually consist of three waves. They come in two different categories: the simple correction and the complex correction. If wave 2 is a simple correction then expect wave 4 to be a complex correction. If wave 4 is a simple correction then expect wave 2 to be a complex correction.

THE SIMPLE CORRECTION

The simple correction that which has only one pattern which is the zigzag correction. This is an a, b, c correction. Wave b will correct 1/2 - 3/4 of wave a. If it exceeds that correction then it is not a simple correction, but a complex correction. Wave a will always have a 5 wave pattern in the direction of the correction. Wave c will go below wave a. Wave c will be equal to wave a or 1.5 to 2.5 times of wave a. The way to know if you are in a zigzag correction is to determine if wave a has a five wave pattern.

THE COMPLEX CORRECTION

The complex pattern consists of three different patterns:
    a) The flat correction where each wave is equal in length

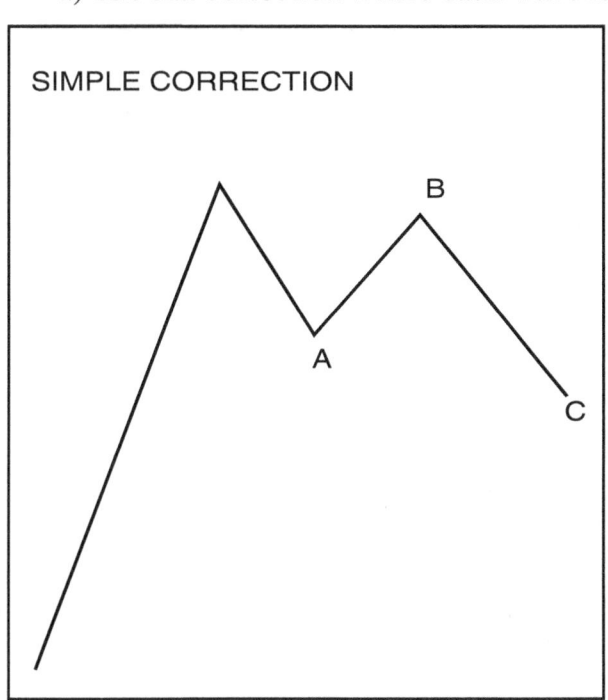

EXHIBIT 7.5 Simple correction

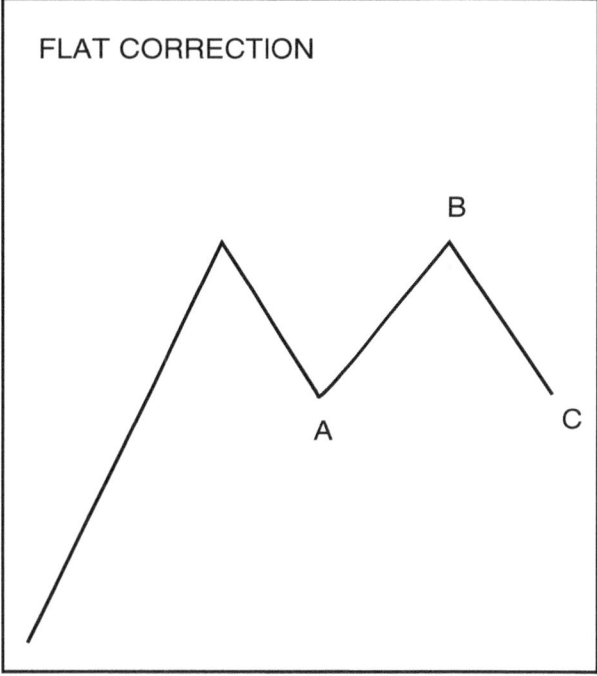

EXHIBIT 7.6 Flat correction

b) The irregular correction where wave b makes new high then drops to the beginning of wave a or below it. Wave b equals 1.125 - 1.25 of wave a. Wave c equals 1.5 - 2.5 of wave a.

c) The triangle is where there are 5 subwaves of a, b, c, d, and e in the correction. Triangles are usually associated with wave 4. When the market breaks out of the triangle, it usually does it with a big thrust in the same direction as wave three.

USING WAVE MEASUREMENTS

Wave 1 is the base measurement.
Wave 2 is usually equal to
.25
.33
.50 (most common)
.66
.75
of wave 1
Wave 3 is usually equal to
1.25
1.33
1.5
1.66 (most common)
1.75
2.0
2.5
2.66 (most common)

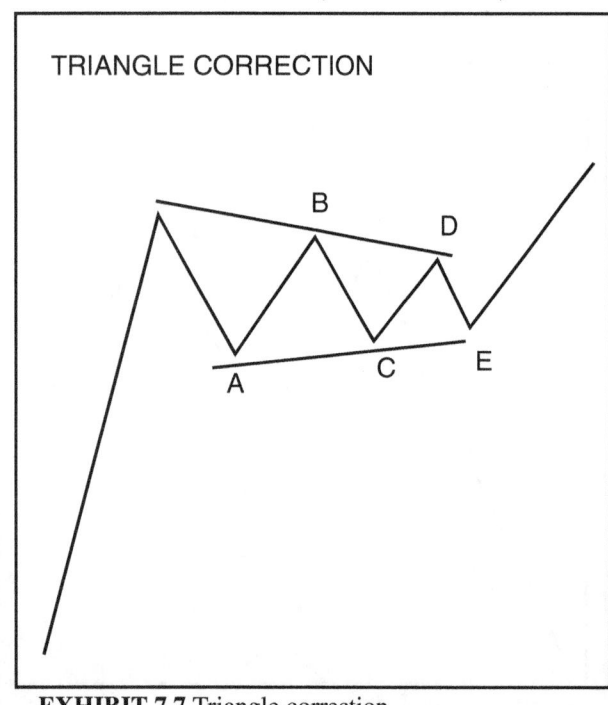

EXHIBIT 7.7 Triangle correction

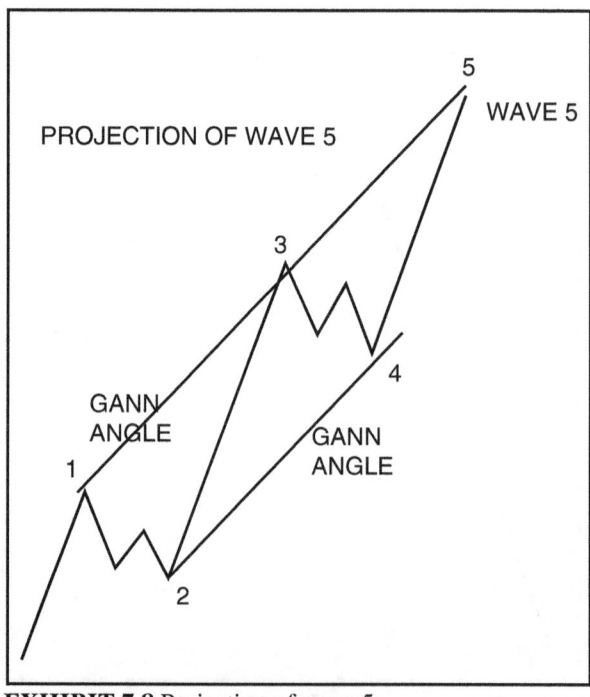

EXHIBIT 7.8 Projection of wave 5

2.75
3.00
3.25
3.33
3.50
3.66
3.75
4.00
4.25 times wave 1
Wave 3 is smaller than wave 1 only 5% of the time
Wave 3 is 1.66 - 1.75 of wave 1 50% of the time
Wave 3 is 1.00 - 1.50 of wave 1 15% of the time
Wave 3 is 1.75 - 2.66 of wave 1 30% of the time
Wave 3 is greater than 2.66 only 8% of the time
Wave 4 is equal to
.25
.33 (most common)
.50 (most common)
.66
.75 of wave 3
Wave 4 is .25 of wave 3 only 15% of the time
Wave 4 is .33 - .50 of wave 3, 60% of the time
Wave 4 is .50 - .66 of wave 3 only 15% of the time
Wave 5 is equal to
1.25
1.33

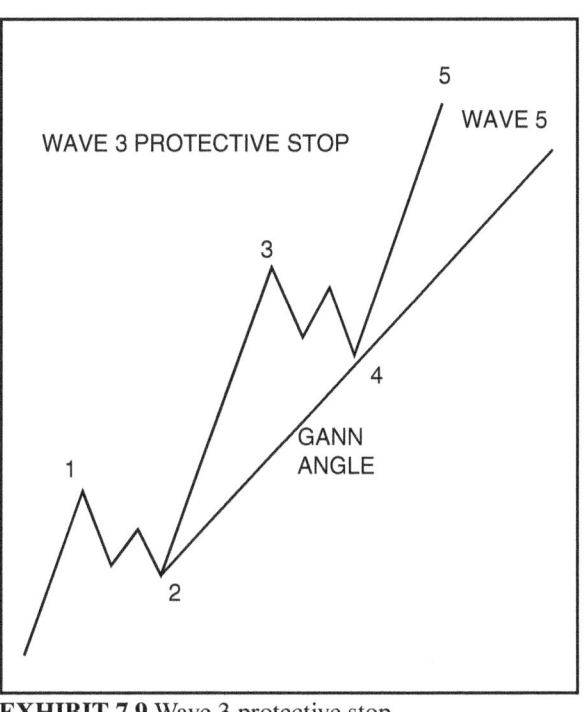

EXHIBIT 7.9 Wave 3 protective stop

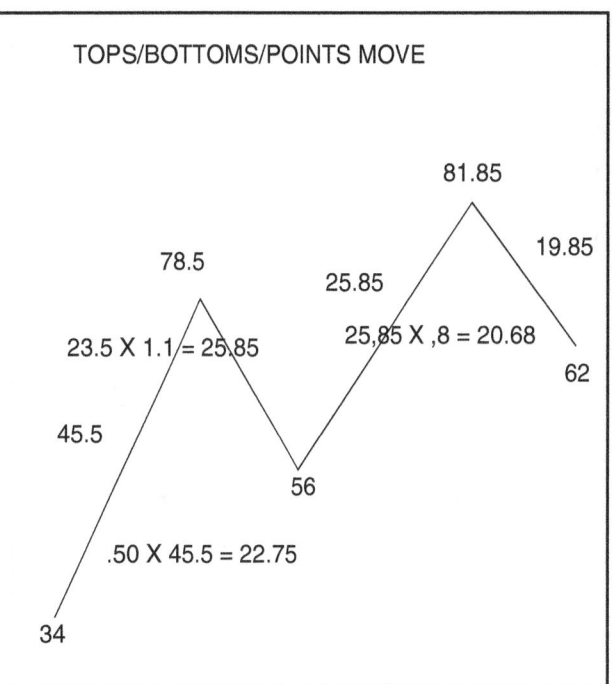

Exhibit 7.10 Tops/bottoms/points move

1.5
1.66 (most common)
1.75
2.0
2.25
2.33
2.50 of wave 1.
When wave 3 is less than 1.75 of wave 5 then wave 5 will equal
.66
.75
1.0 (most common)
1.33
1.5 (most common)
1.66 of the bottom to the top of wave 3.

ANGLE PROJECTION

Gann projection of wave 5. After wave 4 has ended and wave 5 starts draw a Gann angle that connects wave 2 and 4. Now draw that same angles on the top of wave 3 to project the top of wave 5. (See Exhibit 7.8)

If wave 4 breaks key Gann angles or retracement points then the chances of a big 5 wave rally will be slim. How much it breaks determines the strength of wave 5.

You can use Gann angles and retracement levels to protect profits on wave 3 as a stop. (See figure 7.9)

When waves complete themselves on key Gann time and price points you can take action with a trade.

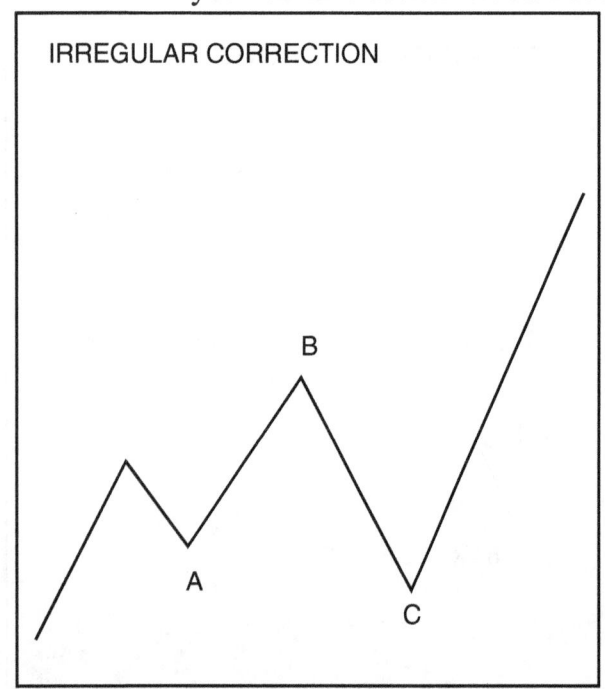

EXHIBIT 7.11 Irregular correction

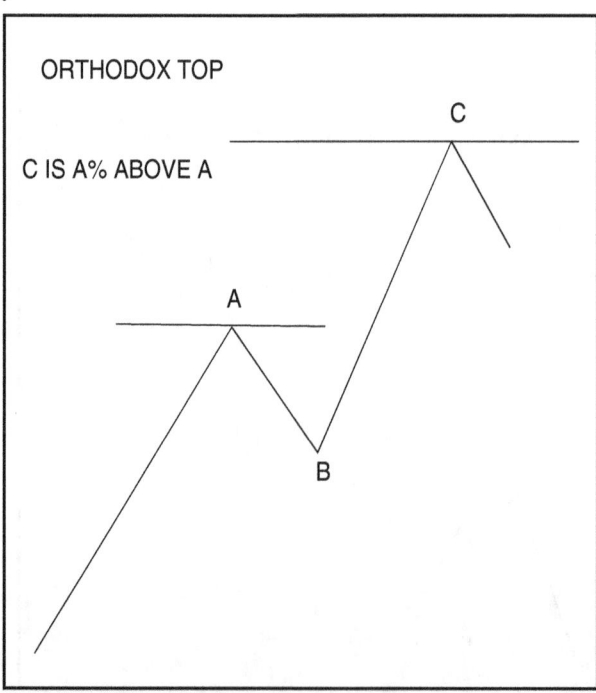

Exhibit 7.12 Orthodox top

It is necessary to look at the monthly, weekly and daily charts to determine where you are in the big picture.

% OF PRIOR WAVE

All waves are a Gann % of the prior wave. For example wave 3 is the following of wave 2 the prior wave:

Ratios to use with short term (3 months) and intermediate wave (3 months - 12 months).

.25
.33
.50
.66
.75
1
1.25
1.33
1.50
1.66
1.75
2.0
2.25
2.33
2.50
2.66
2.75
3.00
3.25
3.33
3.50
etc.

Ratios to use with waves over 12 months:

.10
.20
.30
.40
.50
.60
.70
.80
.90
1.00
1.10
1.20
1.30

1.40
1.50
1.60
1.70
1.80
1.90
2.00

You will find that each stock or commodity has its own characteristics and what ratio it used before, it will use again. Go back and check the records and you will find this statement is true.

ORTHODOX TOP OR BOTTOM

You will find that after a stock or commodity has made its top, many times the market will make an irregular high or low stopping out many traders. In most cases the market will run a certain percent above the prior wave. These are for short and intermediate term waves:

4%
6%
8%
10%
12%
14%
16%
18%
20%
22%
24%
26%
28%

Each market will have it own characteristics, check back on past records to see that the market has done before.

For long term waves use
1%
2%
3%
4%
5%
6%
7%
8%
9%

Check back on a certain market to see what it has done before to find its normal orthodox percentage move of the prior wave.

USING EXTREME HIGHS AND LOWS
It is important that you use the extreme highs and lows in calculating all moves. Do not use closes as many Elliott wave technicians do. Gann always used the exact extreme high or low to calculate the correct move.

ELLIOTT WAVE EXAMPLE - DEC 91 CORN
Now lets look at an example which is the Dec Corn Exhibit 7.13. The market topped out in the beginning of March and began to fall. Wave 1 moved down approximately 15 cents. Each square equals one cent of corn in this example or $50.00. The market bottomed out on the bottom of wave 1 down and then had a violent move up. This meant that traders that were long felt that the market would go up. They bought and added to long positions. They put sell stops below wave 1 bottom. The market did not make a new high and then started to falter. That was an indication the market might fall. Since wave 2 rallied more than 75% of wave one, it had to be an complex correction. What actually developed was a flat wave pattern. All waves being equal. The market quietly declined until it hit the bottom of wave 1. When it got through wave 1, the market gapped down two different times with extreme weakness, indicating long were getting stopped out and other people were shorting. Even the longs that got stopped out started to short to get their money back. The market declined quickly. It dropped 26 cents to the bottom of wave 3. This equaled 1.75 of wave 1, the most popular count of wave three. The market then went into a simple correction since wave 2 was a complex correction earlier on. After the ABC correction completed itself, corn then dropped to new lows down to wave 5 to make a bottom. Since wave 3 is less than 1.75 of wave 5 then wave 5 will probably equal 100% of the top to the bottom of wave 3 which was 28. Actual count of wave 5 was 30 cents.

In this example a protective stop for shorts could be placed above the 3 X 1 line coming off the top of wave 2. The 1 x 3 coming off of the exact top also restricts the wave 4 rally. The 2 x 1 coming off the bottom of wave 1 and wave 3 also tells where the wave 5 objective was.

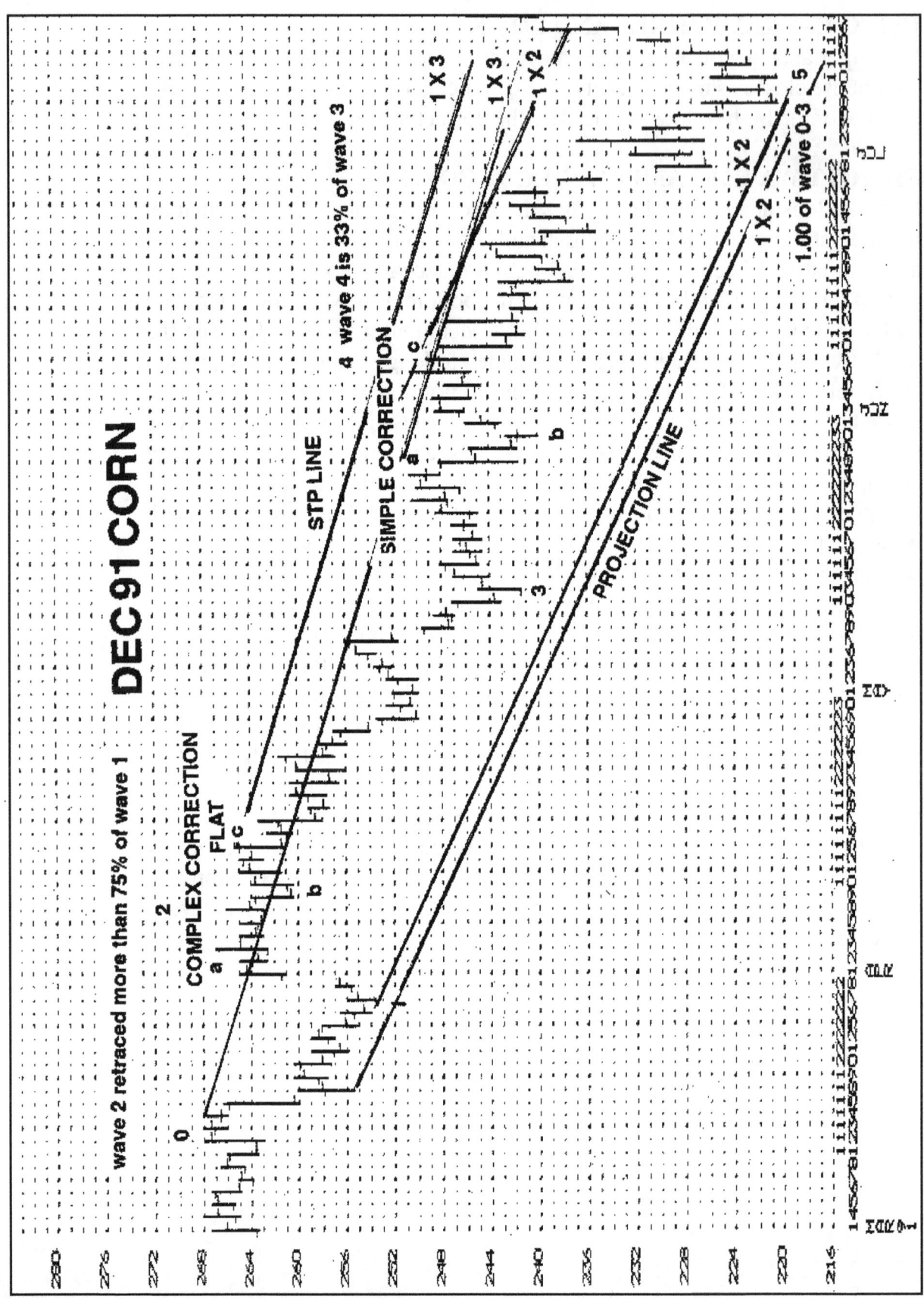

EXHIBIT 7.13 Dec 91 corn example

CHAPTER 8

THE TIME FACTOR

Gann said that time is the most important factor.

The most important factor in determining market movements is time. Time tells the trader when the market stops its trend and goes the other direction. If you know the time changes in the markets, your chances of success will be increased many times.

All time is determined from the circle of 360 degrees:

Divide the circle by 4 parts and you get:
360
270
180
90

You can break these numbers down even further:
45
22.5
11.25

Divide the circle by 3 parts and you get:
360
240
120

You can break these numbers down even further:
60
30
15
7
3.5

3 Times the odd and even numbers and doubling them is very important. Take 3 x 3 (the odd low number) and double them to get the following important numbers:

9
18
36
72
144
288

Take 3 x 4 (the even low number) and double them to get the following important numbers:
12
24
48
96
192

The number 9 is very important as it is the number that ends your count before you start over, see the following:
1 2 3 4 5 6 7 8 9
add 1 to get the next set
10 11 12 13 14 15 16 17 18 19

The number 7 is also very important. Many counts start over after the number 7. Also the following multiples of the number 7 are important:
7
14
21
28
35
42
49 very important

Minor time trend changes will therefore occur every:
3.5, 7, 9, 11.25, 14 15, 18, 21, 22.5, 24, 28, 30, 35, 36, 42, 45, 48, 49, 54, 60, 72, 90, and 96 days

Intermediate time trend changes will therefore occur every: 120, 144, 180, 240, 270, 288 and 360 days.

Long term time trend changes occur every 3.5, 7, 11.25, 15, 22.5, 30, 45, 60, and 90 years.

BUILT UP FORCES
If a market moves sideways for several months the accumulated force of volume will push the market rapidly to catch price up with time. Watch carefully for breakouts out of long sideways ranges. When markets breakout they will often run up to 49 days rapidly in one direction.

HARMONICS
When you find what long term time cycle a commodity is working in you can easily see the harmonics of the moves. For example on a 90 year cycle every 9 years will give a good harmonic high or low. On a 60 year cycle every 6 years will give a good harmonic high or low. This is another check to see what time cycle you are really in.

Check back on the harmonic time cycle years to determine what the market might do today. For example, if you are following a 90 year cycle, pull up charts every 9 years back, to see what the market did in the past on these harmonic years. Many times the market will make an exact high or low on the exact date of the prior year.

MONTHLY MOVES
Markets often move on the basis of one year. Therefore it is important to watch divisions of the year. Divide the year into 4 parts. Watch for changes on the end of 3 months, 6 months, 9 months and 12 months. Many changes occur between the 9 and 12 month period.

PRICES MOVE FASTER THE HIGHER THEY GO
As prices get higher, they will move faster and faster and have wider swings. When prices drop to new lows, they will have lower volume and smaller ranges. If you look at the circle charts in a later chapter and the angles that extend out from the center, you will notice that prices have wider swings between the angles as you go out from the center.

CHANGES IN TREND
The trend of a market is determined by three different factors either by breaking angles, tops or bottoms. When these are broken important time factors should be nearing their end. When a daily point is broken the market will often move 3 to 10 days. When a weekly market is broken the market will often move only 3 weeks. When a monthly trend is broken the market will move at least 3 months. When a yearly trend is broken the market may move up to 3 years in the other direction.

LOST MOTION
When a market is very slow, it may not have enough motion to get to a time and price point. On the other hand when a market is very fast, it will exceed the time and price points temporarily.

MARKET IN STRONGEST OR WEAKEST POSITION
The market is in its strongest position when its price equals the square of its time. When the market tops at 54 and drops 54 days, 54 weeks or 54 months it will square itself. You can expect the market to reverse if it stops at that level and moves sideways for 3 to 4 days and goes the other way. When the market gets above the square price and does so with velocity you can expect a big move in the same direction. If you use trend lines which are created as time lines, they will tell you what position the market is in. If you have the market set up in a perfect dollar ratio, for example 1 square = $10, 100, 1000 etc. then the 45 degree angle when broken will indicate a major change of trend.

LIFE OF THE CONTRACT
When you know the exact life of a futures contract you can also break that cycle up into odd and even numbers. You will find important time changes occur during the intermediate divisions of a contract.

DIVISIONS OF THREE, FIVE AND SEVEN
The third, fifth and seventh period of anything very often is a major trend change and the market goes the other way. Watch carefully for 3, 5 or 7 days, 3, 5 or 7 weeks, 3, 5 or 7 months or 3, 5, or 7 years. When a market has moved up quite a lot and slows down watch for the 3,5 or 7 day for a change in trend.

OVERBALANCING OF TIME AND SPACE MOVEMENTS
Time and space movements can be used in conjunction with time factors to determine changes in trend. For an example of space movement - when a contract of corn has been dropping 14 cents on prior reactions and this reaction it drops 20 cents, look for a change of trend. For an example of time movements - when a contract of corn has been dropping 12 days on prior reactions and this time it drops 23 days, look for a change of trend. These changes are very important to watch. They can give you an early warning signal that a change in trend is beginning to happen.

SQUARE OF SPACE AND TIME
When the market goes up 30 cents in corn in 30 days then the market has squared itself. The squaring of a time or bottom when using the odd and even circle numbers will many times indicate a major change of a time cycle.

DURATION OF TIME MOVEMENTS
Go back and check how long a market normally moves. For example, some markets make a practice of moving at least 5 months. You can break the normal movement of a market into 4 parts to determining when it might end. The fastest part of the move will begin in the 3 or 4 section.

GEOMETRIC ANGLES
Geometric angles will tell you what time cycle the market is moving in. When a market breaks an important angle the market will start a new time cycle. It is important to note that the new time cycle may start a different time than the one ending.

CYCLES OF THE MARKET
Check back on the market you are studying it to see what cycles it normally trades in. What cycles it has been trading in will be the same as today. These numbers give you approximations of where the market stops and starts in its time cycles.

DEC CORN (EXAMPLE) SECTIONS
Now let's look at the December Corn example. (See Exhibit 8.1) The entire contract is printed from Beginning to End. The contract is divided into odd 4 and even 3 sections (see the vertical words BEGIN OF LIFE OF CONTRACT SECTION 3 and 4. Notice, right after the beginning of each section you can draw horizontal lines on top and bottom of the range for the first few days. When it breaks out of the range the contract will usually continue in that direction. In many cases the trend started will continue to the next same section line. The SECTION 4 will go to the next SECTION 4 and SECTION 3 will go to the next SECTION 3. If you combine both sections you will get cross currents of two different trends. Some times you will get two confirmations of the same trend. See the dates of SECTION 4 in late July and SECTION 3 at the beginning of September. Both trends were pointed down.

45 DAY CYCLE
The 45 DAY CYCLE will usually give you a clear indication of the direction of the market. When prices drop down into a 45 DAY CYCLE the prices should then rise. See the 45 DAY CYCLE on October 12. When prices go up into a 45 DAY CYCLE the price will then turn down after the cycle hits. See the 45 DAY CYCLE high on December 14.

DIVISIONS OF 3, 5, 7 DAYS/WEEKS
The market will usually run up or down and stop on 3, 5, or 7 days or weeks. Each commodity has its own characteristics. In the December Corn example

the market dropped 7 weeks down into a market low on August 10 and November 13. The market rallied 7 weeks into the high of April 20. The market dropped down 5 weeks into the date of October 14 and December 30. When the market runs up into the 3, 5, or 7 days or weeks watch the market carefully to see if it is running out of steam. If it starts to turn the trend will usually go the opposite direction and reverse.

SQUARE OF SPACE AND TIME

When the market makes an important high or low it will square itself with time in the future in days, weeks or months. In this example the market topped at an important high on May 29 at 285. That means that the market will cycle 285 days, weeks or months from that point. You can also divide those numbers into 10 equal parts to get the harmonics sections of the market. See in this example the harmonic points labeled 1/28 through 10/28. Notice near the end at points 9/29 to 10/28 the market ran out of downward pressure and started to rally indicating an end to the long 285 day downtrend.

OVERBALANCE SPACE AND TIME

In this example the market started to show signs of a bottom on November 23 when the market rallied 14 cents in 21 days which is more than the previous rallies. This again happened on July the 19 when the market rallied 36 cents in 20 days indicating the end to the 285 day downtrend.

DEC CORN HARMONICS 60 YEAR CYCLE

The example of the 60 year harmonic cycle for corn is very important. Divide 60 years by 10 to get the 6 year harmonic cycles. Now take the year of 1993 and go back every 6 years. Print out the charts and overlay them on top of each other. You will find many times that lows or highs occur the same time periods. When you find every year that has a low exactly on the same area you have a winner. See the lows that occur every harmonic year between February and March. That is a trade that you can bank on. You will see that in other parts of the charts that inversions occur. That means that some years may have a low at that time period and other years may have a high. You can use this to your advantage. When the market does this it will usually go the opposite direction. So when it drops into a low buy and when it rallies into a high, sell it. It can be very profitable. As always use this with all your other Gann tools you have learned in this course.

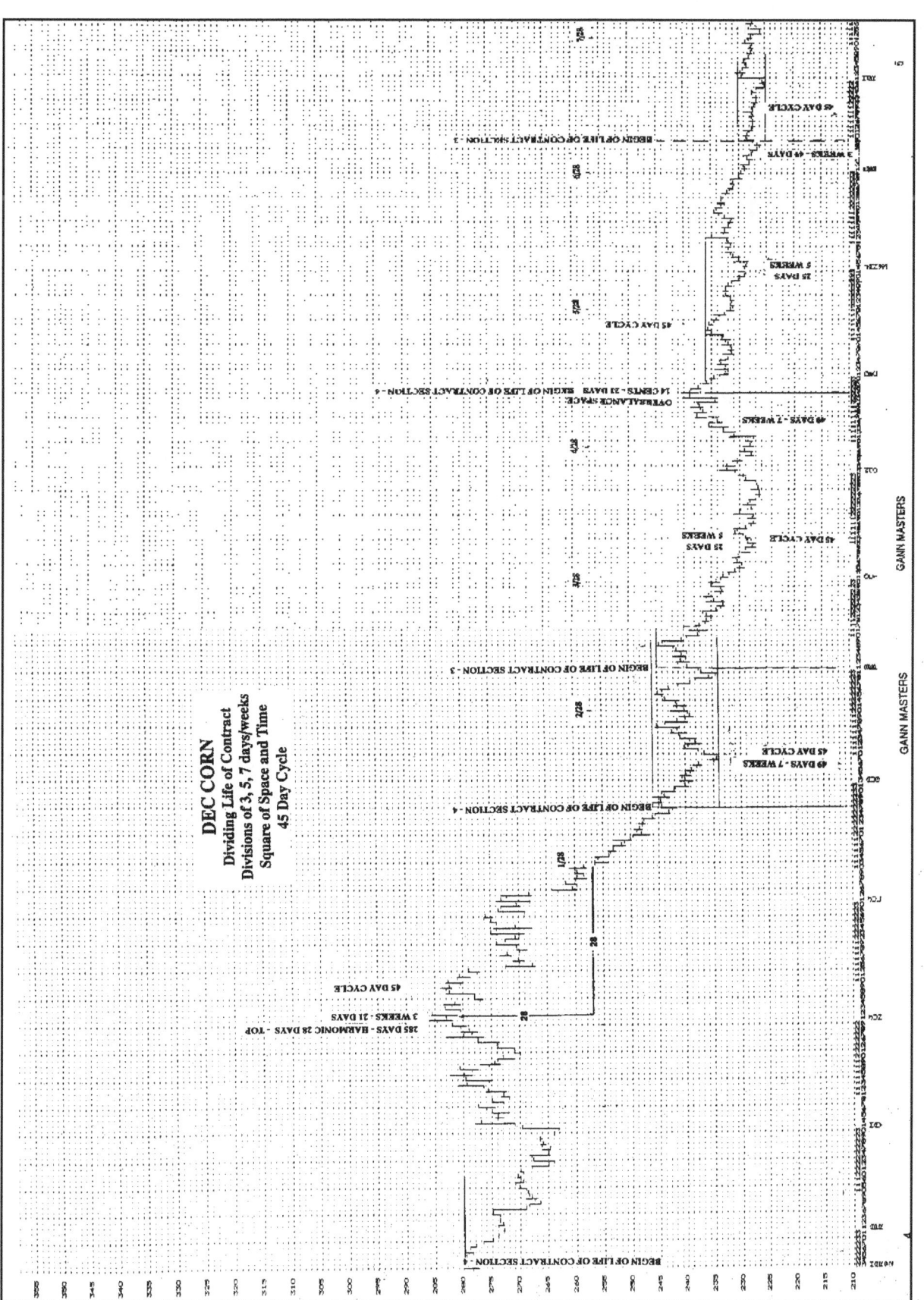

EXHIBIT 8.1 December Corn Example

CHAPTER 9

SUPPORT & RESISTANCE

Markets move between support and resistance.

In trading the markets, it is very important to know the important force of both support and resistance. Every top or bottom in the market has some relation to some prior top or bottom and it is mathematically based on that prior top or bottom. By using trend lines and time cycles with support and resistance levels, you can do much better in trading and know where to put your stop loss orders.

RANGE

Take the high price and the low price and divide it by odd and even or 3 or 4. If you want to go down another degree divide it by 6 or 8 or even 12 or 16 levels. When the market approaches these levels of support or resistance and is starting to show a possible change of trend, it is a place to either buy or sell. The halfway points are always the most important. The market will many times hold at these levels for 3, 5 or 7 days, 3, 5 or 7 weeks or 3, 5 or 7 months and give you a chance to buy or sell it. It depends on if the trend is minor, intermediate or major.

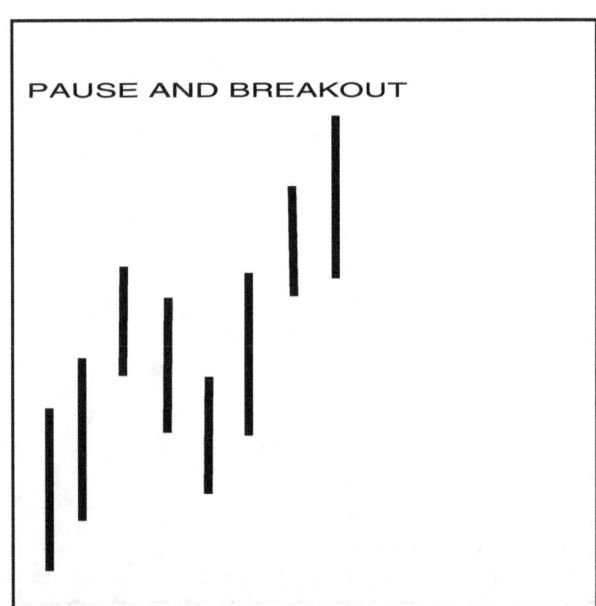

EXHIBIT 9.1 Pause and breakout

EXHIBIT 9.2 Failure & reverse of move

HOW THE MARKET TOPS OR BOTTOMS

When the market moves up to a resistance level or comes down to an important support level its volume and price activity will slow down for several days. The price pattern is usually in a narrowly traded range. Watch the activity closely for a change in trend. It will usually make its move in the direction that it will be going. You should then go with the trend. (See Exhibit 9.1 and 9.2)

HIGHEST PRICE EVER

You can also divide the highest price the stock or futures ever sold at. Divide it by odd or even numbers to get the support and resistance levels. Again the halfway points are the most important.

If the market ever breaks through it's all time high, the market has no overhead resistance and it many times surges with tremendous strength and volume. Whenever the market breakout out into new highs go with the trend as there is no resistance. In the stock market it is a profitable practice to buy the stocks that are making new highs as these are the strongest stocks in the market.

LOWEST PRICE EVER

You can take odd and even multiples of the lowest price the market ever sold at for support and resistance levels. If the markets all time low is 133 then multiply it by 2 to get 266. If that is in the current price range area, then use the number. If it's not in the current price range then multiply 133 by 3 or 4 to get the next price levels.

If that market ever breaks into all time lows it usually is a good idea to short the market and go with the weak trend. The market is in its weakest position when it is making new lows. Everyone that is long the market has a loss and is anxious to get rid of their position when ever the market rallies. Many times the market does not rally when it makes new lows, it just goes lower. Many longs panic and get out of the market and the prices even go lower.

PENETRATION

When a market is very fast, it will often penetrate a resistance level temporarily and then bounce back. This often happens at the 50% midpoints of the market. If the market stays above the 50% market, then their is a good chance the market will hold and start to rally when time factors turn up.

PAST PERFORMANCE

Study past action of important support and resistance levels to determine what it will do in the future. The best past action to study is previous same price levels. Also study previous same harmonic time areas such as every 6 years, if the market is following a 60 year cycle. If this is a 45 day cycle low, then you also need to study previous 45 day cycle lows to see how they bottomed.

PREVIOUS FUTURES CONTRACTS HIGH/LOWS
It is very important to know when the market has gone through a previous contract high or low. For example, December 1992 Corn vs December 1993 corn. When prior bottoms or tops are crossed, look for a change of trend. When a previous top which was resistance is crossed, it then becomes support. When a previous bottom which was resistance is penetrated, it then becomes resistance.

OPENS/CLOSES
Opens and closes are important to determine support and resistance levels. In strong bull markets there are never more than 2 days, weeks, months prices closing lower than the open. The market comes back to close higher than the open and continues its trend. In bear markets there will never be more than 2 days, weeks, months prices closing higher than the open. The market will usually close lower than the open to continue its trend. Watch the opens and closes especially near important support and resistance areas.

BEGINNING TIME RULE
Watch carefully at the beginning of the year in January or in the mid point of the year at July for changes of trend. Watch the first 3, 5, 7 days of the period. If the trend is sideways for those few days and then breaks out, go with the trend. That is the direction of the market. The trend started then will usually last from 3 - 4 months.

EXTREME HIGH OR LOW PRICE
Watch the years of extreme high or low prices. These years are very important for support and resistance and determine future movements usually in some important harmonic time measurement. Look carefully at the last number of the year. For example, many times a market will make highs or lows with the same last digit. For example the market might make highs on years that end with 9. See the years 1969, 1979 and 1989. If the market made highs on those years then look for the year 1999 to be a high also. Every market is different so always check back on your long term historical data.

LONG SIDEWAYS MOVEMENTS
Watch these time periods carefully. The market is usually just marking time while it squares out some prior top or bottom. When the market breaks out of this range, it usually is a major change of trend.

DEC CORN (EXAMPLE) SUPPORT AND RESISTANCE LEVELS
In Exhibit 9.3 of December Corn we take the all time high of 400 less the all time low of 112 3/8 to get a range of 287 5/8. If you notice this is close to the Gann number of 288 or 2 x 12 x 12. The halfway point between the all time high and low is 256 which we have drawn a horizontal line on the chart.

ALL TIME HIGH
In all markets you should find the all time high and divide it either by odd 3 or even 2 or 4 to get important support and resistance areas. In this example we divided it by 3 to get 266 which is a price in our trading range. Notice how the price of 266 keeps a top on this market. You can use this line as a resistance area.

ALL TIME LOW
You should also multiply the all time low by either odd 3 or even 2 or 4 to get important support and resistance areas. In this case the all time low was 112 3/8. Multiply this by 2 to get 224 3/4. This area of support on this chart occurred two times in November and in July. This became the real support of the overall corn market through this contract.

SIDEWAYS RANGE
The all time high divided by 3 to get 266 and the all time low 112 3/8 x 2 to get 224 3/4 became the major support and resistance for this entire contract. See how important it is.

HIGH/LOW RANGES
Inside the contracts movement you can see the ranges and divisions thereof. The long sideways range that occurred from January to July was 26 points from top to bottom. The smaller range from August to November was exactly half of this 13 points. Watch carefully for breakouts of long sideways ranges. If it happens with gaps and big volume, it can mean a big move is coming.

ANGLES
Support and resistance lines and halfway points can often be used to draw Gann angles. If you have an important high or low you can put your Square of 90 overlay on a high or low and move it up or down to the various support and resistance line. You will be surprised how the Gann angle lines then hit. See the 45 degree angle that was drawn on March 28. When it broke, the market took a large drop into July.

76 Gann Masters

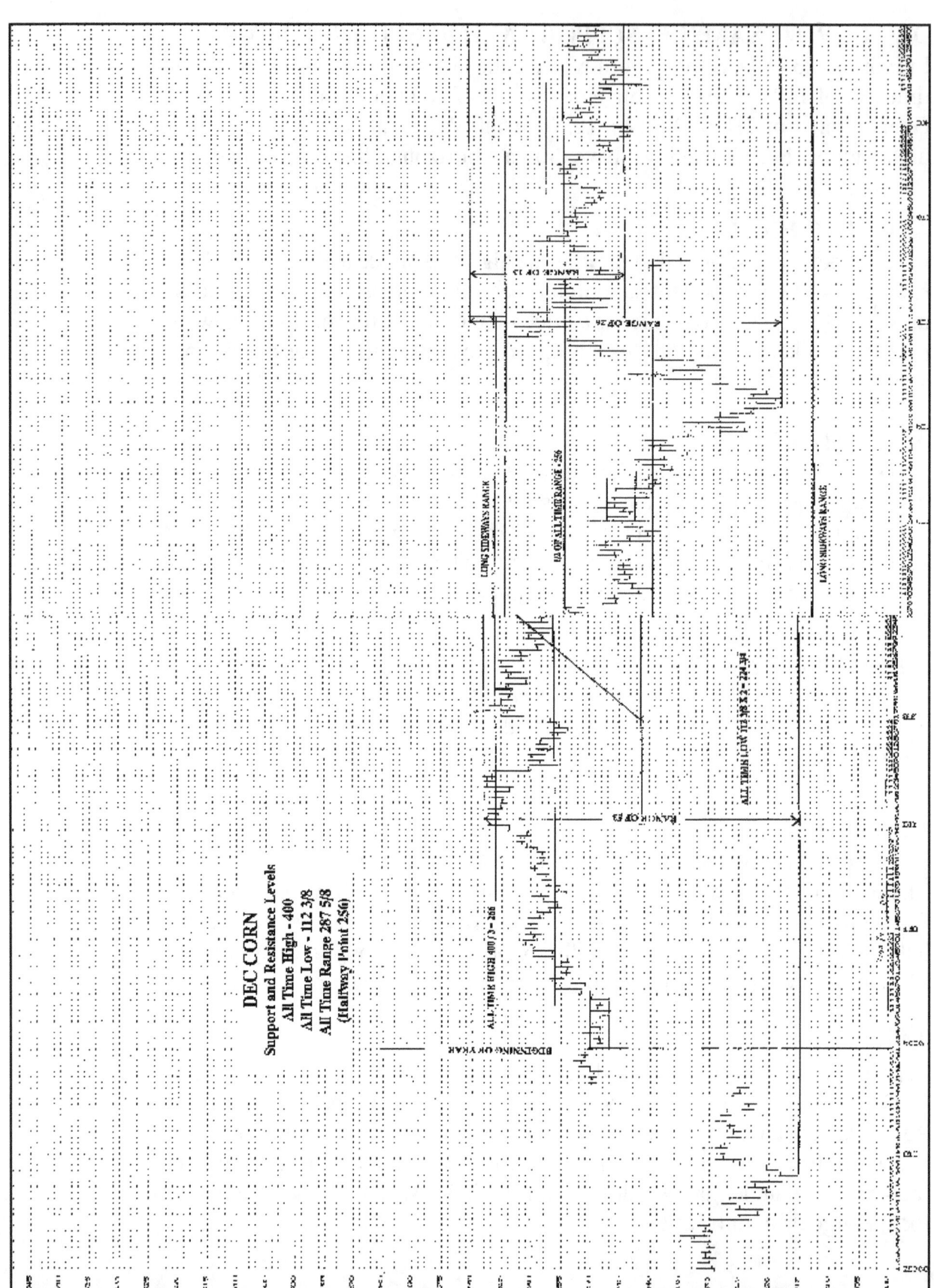

EXHIBIT 9.3 Dec corn

CHAPTER 10

TIME & PRICE OVERLAYS

"Gann's most important discovery"

In his last years, W. D. Gann said that one of his most important discoveries was the time and price overlay. By using it you could save enormous time in doing your calculations for determining the trend of the market. This chapter explores this most important tool.

When W.D. Gann discovered the important tool of the time and price overlay, we did not have computers. All charts were done by hand. It was very difficult to make a nice long term chart that you could effectively use overlays on. Today we have programs such as GannTrader and MAX:CHART. Both of these programs produce excellent precision paper charts which can be used nicely with overlays.

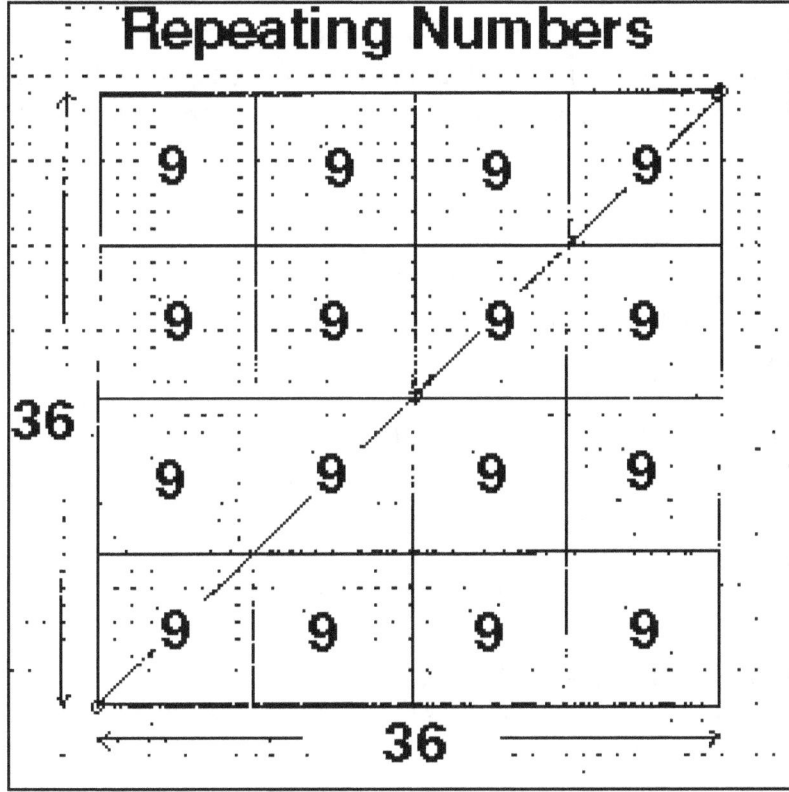

EXHIBIT 10.1 Repeating numbers

By studying and learning how to apply time and price overlays to the various markets one can forecast market price and time swings long into the future. It is necessary to obtain long term historical market data such as in the form of Gann style charts which would include the open, high, low and close of the market. This should be on a daily, weekly, monthly and yearly basis. This information can be obtained from commodity year books, or any of the many historical data services. It is important that the data be linked together correctly. The most effective format of data is the Gann style which links data together from year to year. This means that December 1992 corn would be linked to December 1993 corn and December 1994 corn would be linked to the December 1993 corn on a continuous basis. Nearby contintious charts link the nearest futures contracts together. This provides a chart similar to the cash markets, but is not as effective in using the overlays. The cash markets and stocks are do not need any linking method. They both work very nicely with overlays.

TYPES OF OVERLAYS
There are two kinds of time and price overlays one can construct to indicate resistance points in the markets. They are the permanent and the variable type. They can be used separately or together to indicate time and price resistance points. The following is a description of each. Permanent time and price overlays give natural resistance points. These resistance points are fixed and based upon key important natural numbers. These overlays help one understand why markets move the way they do. The time and price resistance points formed from these overlays are permanent and do not change. You will learn through trial and error which permanent overlays should be applied to which stock or commodity.

THE VIBRATION NUMBER
Every stock or commodity has its own vibration number and that is what usually sets the square it works in. It will trade within the square of the number. The number is based on one of several factors. The most common is the birth data or incorporation of the stock or commodity. It the stock was incorporated on December 21, 1945 its number would be 3 determined from adding 2 + 1. This data is usually hard to find, but can be found in exchange or corporation records. The next possible basis for the vibration number is the first day of trade on the exchange. It is also possible the number might be found from the all time low or high of the stock or commodity.

COMMODITY ALL TIME HIGHS AND LOWS
Exhibit 10.2 is a listing of some of the all time high and low price for many of the actively traded commodities. The source is the Chicago Board of Trade.

Commodity	All Time High	All Time Low
Mar Wheat	645 - 02/26/74	43 - 12/28/32
May Wheat	636 - 02/26/74	43 1/4 - 12/28/32
Jul Wheat	585 - 02/26/74	43 3/8 - 12/28/32
Sep Wheat	582 - 02/26/74	45 1/4 12/29/32
Dec Wheat	582 - 02/26/74	41 1/2 - 11/25/32
Mar Corn	409 - 10/04/74	21 - 02/27/33
May Corn	413 - 10/04/74	22 3/4 - 05/09/1897
Jul Corn	411 - 10/4/74	23 1/4 - 05/29/1897
Sep Corn	388 1/4 - 10/04/74	19 1/2 - 09/08/1896
Dec Corn	400 - 10/04/74	20 3/4 - 12/23/32
Mar Oats	207 - 10/04/74	15 1/4 - 02/27/33
May Oats	208 1/2 - 07/30/74	15 3/4 - 03/02/33
Jul Oats	202 1/2 - 06/14/76	14 7/8 - 06/30/1896
Sep Oats	198 1/2 - 7/30/74	14 1/2 - 09/08/1896
Dec Oats	203 - 07/30/74	13 7/8 - 12/03/32
Jan Beans	961 1/2 - 10/04/74	171 - 12/24/41
Mar Beans	969 - 10/04/74	200 - 06/28/49
May Beans	1076 1/2 - 04/22/77	67 - 07/26/39
Jul Beans	1290 - 06/5/73	75 1/2 - 06/17/40
Aug Beans	1175 - 06/26/73	238 1/2 - 08/07/62
Sep Beans	1010 - 07/25/73	241 1/4 - 08/20/53
Nov Beans	956 - 10/04/74	191 1/4 - 02/06/50
Jan Bean Oil	4787 - 10/04/74	700 - 09/30/68
Mar Bean Oil	4676 - 10/04/74	707 - 10/09/68
May Bean Oil	4588 - 10/04/74	715 - 10/09/68
Jul Bean Oil	4512 - 10/04/74	700 - 07/09/68
Aug Bean Oil	4740 - 07/31/74	711 - 07/09/68
Sep Bean Oil	4490 - 07/30/74	705 - 10/08/68
Oct Bean Oil	5100 - 10/01/74	691 - 10/11/68
Dec Bean Oil	4885 - 10/04/74	695 - 10/09/68
Jan Meal	29000 - 08/14/73	4260 - 01/13/58
Mar Meal	28300 - 08/14/73	4320 - 01/13/58
May Meal	32150 - 05/10/73	4370 - 05/21/57
Jul Meal	45100 - 06/05/73	4335 - 06/25/57
Aug Meal	41350 - 06/05/73	4375 - 06/19/67
Sep Meal	36500 - 06/26/73	4290 - 01/23/58
Dec Meal	29700 - 08/18/73	4280 - 06/19/57

EXHIBIT 10.2 Commodity all time highs and lows

It is necessary to experiment with several of the possible numbers that one finds. Use trial and error with several numbers until you find the one that an overlay works with best. You can do that by laying an overlay over a price chart and visually seeing the prices fit in a square.

NATURAL RESISTANCE LEVELS
Permanent time and price overlays are based on divisions of the circle. They can be applied to the measurement of both time and price. The following is a list of the most important resistance levels:
Divisions of the circle by 2, 3, 4, 5, 6, 7, 8, 9, and 12.

$$360 / 1 = 360$$
$$360 / 2 = 180$$
$$360 / 3 = 120$$
$$360 / 4 = 90$$
$$360 / 5 = 72$$
$$360 / 6 = 60$$
$$360 / 7 = 51$$
$$360 / 8 = 45$$
$$360 / 9 = 40$$
$$360 / 12 = 30$$

Overlays can be created based on the above numbers. Some traders have the entire set of overlays made up. They overlay each one on top of prices to find the one that best fits. Some times more than one overlay works. So it maybe necessary to use 2 - 3 overlays to guide you to the price trend.

The following is a listing of the most popular overlays which are based on the above circle numbers:

Description	Base Number
Square of 12	3
Square of 19	4.75
Square of 27	9
Square of 36	9
Square of 40	10
Square of 45	9
Square of 52	13
Square of 90	9
Square of 180	9
Square of 360	9
Square of 144	12

The basic square is drawn by dividing a square from all corners and sides into equal divisions. The corners are divided by odd number angles 3, 5, 7, 9 etc. This is because time is based on odd numbers The sides are divided by even numbers of 2, 4, 8, 16, 32, 64 etc. Sides represent price which is divided by even numbers. In most cases it is not necessary to go all the way out in divisions. The following is an example of a basic square. It is the square of 40 which is 40 squares up and 40 squares across. The square was drawn on 12 x 12 to the inch chart paper produced by MAX:CHART. The software program that plots precision Gann charts.

PERMANENT TIME AND PRICE OVERLAYS

Most permanent time and price overlays are based upon the numbers 1 to 9, but more specifically on the number 9 which is the number that represents the end of the number series upon which all numbers are based upon. In other words beyond the number 9 all ordinary numbers are just a repetition of the first 9. For example, the number 10, as the zero is not a number, it just becomes a repetition of the number 1. The number 11 repeats the number 2, 12 repeats 3, 13 repeats 4 and so on. Exhibit 10.1 shows why all numbers are just a repetition of the numbers 1 through 9.

Overlays with other base numbers are based on time numbers such as 12 for the 12 months of the year or 52 for 52 weeks of the year. These give you a three dimensional time view of the market.

```
            Basic Numbers 1 - 9
           1 = 10 reason ( 1 + 0 = 1)
           2 = 11 reason ( 1 + 1 = 2)
           3 = 12 reason ( 1 + 2 = 3)
           4 = 13 reason ( 1 + 3 = 4)
           5 = 14 reason ( 1 + 4 = 5)
           6 = 15 reason ( 1 + 5 = 6)
           7 = 16 reason ( 1 + 6 = 7)
           8 = 17 reason ( 1 + 7 = 8)
           9 = 18 reason ( 1 + 8 = 9)
```

The fact is the squares that really work well are based on the repeating number of 9. See Exhabit 10.5 of the square of 43. Let's take an example for this repeating number square. Say a commodity bottoms at 42.6. If you add these numbers together (4 + 2 + 6 = 12 and 1 + 2 = 3) if you place the left bottom on that price, the top right will land on 49.80. Now ad this number. (4 + 9 + 8 = 21 and 21 = 3). That's the same number as the bottom.

VARIABLE TIME AND PRICE OVERLAYS
Variable time and price overlays are developed around major tops and bottoms for a particular commodity or stock. Variable time and price overlays can be used together with permanent time and price overlays for time and price resistance levels and movement for a particular commodity or stock. You should study these overlays carefully and learn how the resistance and support point act on them at different levels.

SETTING UP VARIABLE LOW SQUARES
Squares can be worked up for a specific commodity or stock based upon their contract low. For example, on December 28, 1932 March Wheat had a low at $.43 per bushel. The square or balancing of this price was 43 days, 43 weeks, 43 months. The square of 43 (43 up and 43 across) can be worked up for March Wheat to use for time and resistance points.

SETTING UP VARIABLE HIGH SQUARES
Besides using lows to set up squares one can also use contract highs. Use the all time high of a particular contract for it's balancing square. For example,, March Wheat had a high of $645 on February 26, 1974. Therefore use the square of 81 ($6.45 / 8 = .80625) as its balancing square of this top.

SETTING UP CONTRACT RANGE SQUARES
Besides using contract highs and lows, contract ranges can also be used to set up balancing squares. March Wheat had an all time high of $6.45 - an all time low of $.43. The difference between the two is $6.02. Therefore a balancing square of $.70 ($6.02 / 8 = $.7525 per bushel can be setup to indicate resistance points).

COMBINING SQUARES FOR RESISTANCE POINTS
It is important to combine the natural squares, especially the square of 9 and 13 with the contract high, low and range squares to indicate the time and price resistance points for each stock or commodity. When natural time square points complement the same points given by the variable squares it creates an extra strong points for resistance. In other words if a commodity was working in the permanent square of 144 and the variable square of 43 and they both hit a day the same time, it would be considered a very important turning point.

ODD SQUARES AND HALFWAY POINTS
Odd and even squares and halfway points usually give strong resistance points for time and price. The following is a listing of some of these points. See Exhibit 10.4.

ODD SQUARES AND HALFWAY POINTS

Sq Of	Is	Halfway
9	3	
		17
25	5	
		37
49	7	
		65
81	9	
		101
121	11	
		145
169	13	
		197
225	15	
		257
289	17	
		326
361	19	

EVEN SQUARES AND HALFWAY POINTS

Sq Of	Is	Halfway
4	2	
		10
16	4	
		26
36	6	
		50
64	8	
		82
100	10	
		122
144	12	
		170
196	14	
		225
256	16	
		289
400	20	

Exhibit 10.4 Odd and even squares

WHERE TO GO FROM HERE

It is important that one uses the proper materials in developing his charts and overlays. The following will give you an idea of where to start.

CHART SCALES

To make plastic transparency overlays use Exhibit 10.2 illustrated in this chapter. The pattern is in the scale of 12 x 12 to the inch and was created by the MAX:CHART software program. If you use different grid paper or a chart service using another scale, you will have to modify them to adjust for the change of scale. Always try to use graph papers with square grid and avoid rectangular grid. It is advisable to use either MAX:CHART or GannTrader to produce the charts for overlays because they save a lot of time and they are more accurate. If you want to charts by hand, the following K&E graph papers are recommended:

#470780	10 x 10 to the inch
#471020	12 x 12 to the inch
#471120	16 x 16 to the inch
#471320	20 x 20 to the inch

The papers are 100% rag stock and come 100 sheets per box. Their size is 11 x 16 1/2". They can be purchased from Gann Masters.

CONSTRUCTION MATERIALS

You will find it necessary to obtain construction materials to create the vari-

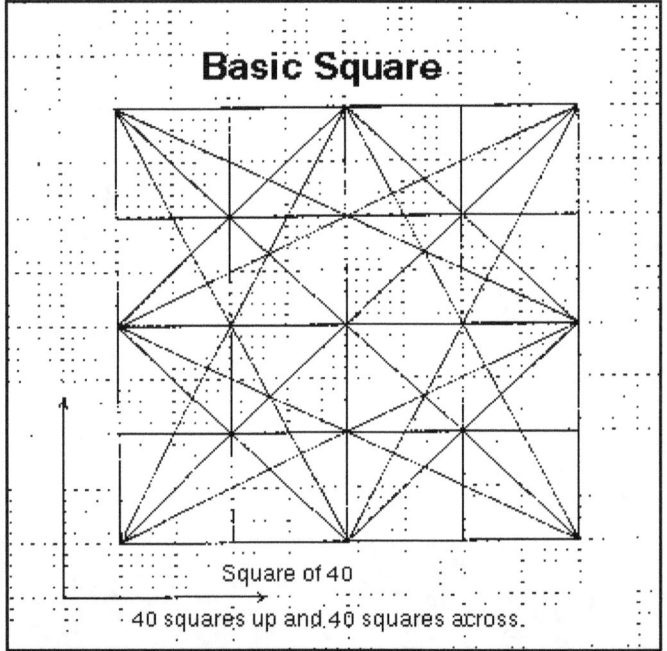

EXHIBIT 10.4 Basic square

ous overlays you will require. Materials can be ordered through Gann Masters. The plastic overlay material comes in rolls and it is recommended that you purchase SCUF permanent marker pens for drawing angles on the overlay materials.

THE IMPORTANCE OF CHARTS

It is important again to stress that the bar charts you set up must be done according to time and price guidelines. That means the price per grid should be based on Gann numbers. For example, 10, 20, 40, 50, 80 or 100. The prices should be set up on a open, high, low and closing basis. Holidays and weekends on the charts should be omitted. That means do not leave spaces for them. The charts are set up on trading basis only.

IMPORTANT FUTURE MONTHS

The important future months should be watched for key signals. A good set of charts should include the key months of future contracts of the year in commodity future contracts. For example, in most commodities the 12th and 6th positions of the cycle of the year are important. These are December and June. The next important commodities are the 3rd and 9th positions which are March and October.

SCALE

The scale is very important. The correct scale on a chart can be determined by how the overlays fit it. The 1 x 1 angle should usually hit the 50% reaction exactly.

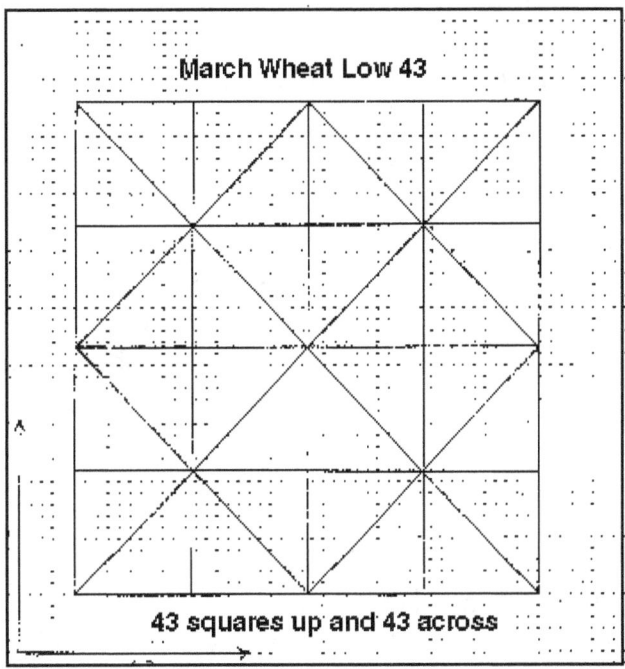

EXHIBIT 10.5 Square of 43

TIME INCREMENTS
The time increments are important. When trading correctly, you should have daily, weekly, monthly and yearly charts. If possible the chart should go back to the beginning of the contract. If that is not possible then you should at least have the all time high or low on the chart. Weekly charts are the most useful for long range trading.

TIME AND PRICE LABELS
The calendar should be correctly labeled at the bottom of the chart indicating year, month and day. The price should be correctly labeled on the side with price divisions related to circle numbers if possible. Price divisions are the heavy horizontal guide lines on a chart.

UPDATE SPACE
It is very important to have the necessary update space on your chart so you can do long range forecasting. On a daily chart the update space should go out 1 year. On the weekly chart the update space should go out for 2 years and on a monthly chart the update space should go out for 5 - 10 years.

TIME FRAMES
Man has learned to measure time with calendar periods. The larger the calendar period, the more important it is. Different time periods should be used to get the trend of the market. You should always know what direction each of the time periods is in. It will make you a much more effective trader. Watch closely for a change of trend in each time frame and trade accordingly. In order of importance the following are calendar periods most used:

IMPORTANT TIME FRAMES

> Yearly - for long term
> Monthly - for long term
> Weekly - for intermediate and long term
> Daily - for short term
> Hourly - for short term
> 60 minute - for short term
> 30 minute - for short term
> 15 minute - for short term
> 5 minute - for short term

HOW TO USE THE OVERLAY
It is recommend that you get monthly, weekly and daily charts of the markets you want to trade. These are the charts that W.D. Gann used. All these charts

must have adequate update space to the right of the chart for updating and forecasting future trends. By using all of these charts your perspective of where the market is will greatly improve.

MONTHLY CHARTS
These charts should be back for at least 30 years. They should have update space for at least five years. They are the best charts to use for effective long term time counts. They also give you excellent price support and resistance levels. These charts often change every 3 months.

WEEKLY CHARTS
The weekly chart is probably the best long term chart to trade from by the average trader. The chart should have 5 to 10 years of data on it and at least 2 years of update space. You will find that these charts often will change trend every 3 - 12 weeks. This is an excellent chart to use verify that the monthly charts are changing trend.

DAILY CHARTS
The daily charts are used by most traders, from computer programs to chart services. These charts should be at least 3 years in length and have update space of 1 year. Most losses occur because of these charts because people do not know how to trade them. These are the charts that you will use to enter and exit the market after both the monthly and weekly charts have changed trends. The scale on these charts is very important. Gann tried to use a 1 to 1 scale in most cases. You will have to experiment with the scale so it is right. Commodities like corn, wheat, oats, and the S&P might be on a scale of 1 to 1. You'll have to experiment with this scale by to get it right.

INTRADAY CHARTS
The intraday chart is the most difficult chart to trade with. More people lose money using this chart than any of the others. For the beginner 60 or 30 minute charts are recommended. Used properly they can help your entry into the market. After the monthly, weekly, daily charts have all changed trends, use these charts to enter or exit the market with precision. For these charts, you'll have to have real time or delayed data from an on on-line service such as Signal.

ADVANCEMENTS IN COMPUTERS AND SOFTWARE
There have been some advancements in computers that have helped to narrow the edge chart paper has. The speed of the new machine are awesome. They can pull charts up in split seconds. This save significant time and greatly aids the researcher and the trader. These computers use the new PCI bus. This

allows increased speed with hard disk drives for pulling up data faster. It also allows for faster on screen redrawing of charts.

MS WINDOWS SOFTWARE

Many new programs are being developed on this platform. The windows platform is easy to use and gives the advantage of high resolution screen output. Window programs such as SuperCharts and Trade Station are excellent and give you many of the tools you need to trade with. See the charts in this book, they were produced with SuperCharts and Trade Station. The Number Nine video card is a wonderful video card is capable of giving you big charts on your monitor almost as good as long term paper charts. See Exhibit 10.6. It has the advantage of giving you monthly, weekly, daily and intraday charts of any time scale. The resolution of this card can go as high as 1600 x 1200 with a virtual screen 2 to 4 times as large. This card gives you a portal view on a much larger virtual screen. Through this port, you can scroll around with a hardware pan with the use of your mouse. This will give you a screen chart which in most cases is as large as chart paper printed on long term grid paper.

17" FLAT COMPUTER MONITOR

The excellent and bright new monitors are wonderful. They provide a tight dot pitch of .26 - .28 and their screens are almost flat. Some traders actually lay rulers over the front of the screens. The NEC brand is usually the most recommended by Gann Masters.

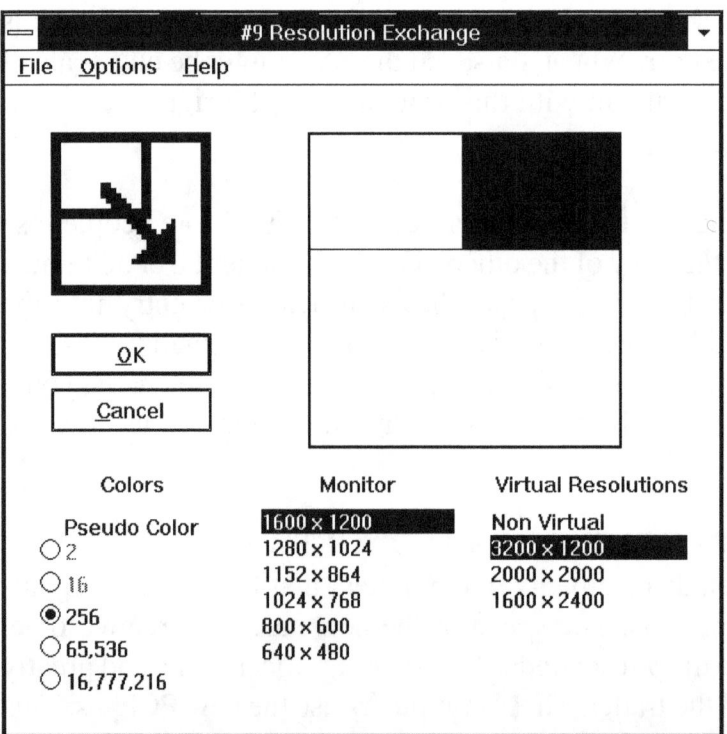

Exhibit 10.6 Number nine virtual screen on screen adjustment

HOW TO USE THE PLASTIC SQUARE OVERLAYS

The plastic square overlays should be overlayed over price charts in the followng fashion (See Exhibit 10.7)

    1. The bottom/left corner of the square should be placed below the exact bottom on the date of the bottom. This will show the important support angles pointing up.

    2. The top/left corner of the overlay should be placed above the exact highs on the date of the high. This will show the important resistance angles running down from the top.

    3. The square overlay can also be placed on 1/2 of the highest high. It can also be placed on an important circle number or a table number.

    4. It can also be placed on 1/2 of the range. The angles will indicate support or resistance where they hit price.

    5. The bottom/left corner can also be placed on the 0 low under and major high or low.

    6. It you use an MACD oscillator the square can also be placed on a momentum high or low which not necessary the price high or low.

    7. The top/left high can also be placed over the anniversary date or 1/2, 1/4 or 1/3 of the anniversary of a high 1, 2, 3, 4, 5 etc. years out.

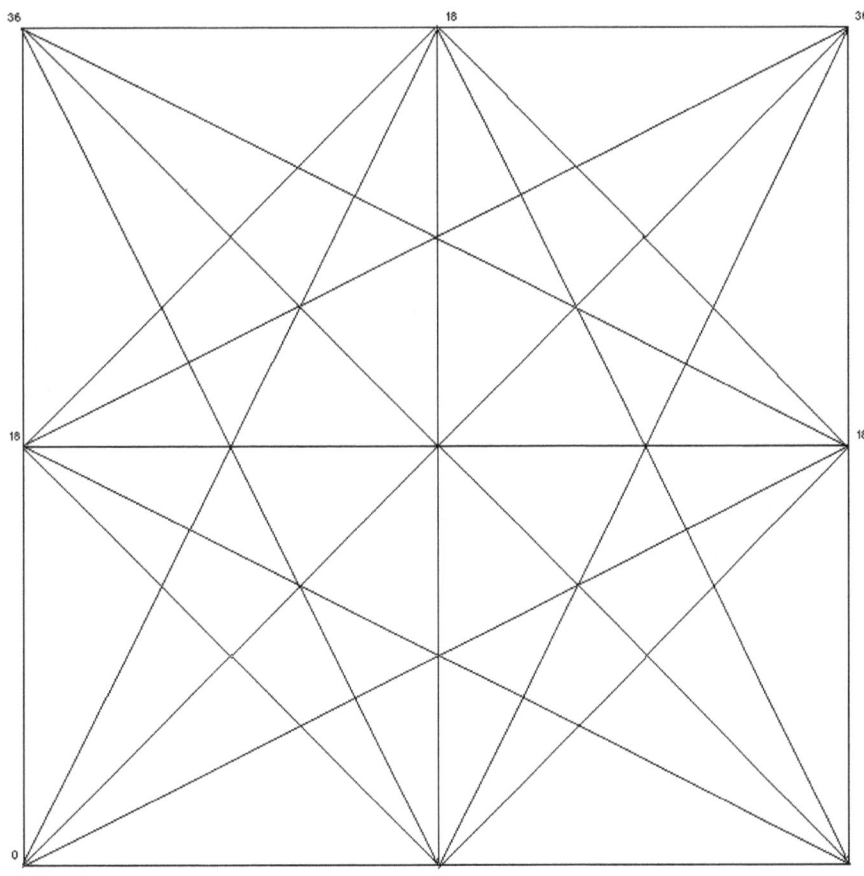

Exhibit 10.7 The Square of 36 overlay

CHAPTER 11

TABLE CHARTS

••

"The secret behind time and price moves"

This chapter on table charts has been developed from long experience, cultivation and studious research designed to unravel, at least to some extent, the mysteries of the subject of table charts on which many students of Gann have floundered.

It is admitted by all that the theory of application of table charts for time and price forecasting has been the one side of technical analysis that has been least explored or investigated.

This chapter is designed for the serious-minded student of the commodity and stock market. Presented herein will be the often misunderstood and mysterious table charts that most traders have so much trouble understanding. The table charts are presented in two different forms. The most used is the square table form, the second is the tritable. The ideas on how to use these table charts will remain ideas unless one spends many hours studying each one and proving to his own satisfaction that they work.

All the table charts in this chapter are produced with the Microsoft Excel spread sheet program. The template for this program is available free with this course. This is an excellent piece of software that can save you many hours in constructing these variations of table charts rather than doing them by hand.

Time and price forecasting are the essential ingredients for success in trading the markets. One who can predict time and price movements of the markets can reap enormous financial rewards. Proper interpretation of the table charts should help one anticipate many of the fundamentals that one

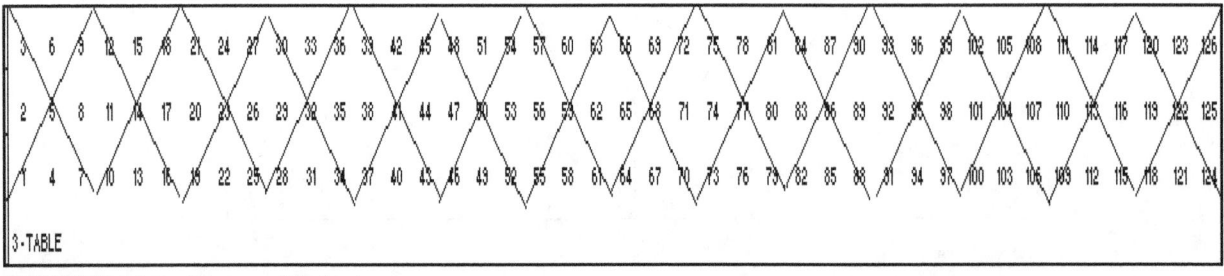

EXHIBIT 11.1 - Square of 3 chart

needs to know long before they become known to the general public. Table charts give a mathematical view point of how a market should move with respect to both time and price. With the knowledge table charts gives you, can easily spot the important support and resistance points.

By studying and learning how to apply table charts to the various markets one can forecast market price and time swings long into the future. It is necessary to obtain historical market information such as the first trade day of a commodity or stock, major high and low prices with dates of each. This information can be found from commodity year books, historical data, chart services and from company records.

The more you study commodity or stock price movements, the better you will understand the markets. Working with table charts will help you understand the interplay of the underlying economic forces of supply and demand in the market. This chapter will attempt to help you develop an understanding of price and time movements and provide you with fertile seeds which, if properly nurtured, should yield success in the field of stock and commodity speculation.

With these few words as a preface, I will endeavor to make the theory and application of table charts so clear that I hope anyone of ordinary education may be able to follow and experiment with certain rules which will be treated in the following chapters.

BASIC NUMBERS

The table charts presented in this chapter are mathematical sequences of numbers presented in various forms of design to aid the technician in the forecasting both time and price movements in the stock and commodity markets. The charts are based upon the numbers 1 to 9, but more specifically on the number 9 which has to be regarded as the end of the series of numbers, upon which all of our materialistic calculations are built upon. Beyond the number 9 all ordinary numbers are just a repetition of the first 9. For example, the number 10, as the zero is not a number just becomes a repetition of the number 1 The number 11 repeats the number 2, 12 repeats 3, 13 repeats 4 and so one. The

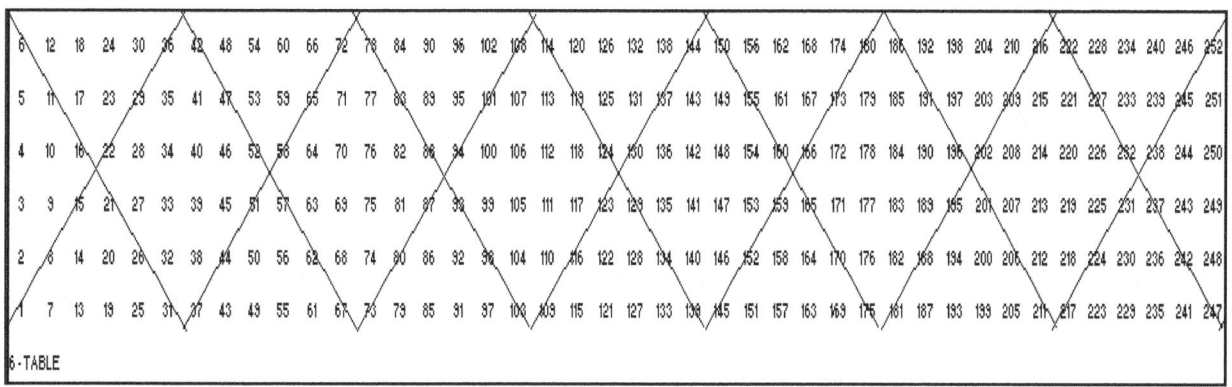

EXHIBIT 11.2 - Square of 6 chart

following illustration shows why all numbers are just a repetition of the numbers 1 through 9.

BASIC NUMBERS 1 - 9

$$1 = 10 \text{ reason } (1 + 0 = 1)$$
$$2 = 11 \text{ reason } (1 + 1 = 2)$$
$$3 = 12 \text{ reason } (1 + 2 = 3)$$
$$4 = 13 \text{ reason } (1 + 3 = 4)$$
$$5 = 14 \text{ reason } (1 + 4 = 5)$$
$$6 = 15 \text{ reason } (1 + 5 = 6)$$
$$7 = 16 \text{ reason } (1 + 6 = 7)$$
$$8 = 17 \text{ reason } (1 + 7 = 8)$$
$$9 = 18 \text{ reason } (1 + 8 = 9)$$

The above are sequences of numbers that add up to the indicated based number. Look them over and use the following pages as a reference to those numbers.

KINDS OF TABLE CHARTS

There are two kinds of table charts one can construct to represent support and resistance points for both time and price in the markets. They are the permanent and the variable number table.

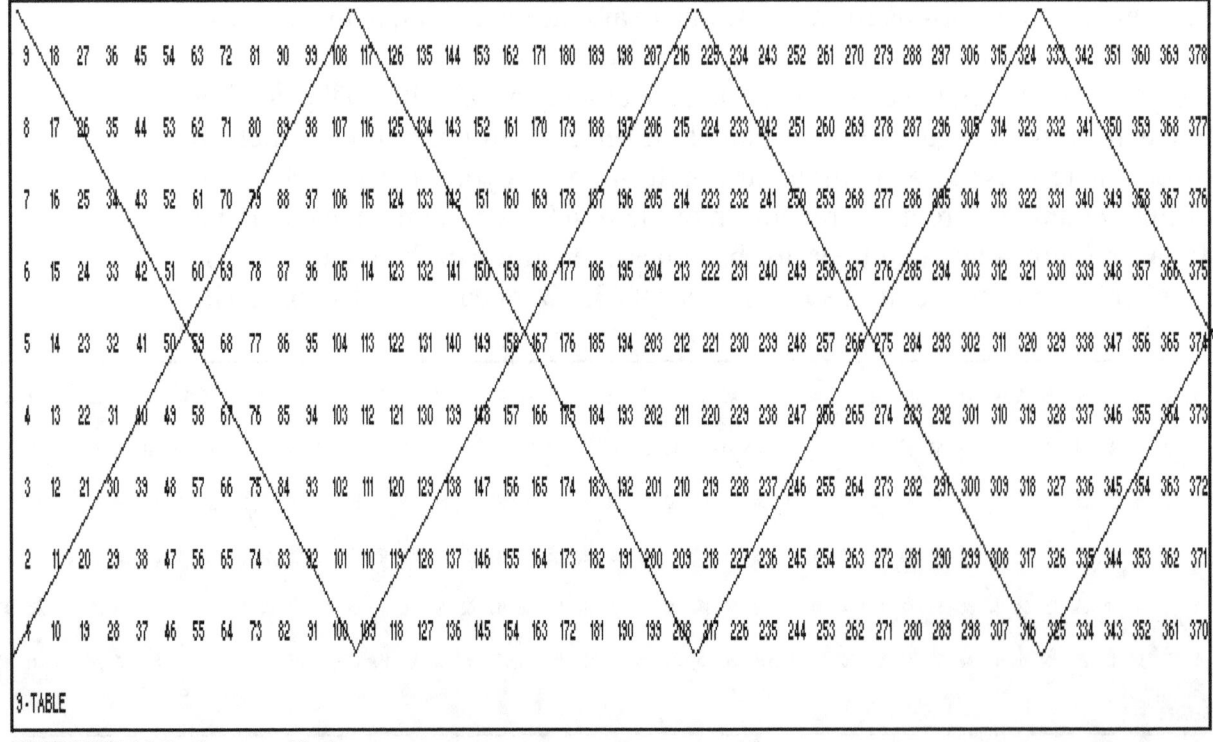

EXHIBIT 11.3 - Square of 9 chart

THE FIXED CHART

The fixed chart gives you natural resistance points. These natural resistance points are fixed and based upon key important numbers. These tables help one understand why markets move the way they do. The time and price resistance points formed from these fixed charts are permanent and do not change. You will learn through trial and error which table charts should be applied to which stock or commodity. Every stock and commodity has its own square of a number that it works in and that number will never change. The following is a listing of the most commonly used fixed tables.

SQUARE TABLE CHARTS

Square of 3
Square of 4
Square of 6
Square of 9
Square of 12
Square of 19
Square of 20
Square of 24
Square of 27
Square of 36
Square of 52
Square of 90

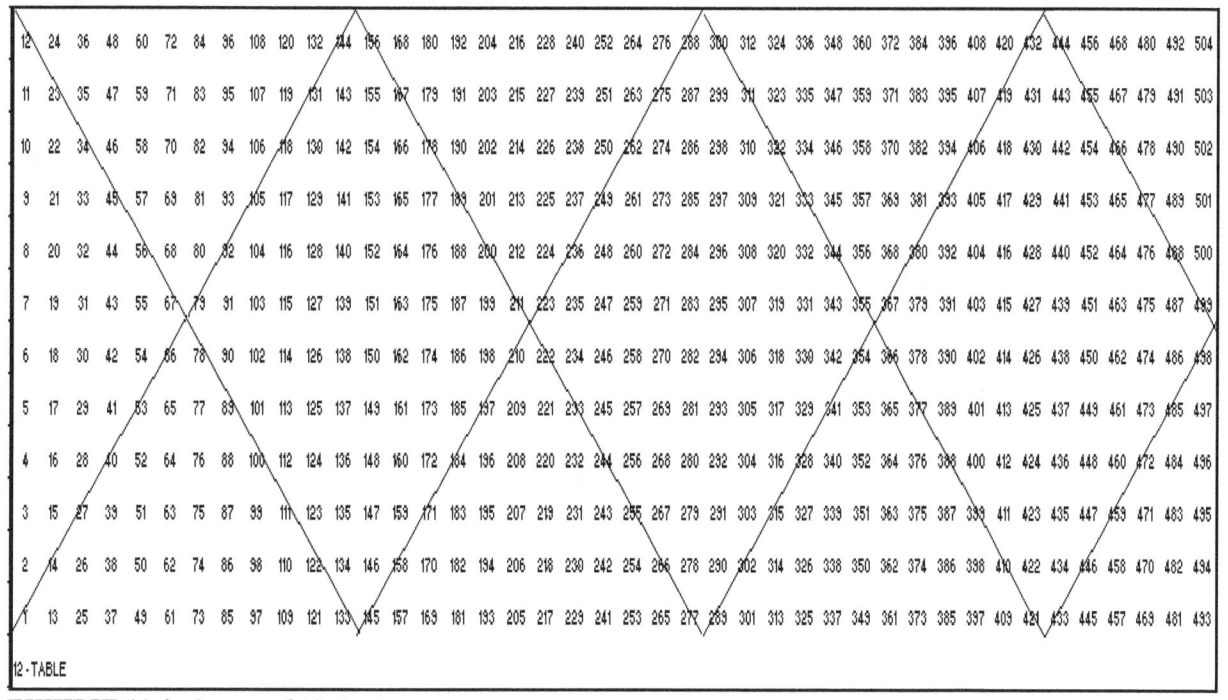

EXHIBIT 11.4 - Square of 12 chart

THE VARIABLE CHART

Variable table charts are developed around key individual market data beginnings, and major price tops and bottoms for a particular commodity or stock. Variable table charts can be used together with fixed table charts for time and price resistance levels and movements for a particular commodity or stock. Variable table charts can be used together with fixed table charts for time and price resistance levels and movement for a particular commodity or stock. You should study these charts carefully and learn how the resistance points are formed and how to apply them.

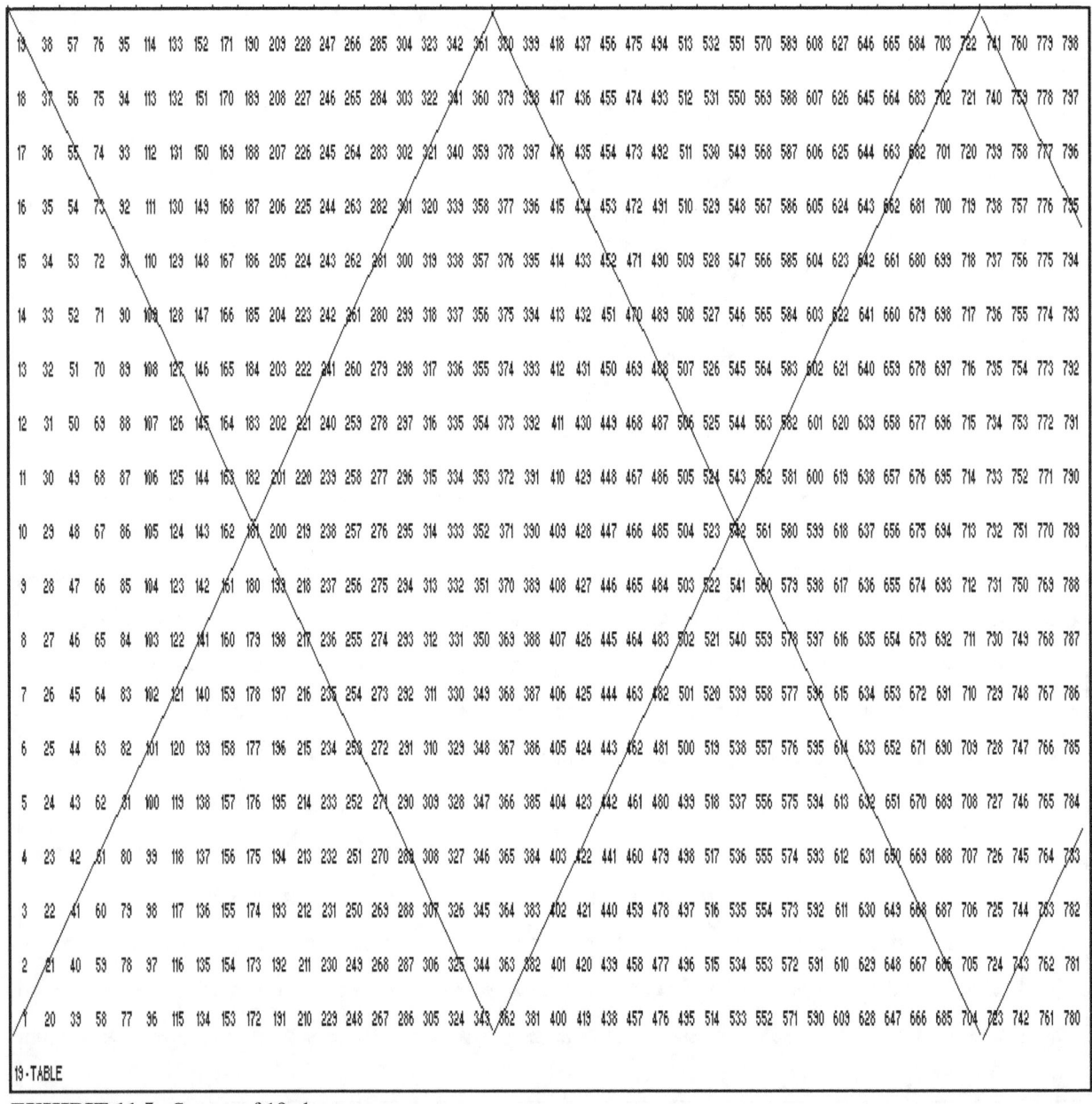

EXHIBIT 11.5 - Square of 19 chart

/ Gann Masters   95

THE SQUARE TABLE CHART
The square table chart is the most commonly used forecasting table of all the types available. It has a basic square or rectangle construction. The charts start out in the lower left corner going up in number progression to the top of the square. It then restarts back down at the bottom in row two and starts up again and so on. The following is a description of several of the more popular squares.

THE SQUARE OF 3 CHART
Exhibit 11.1 shows the square of three table chart 3 up and 3 over. It is the most basic of table charts and represents the importance of the number 5 as

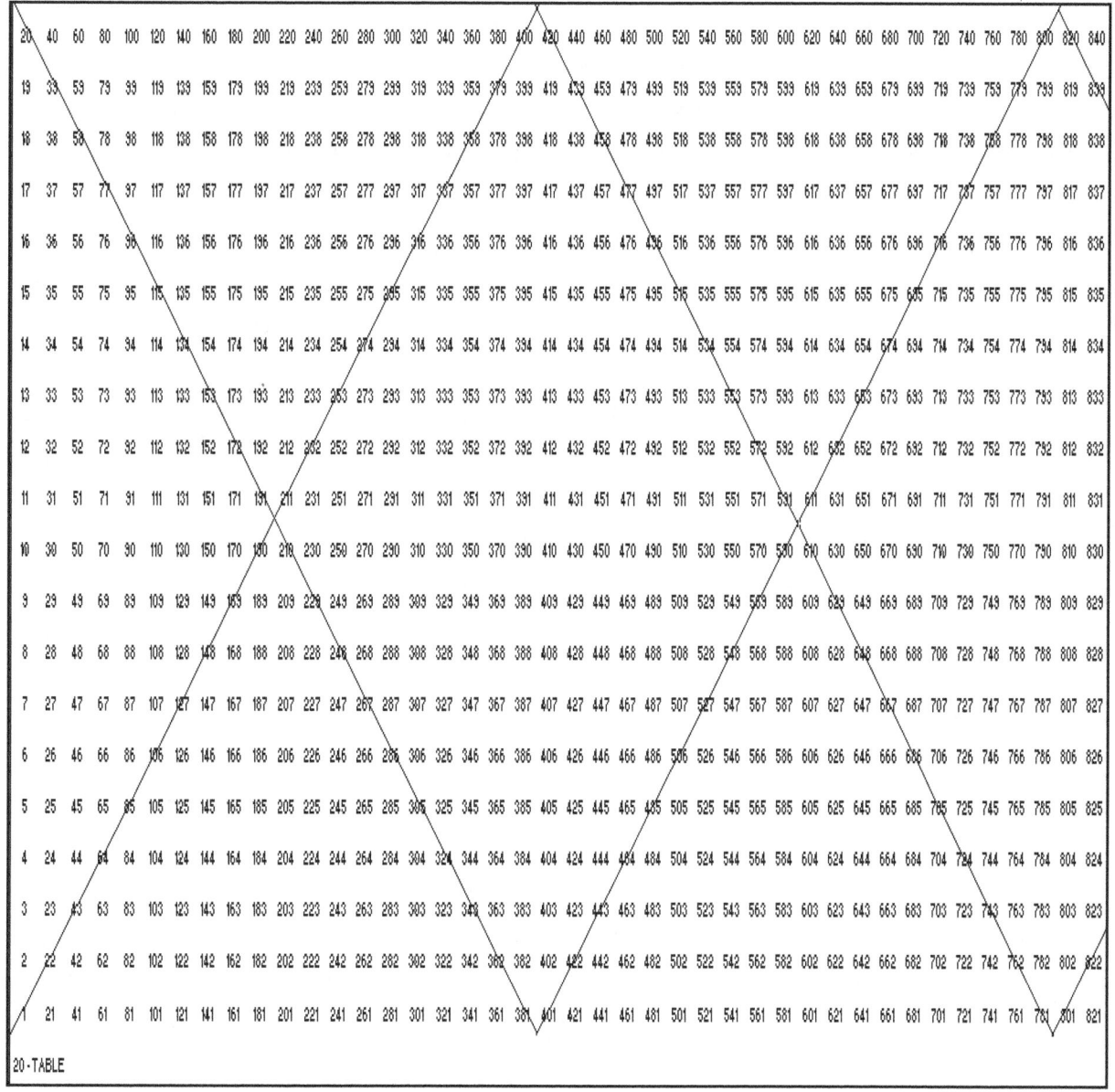

EXHIBIT 11.6 - Square of 20 chart

the mid point or halfway point of our basic 1 to 9 number system. The number 5 is surrounded on all sides by 4 numbers, the numbers 2, 4, 6, and 8. This table chart is the most basic of all and is the basis of all numbers.

THE SQUARE OF 6 CHART

Exhibit 11.2 shows the square of 6 chart 6 up and 6 over ending at 36. This first square of 36 is very important for time and price measurement. Six represents one quarter of the hours in the day. Six months is one half of the year. Six is a division of the circle 6 x 60 = 360 degrees.

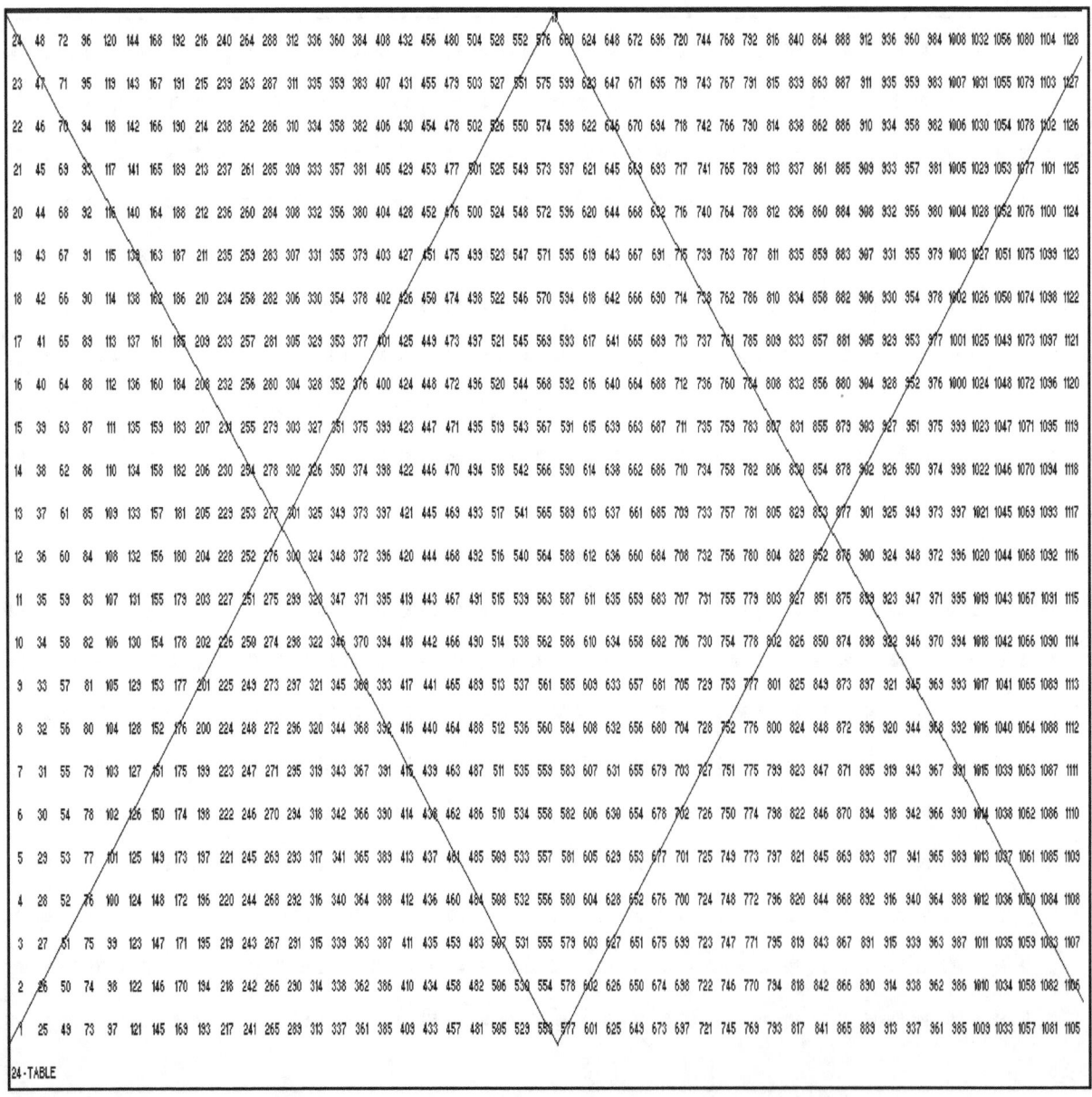

EXHIBIT 11.7 - Square of 24 chart

THE SQUARE OF 9 CHART

Exhibit 11.3 shows the square of 9 chart which is very important in measuring time and price moves. As we stated earlier in the course the number 9 in our mathematical system is very important. You cannot count beyond 9 without starting over with the number 0. In the square 9 x 9 which equals 81 which completes the first square of 9. The second square of 9 is completed at 162, the third square of 9 is completed at 243 and the fourth square of 9 ends at 324. Completing five squares gives us the important number of 360.

THE SQUARE OF 12 CHART

Exhibit 11.4 shows the square of 12 chart which is a very important table chart. It is important because of its relationship to the 12 months of the year. It consists of a chart which is 12 up and 12 over which makes the first square

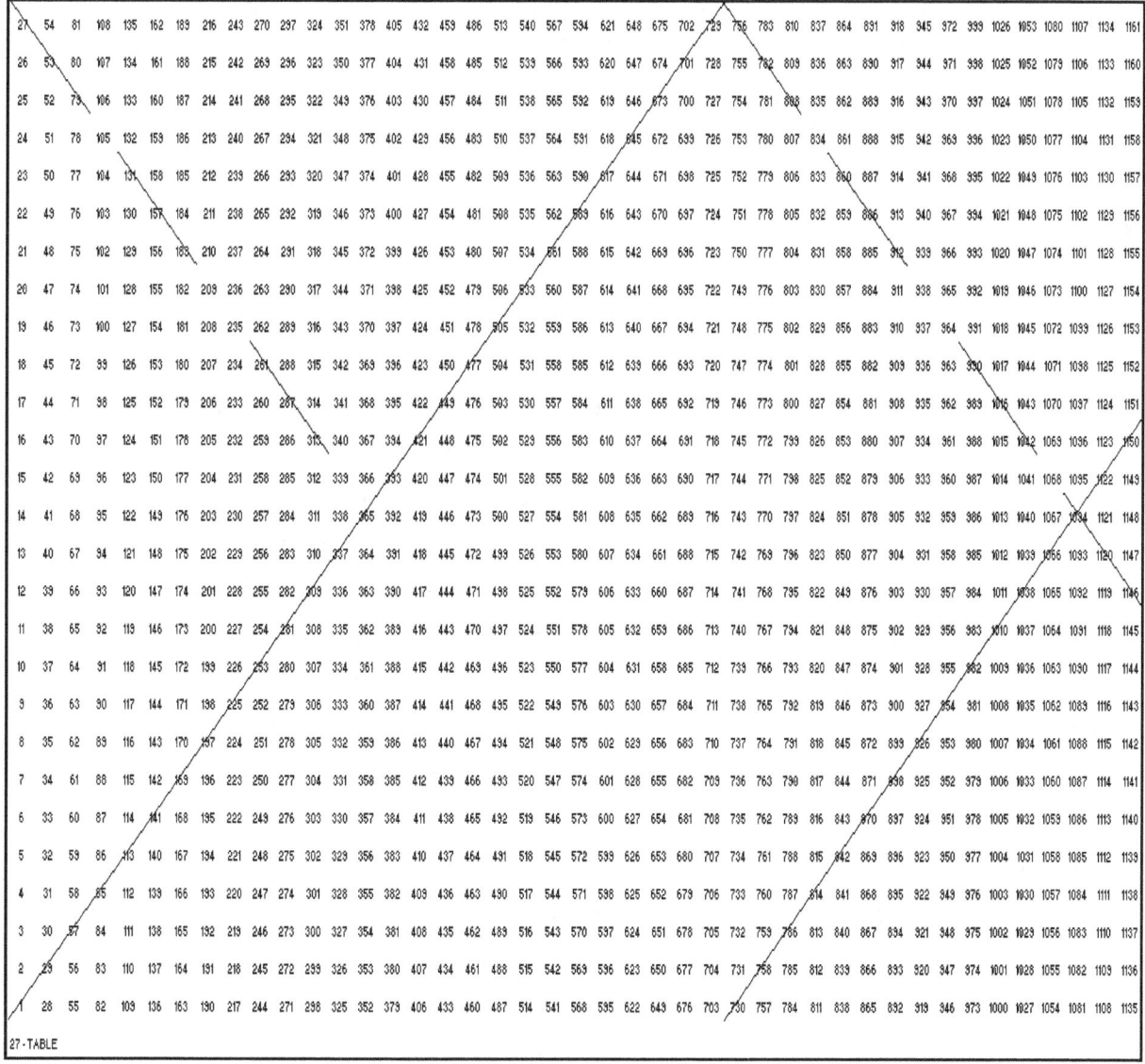

EXHIBIT 11.8 - Square of 27 chart

98   *Gann Masters*

of 144 and the fourth square at 576 - all key mathematical resistance numbers. The squares all end on the important 9 numbers. There is (1 + 4 + 4 = 9), (2 + 8 + 8 = 18) and so on. The number 9 is the finality on which all our number calculations are built. This important square can be used to measure both time and price movements. That is, the number of time or price points up or down in units days, weeks, months our years. You can make as many squares as you want to cover any price or time movement. Now lets list and analyze the important areas of resistance in the first square.

1) The Major Center is where the strongest resistance is met. These are the four number in the center of the square - 66, 67, 68 and 69. A stock or commodity going up or down should meet strong resistance here.

2) The Diagonal Resistance Numbers are the second strongest resistance points. One diagonal these are the numbers 1, 14, 27, 40, 53, 66, 79, 92, 105, 118, 131 and 144. On the other diagonal are the numbers 12, 23, 34, 45, 56, 67, 78, 89, 100, 111, 122, and 133.

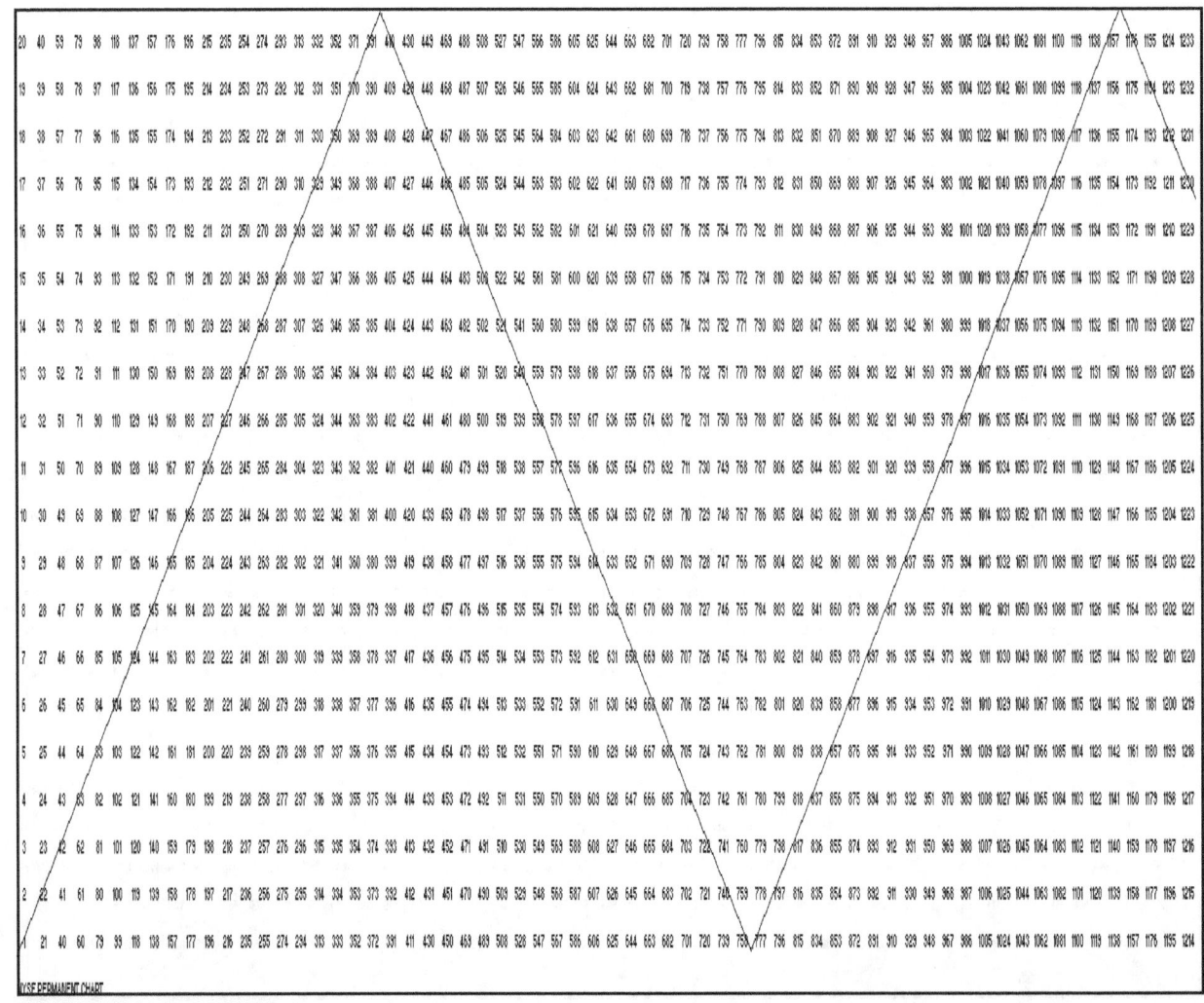

EXHIBIT 11.9 - NYSE Permanent chart

3) The Diagonal resistance Numbers of Quarter Squares are the third strongest resistance points. These are the numbers 7, 20, 33, 46, 59, 72, 6, 17, 28, 39, 50, 61 and 73, 86, 99, 112, 125, 138, 139, 128, 117, 106, 95 and 84.

4) The Top and Bottom Numbers are next in importance and many times represent important tops and bottoms and halfway points in respect to time and price.

5) The Halfway Point Numbers are next in importance and represent minor tops and bottoms or halfway points in regard to the time and price.

6) The Four Sections of a Square are important for determining resistance of both time and price movement. Divide the square into 4 sections and you get the number 36. Add 0 and you have the number of degrees in the circle. Divide the 36 into 4 minor square and you will get the important number of 9. Divide the number 9 again into four sections and you will get the

EXHIBIT 11.10 - Square of 43 chart

most important minor division of time and space of 2.25. Now, lets go back to the original 4 sections of the square. Moving over one section on the square of 36 you will reach the square of its own place. Next, when you move over two sections to the number 72, it reaches its halfway point. Three sections over to the number 108 it reaches its third resistance point which in many cases is a very difficult point to penetrate. The fourth resistance point is the hardest of all to penetrate which ends with the key number of 144. If it gets through the fourth section it will then be in the second square of 12 which is 145 to 288. If it maintains this price level with falling back into the first square it will then attempt to go through each section of the second square. Price or time movement will continue to move into each consecutive square trying to penetrate each section of the squares until it finally fails. Most bull or bear campaigns usually fail in the fourth square of 12. In every consecutive square

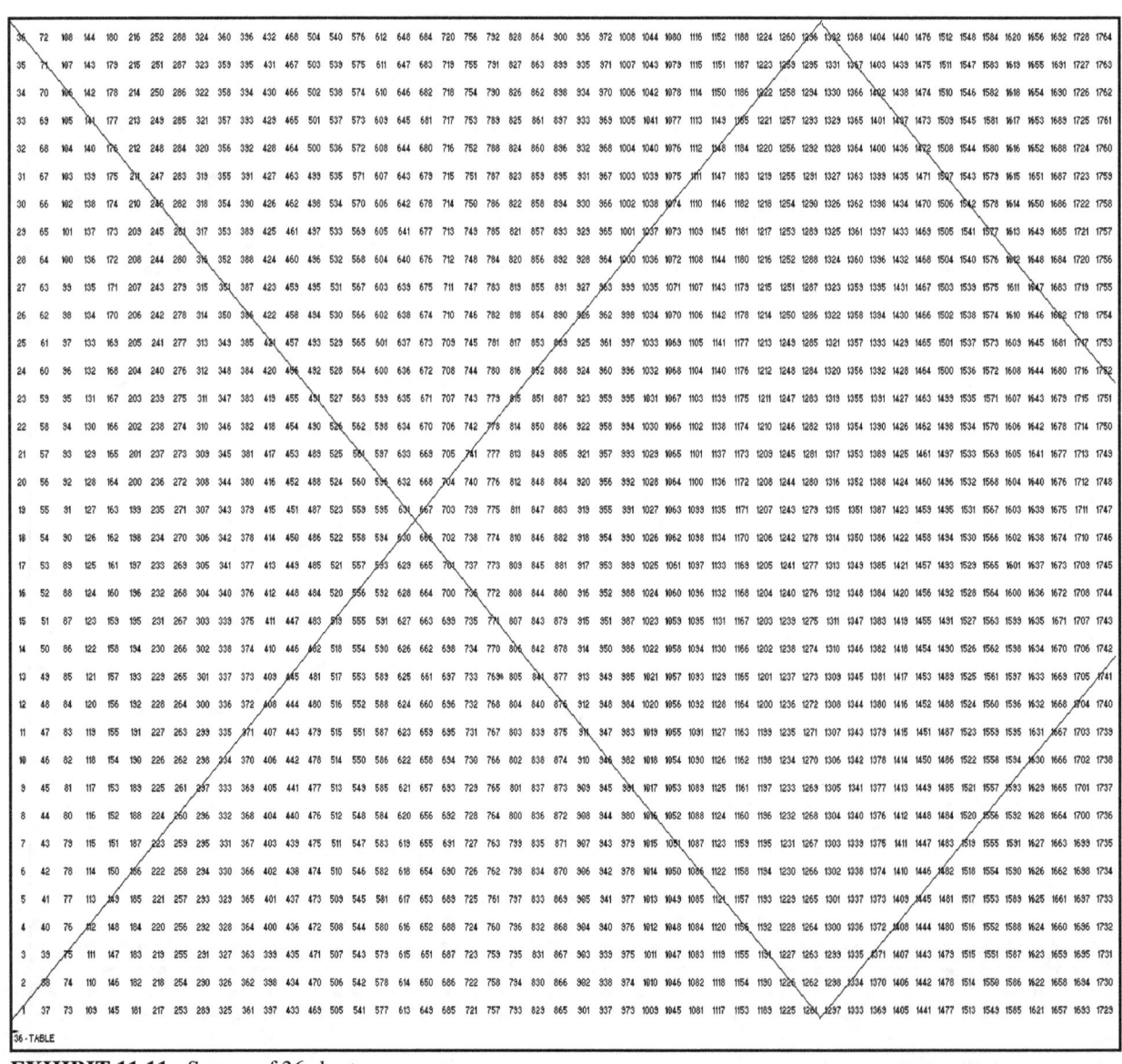

EXHIBIT 11.11 - Square of 36 chart

price and time movement volatility increases proportionally. Which is why many times a market ends its campaign with a price blow off

THE SQUARE OF 19 CHART
Exhibit 11.5 shows the square of 19 chart which is a very important table which is 19 up and 19 over. This square is often called the square of the circle because it proves the circle. The square of 19 x 19 ends at 361 which is just one over the 360 degrees in the circle. At the major center is the number 181 which is one over the half the circle 180 degrees. This illustration shows that when we reach the number 181 we are crossing the center and on the other side of the 360 degree circle. It is important to know that many price movements end with the square of 19.

THE SQUARE OF 20 CHART
In Exhibit 11.6 the number 20 which represents the number of trading days in the normal month, and the 18th division of the circle is quite important for measuring both time and price. The first method of counting by man was probably with his hand which consists of 5 fingers. Finally he probably incorporated his toes which eventually developed into a system of 4 x 5 = 20. It was then finally possible with a combination of finder counting and memory to reach even larger numbers. Many of the civilizations of the world have used a 20 finger number system. This is the chart Gann used for the New York Stock Exchange. He called it his NYSE Permanent Chart.

THE SQUARE OF 27 CHART
Exhibit 11.8 shows the square of 27 chart 27 up and 27 over which ends at 729 is close to 720 or 2 times the circle. The number also adds up to the important number 9 the end of your basic number series. Dividing the square of 12 months gives 60.75 years or 1/6 the circle. Dividing each quarterly square then gives 15.19 years and the halfway point is 7.59 years close to the 7 1/2 year cycle.

THE SQUARE OF 36 CHART
In exhibit 11.11 the square of 36 chart 36 up and 36 over which ends at 1296 is important for measuring all time and price movements and resistance points. It adds up to the important number 9 and adding a zero gives the important 360 degrees in a circle. This is a very important square for determining tops and bottoms of the market. The top of the square numbers tend to be highs and the low and mid point numbers are usually lows in the market.

THE SQUARE OF 52 CHART
The square of 52 chart which is 52 up and 52 across is a very important square

representing the 52 weeks in a year. The square of 52 is 2704, which is 7 years and 5 months very close to the important 7 1/2 year cycle or 90 months.

THE SQUARE OF 90 CHART

The square of 90 chart which is 90 up and 90 across which ends at 8100 is an important square. The number 90 is one quarter of the circle and adds up to the important number 9. Dividing the 8100 by 365 calendar days gives you 22.19 years to work out the vibration of each square of 90. Dividing this by 4 gives you 5.54 years or 287 weeks which ends the second square of 12 and divided by 3 gives 7.40 years which basically is the 7 1/2 year cycle.

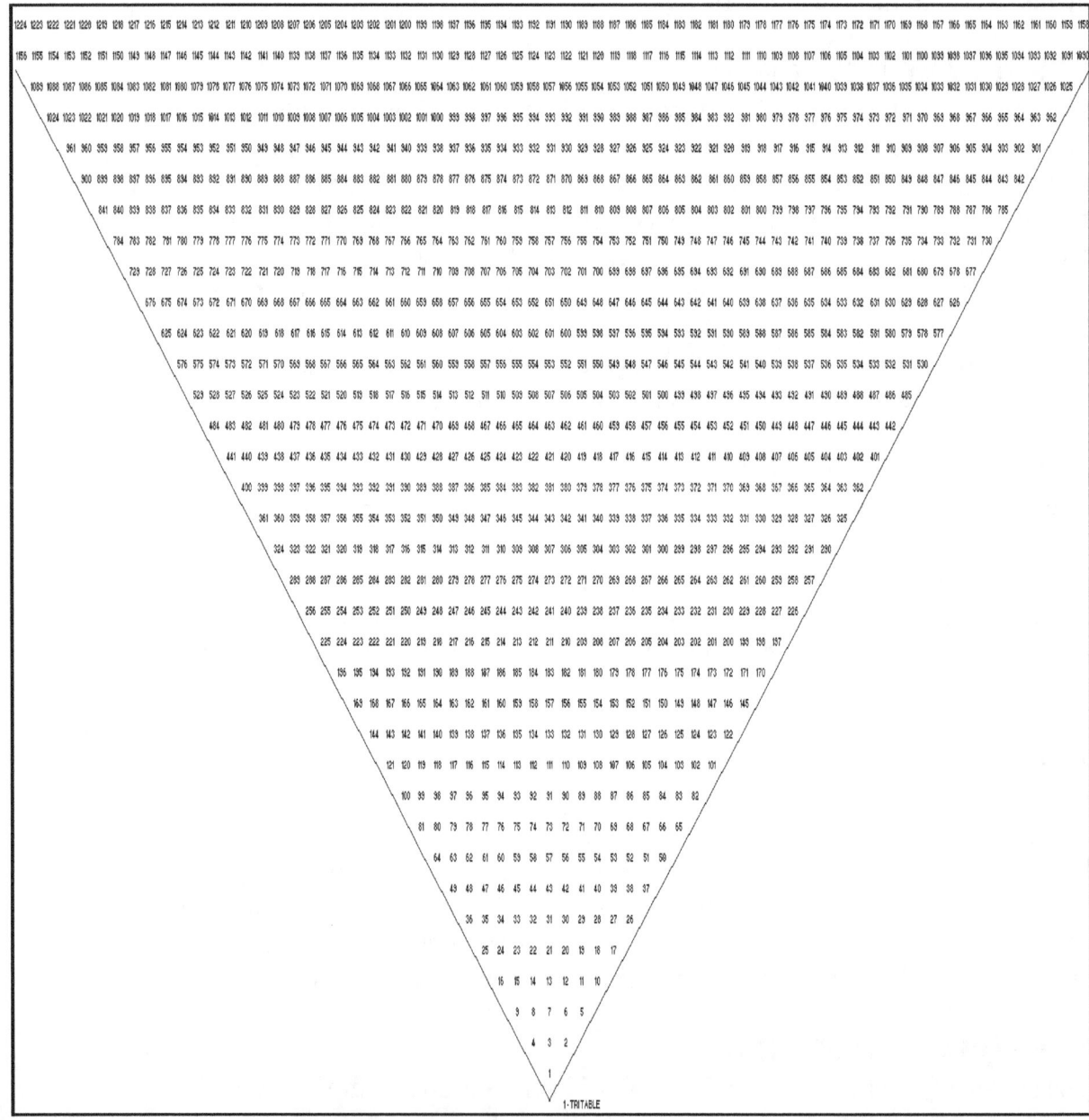

EXHIBIT 11.12 - 1 - Tritable chart

VARIABLE LOW SQUARES

Squares can be worked up for specific stocks and commodities based on their contract low. For example on December 28, 1932 March wheat had a low at 43 cents per bushel. The square or balancing of the price is 43 days, 43 weeks, 43 months. The square of 43 (43 up and 43 across) can be worked up for March wheat to use for time and resistance points. (See Exhibit 11.10) For September Wheat the low was made on December 29, 1932 at 45 1/4 cents per bushel. Therefore for this contract one must use the square of 45 to determine its resistance points.

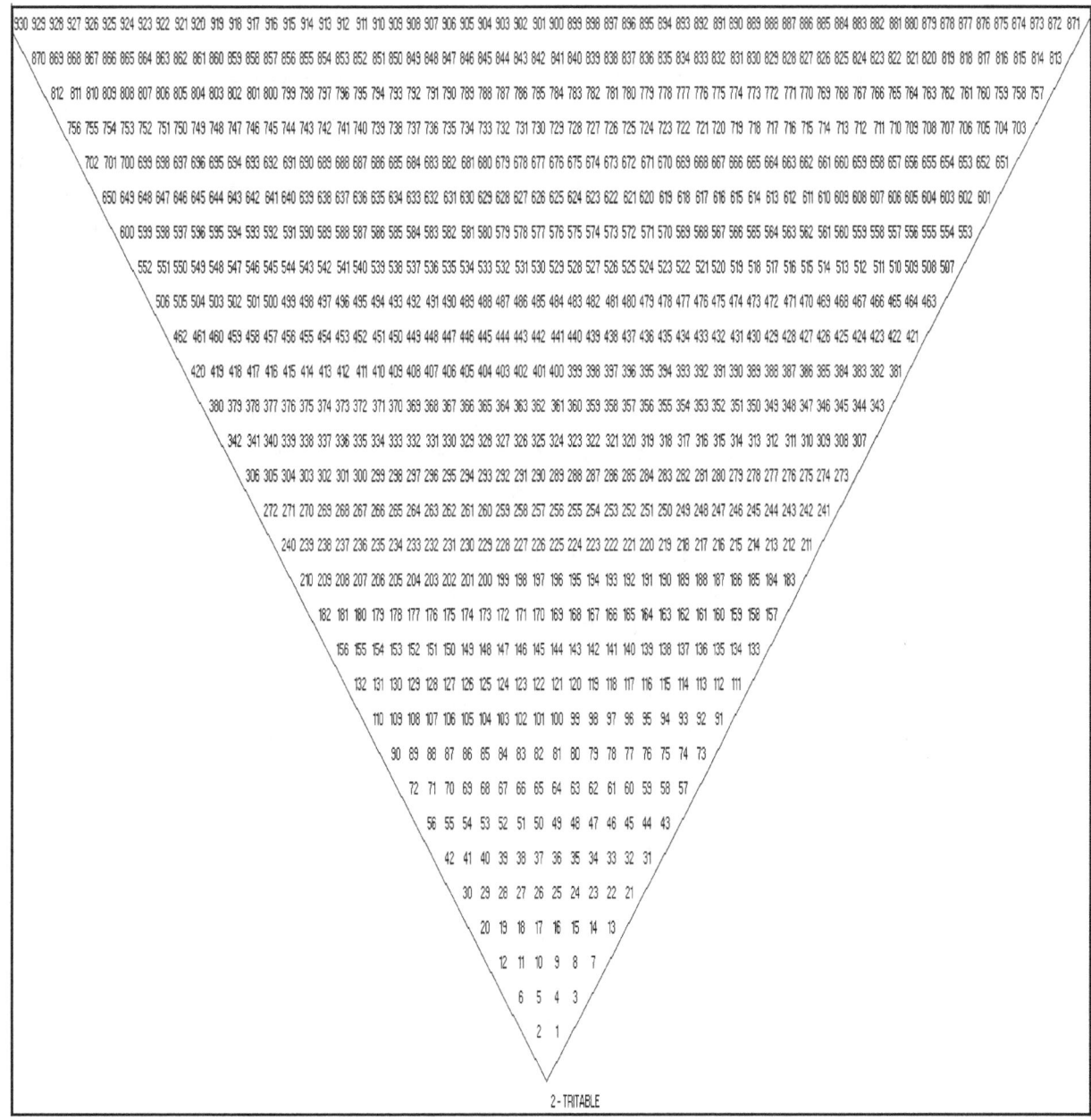

EXHIBIT 11.13 - 2 - Tritable chart

SETTING UP CONTRACT HIGH SQUARES
Besides using lows to set up squares one can also use contract highs. Use the all time high of a particular contract for its balancing square. For example, March Wheat had a high of $6.45 on February 26, 1974. Therefore use the square of 81 (6.45 / 8 = .80626) as it's balancing square for this top.

SETTING UP CONTRACT RANGE SQUARES
Besides using contract highs and lows, contract ranges can also be used to set up balancing squares. March Wheat had an all time high of 6.45 and an all time low of .43. The difference between the two is 6.02. Therefore a balancing square of .70 (5.59 / 8 = .6988) per bushel can be set up to indicate resistance points.

COMBINING SQUARES FOR RESISTANCE POINTS
It is important to combine the natural squares, especially the square of 9 and 12 with the contract high, low and range squares to indicate time and price resistance points for each stock or commodity. When natural time square points complement the same points given by the variable squares it creates an extra strong point for resistance.

LOW/ HIGH NUMBER SQUARES /NATURAL TIME SQUARES
It is possible to use contract low prices to determine intra cycle resistance points within a time period. For example March Wheat had a low on December 28, 1932 at 43 cents per bushel. A square of 12 with an intra cycle of 43 can be set up to determine the monthly future cycle points. Since the low occurred on the 12th month in 1932, label the first row as 1932 and circle the number 12. Therefore every 12 thereafter that occurs in the chart will be an important cycle month. It is also possible to use contract high prices to determine intra cycle resistance points within a time period. For example March Wheat had a high of 645 on 2/26/74. Divide this number by 8 to get it down to a smaller number under 100 to make a square with. This gives the number 80.625 or round to the number 81. Therefore the square of 12 can be set up with an intra cycle number of 81 to give important monthly cycle points.

TRITABLE CHARTS
The triangle table charts illustrated in this chapter were put in Gann's course, but were not explained. We have programmed the Excel spread sheet template to do these charts also. There are two types as illustrated in the examples. The odd type that starts with the number one on the bottom and the even type that starts with two numbers on the bottom. This type of table chart works much the same as the square type. It illustrates support/resistance on the flat top and on the rising sides.

NATURAL TIME SQUARE INTERVALS AND INTRA CYCLES

Intra cycle contract high and low points can be set up within all natural time squares. Squares can be set up on the smallest interval 1/4 hourly points up to larger intervals of monthly points. The following is a listing of some of the most commonly used intervals. It is important to note the low number such as 43 should be monthly points and high numbers such as 645 should be daily points.

    1/4 hourly points - square of 24 (if contract trades 6 hrs per day)
    hourly points - square of 6 (if the contract trades 6 hrs per day)
    daily points - square of 260 (trading days per year)
    weekly points - square of 52 (weeks per year)
    monthly points - square of 12 (months of the year)

NATURAL RESISTANCE LEVELS

Natural resistance levels are based upon natural law and can be applied to the measurement of both time and price. These levels come from base numbers or divisions of the circle. At these points commodities and stocks show strong time and price resistance levels. Table charts can be set up based on these numbers.

BASE NUMBERS

    Base of 5 - 5, 10, 15, 20, 25, 30, 35, 40, 45, 50, 55, 60, 65, 70, etc.
    Base of 9 - 9, 18, 27, 36, 45, 54, 63, 72, 81, 90, 99, 108, 117, 126, etc.
    Base of 10 - 10, 20, 30, 40, 50, 60, 70. 80, 90, 100, 110, 120, 130, etc.
    Base of 12 - 12, 24, 48, 72, 96, 120, 144, 168, 192, 216, 240, 264, etc.
    Base of 20 - 20, 40, 60, 80, 100, 120, 140, 160, 180, 200, 220, 240, etc.
    Base of 25 - 25, 50, 75, 100, 125, 150, 175, 200, 225, 250, 275, 300, etc.

DIVISIONS OF THE CIRCLE BY 2, 3, 4, 5, 6, 7, 8, 9, 12

    360 / 2 = 180, 360
    360 / 3 = 120, 240, 360
    360 / 4 = 90, 180, 270, 360
    360 / 5 = 72, 144, 216, 288, 360
    360 / 6 = 60, 120, 180, 240, 300, 360
    360 / 7 = 51, 102, 154, 206, 256, 309, 360
    360 / 8 = 45, 90, 135, 180, 225, 270, 315, 360
    360 / 9 = 40, 80, 120, 160, 200, 240, 280, 320, 360
    360 / 12 = 30, 60, 90, 120, 150, 180, 210, 240, 270, 300, 330, 360

THE VIBRATION NUMBER

Every stock or commodity will have its own vibration number that it trades by. It will trade within the square of that number. The number is based on one of several factors. The most common is the birthday or incorporation of the stock or commodity. If the stock was incorporated on December 21, 1945 its number would be 3 determined from adding 2 + 1. This is usually hard to find, but can be found in exchange or corporation records. The next possible basis for the vibration number is the first day of trade on the exchange. It is also possible the number might be found from the all time high or low of the stock or commodity. It is necessary to experiment with several of the possible numbers that one finds using the above basis. Use trial and error with several numbers until you find the one that fits best. Once you find it, it will be clear that it works in all cases. See Exhibit 11.14.

NUMBERS GIVEN TO DATES OF THE PERIODS OF THE YEAR

Stocks or commodities that started trading the following dates of the month are ruled by the numbers indicated. They generally will be strongest during their dates or the periods of the year indicated.

Started Trading	Ruling Number	Favorable Period
1st, 10th, 19th, 28th	1	Mar 21 - Apr 19th
2nd, 11th, 20th, 29th	2	Jun 20 - Jul 20th
3rd, 12, 21st, 30th	3	Feb 19th-Mar 27th, Nov 21-Dec 27
4th, 13th, 22nd, 31st	4	Jun 21 - Jul 27, Jul 21 - Aug 27
5th, 14th, 23rd	5	May 21 - Jun 27, Aug 21, Sep 27
6th, 15th, 24th	6	Apr 20th, May 27, Sep 21, Oct 27
7th, 16th, 25th	7	Jun 21 - Jul 27
8th, 17th, 26th	8	Dec 31 - Jan 27, Feb 19 - Feb 26
9th, 18th, 27th	9	Mar 21 - Apr 26, Oct 21 - Nov 27

NUMBERS GIVEN TO DAYS OF THE WEEK

The following are vibration numbers given to the days of the week. Stocks or commodities will be strongest on the day that vibrates their number.

Day	Number
Sunday	1, 4
Monday	2, 7
Tuesday	9
Wednesday	5
Thursday	3
Friday	6
Saturday	8

SAME NUMBER OF YEARS, MONTHS, WEEKS AND DAYS

You should check back in the record of both stocks and commodities and you will find that they advance and decline on the same number years many times up to 3 to 6 to 9 years at a time. For example if a stock advanced during the year of 1915. Add the number 3, 6, and 9 to that data to see if the stock advanced during those years. The dates would be 1918, 1921 and 1924. Some time the market will follow those years exactly to the day, week or month. Sometimes you will have a cycle inversion and the market will do the opposite of those years. You can keep going back 3,6, and 9 years back to 100 years if you have the necessary data. Using this method you can forecast months, weeks and days ahead of time. From this method you can many times determine the weak and strong points of the years based on months, weeks and even days.

```
Year
1915  + 3 = 1918 + 3 = 1921 + 3 = 1924
      + 3 = 1927 + 3 = 1930 + 3 = 1933
      + 3 = 1936 + 3 = 1939 + 3 = 1942
```

Using this method you should print out the charts and overlay them on top of each other to see if you can find similiar trend pattern between the years. Sometimes you will find a slight shift of time. Sometime it will be exact. Anniversary days of major highs and lows many times will come out to the day.

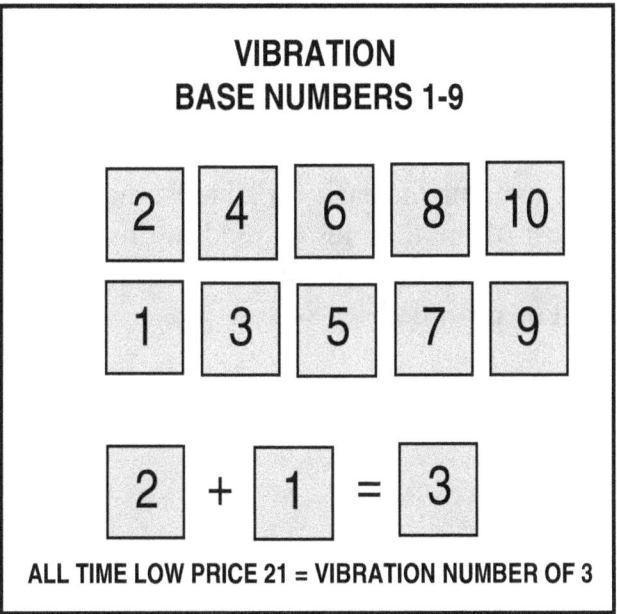

EXHIBIT 11.14 Vibration base number example

COMPOUND NUMBERS AND THEIR MEANINGS

Here is a way to tell whether a day will be favorable or unfavorable for a stock or commodity. It should be of great value to anyone who uses it. Now give your attention and concentration to the following system which I will try to explain as briefly as possible. To find whether a day in the month is favorable or unfavorable to a commodity the simplest rule is to work out the numeric value of the name of the stock or commodity. Determine that value by assigning a numeric value to each letter of the name the commodity is referred to. Add to this number its vibration number and the date of the month and check to see it is a good or bad number. Follow the below charts and example to guide you.

In this example Corn is figured this way.

C = 3, O = 7, R = 2, N = 5 (add 3, 7, 2 and 5 = 17, and 1 + 7 = 8)
Corn = 8
Vibration number = 3
Total = 11

COMPOUND NUMBER CHART
FAVORABLE + AND UNFAVORABLE -

10 +, 11 -, 12 -, 13 0, 14 +, 15 +, 16 -, 17 0, 18 -, 19 +, 20 0, 21 +, 22 -, 23 +, 24 +, 25 +, 26 -, 27 +, 28 +, 29 +, 30 0, 31 0, 32 +, 34 +, 35 -, 36 +, 37 +, 38 +, 39 0, 40 0, 41 +, 42 +, 43 -, 44 -, 45 +, 46 +, 47 +, 48 0, 49 0, 50 +, 51 +, 51 -

Corn	+Vibration Number	+Date	= Total	Expectation
8	3	13th	24	Favorable
8	3	14th	25	Favorable
8	3	15th	26	Unfavorable

CONCLUSION

Table charts are important for understanding the basis for all movement in the stock and commodity markets. Most of the theories learned in this chapter can be transferred to the study of bar charts. Study and apply the principles of this chapter to trading and you will be rewarded.

COMMODITY MARKET BIRTH DATES

The following commodities are given with their first trading day and the vibration number that rules them.

Commodity	Date	Vibration Number
Chicago Board of Trade		
Corn	1877	3
Wheat	1877	3
Oats	1877	3
Soybeans	Oct 5, 1936	5
Soybeans Oil	Jul 17, 1950	8
Soybean Meal	Aug 19, 1951	1
GNMA	Aug 1, 1968	1
Treasury Bonds	Dec 1, 1969	1
Chicago Mercantile Exchange		
Pork Bellies	Sept 18, 1961	9
Hogs	Feb 28, 1966	1
Cattle	Nov. 30, 1964	3
Lumber	Oct 1, 1969	1
British Pound	May 16, 1972	7
Canadian Dollar	May 16, 1972	7
Deutschemark	May 16, 1972	7
Japanese Yen	May 16, 1972	7
Swiss Franc	May 16, 1972	7
Mexican Peso	May 16, 1972	7
U.S. Treasury Bills	Jan 6, 1976	6
Comex Exchange		
Copper	July 5, 1933	5
Silver	Jun 15, 1931	6
Gold	Dec 31, 1974	4
Kansas City Board of Trade		
Wheat	1876	3
New York Cocoa Exchange		
Cocoa	Oct 1, 1925	1

EXHIBIT 11.15 Commodity birth dates

CHAPTER 12

TIME AND PRICE CHARTS

The markets vibrate around these charts.

This chapter goes into the explanation and use of Gann's master time and price charts. Perhaps the most interesting of these charts are the odd and even square charts. The odd chart is commonly known as the square of 9 and the even chart is known as the square of 4. The square of 9 has the number 1 at the center and spirals clockwise around the square. The even chart has four numbers in the center 1, 2, 3, and 4. It spirals counter clockwise around the square. Each of the chart's parameter is divided into dates and degrees of the year that go counter clockwise. Each circle of the square of nine ends with an number that squares out (9, 25, 49, 81, 121, 169, 225, 289 etc.). Each circle of the square of 4 ends with an even number that squares out (4, 16, 36, 64, 100, 144, 176, 256 etc.).

Which of the two charts to use depends on the total days in the contract from beginning to end. You must look up to see when the first day of trade was and look up the last day of trade. If there is an even number of days in the contract use the square of 4. If there are an odd number of days in the contract use the square of 9. There are many different ways to use these charts. One useful way is to set the beginning day of trade at 1 in the center of the square. As the contract trades out in time, you can see resistance at the completion of each circle in the square. You can often tell which chart (odd or even) a commodity is following by where it ends in time. Use calendar days for this timing. The Excel template available to you has the ability to be configured into either entirely dates, numbers or a combination of both. That means you can set the center to the beginning data and price of the contract and easily see all of the resistance dates and prices all the way out. The center can also be set to a major low or high date of price to see all of the resistance dates and prices.

THE SQUARE OF 9

This is a very important chart because nine is our number's system key. Nine is the basis of everything. When we count up to the number 9 we must start the count over to get to 10 (9 +1). Look at the square of nine chart in this chapter. The first major opposition is at 9 x 9 = 81. This completes the first square of 9. The second square of 9 ends at 162, the third square of 9 ends at 243, the fourth square of nine ends at 324 and the fifth square ends at 361 (19 x 19). Watch for these major oppositions when the market is trading in both time and price resistance. Important resistance points are on the fixed cross which is on the horizontal and vertical lines intersecting the center. These are the numbers 6, 19, 40, 69, 106, 151, 204, 265, 334 etc. going to the right. Going to the left are the numbers 2, 11, 28, 53, 86, 127, 176, 233, 298. Vertically the numbers are 4, 15, 34, 61, 96, 129, 190, 249 and 316 and down vertically the numbers are 8, 23, 46, 77, 116, 163, 218, 281 and 352. The cardinal cross numbers are also very important resistance points. These numbers are 3, 13, 31, 57, 91, 133, 183, 241 307, 7, 21, 43, 73, 111, 157, 211, 273, 343, 5, 17, 37, 65, 101, 145, 197, 267, 325, 9, 25, 49, 81, 121, 169, 225, 289 and 361.

The square of 9 chart is an excellent tool to help you forecast the markets. This tool can help you to significantly increase your accuracy in forecasting changes of trend in the market. Look at the square of 9 chart and find the number 496. Moving up on the chart the market finds price support as follows:

Degrees	Support/Resistance
45	485
90	474
120	463
180	452

Moving down on the chart the market finds support and resistance in the following areas in the degrees of 45, 90, 120, and 180.

Degrees	Support/Resistance
45	507
90	518
120	529
180	541

The market will also find support and resistance with dates at those same areas of price. For example on March 21 you will find the following resistance and support on these dates.

Degrees	Support/Resistance
45	May 6
90	June 21
120	Aug 8
180	Sep 23

Look on the chart at the numbers running down from the center to bottom left date of November 7. They are squares of odd numbers and represent support and resistance. The numbers are 1, 9, 25, 49, 81, 121, 169, 225, 361, 441, 529, 625, 729, 841, 961, 1089. The numbers running up from the center to May 6 are even squares of even numbers. The numbers are 4, 16, 36, 64, 100, 144, 196, 256, 324, 400, 484, 576, 676, 784, 900, 1024. The numbers 90 degrees between these squares of both even and odd numbers are midway points of support and resistance in both time and price.

The major trend in both time and price is the year and minor trends are the divisions of the year which the square of 9 chart gives. Major trends will reverse most of the time with the minor trends as follows using the following trends:

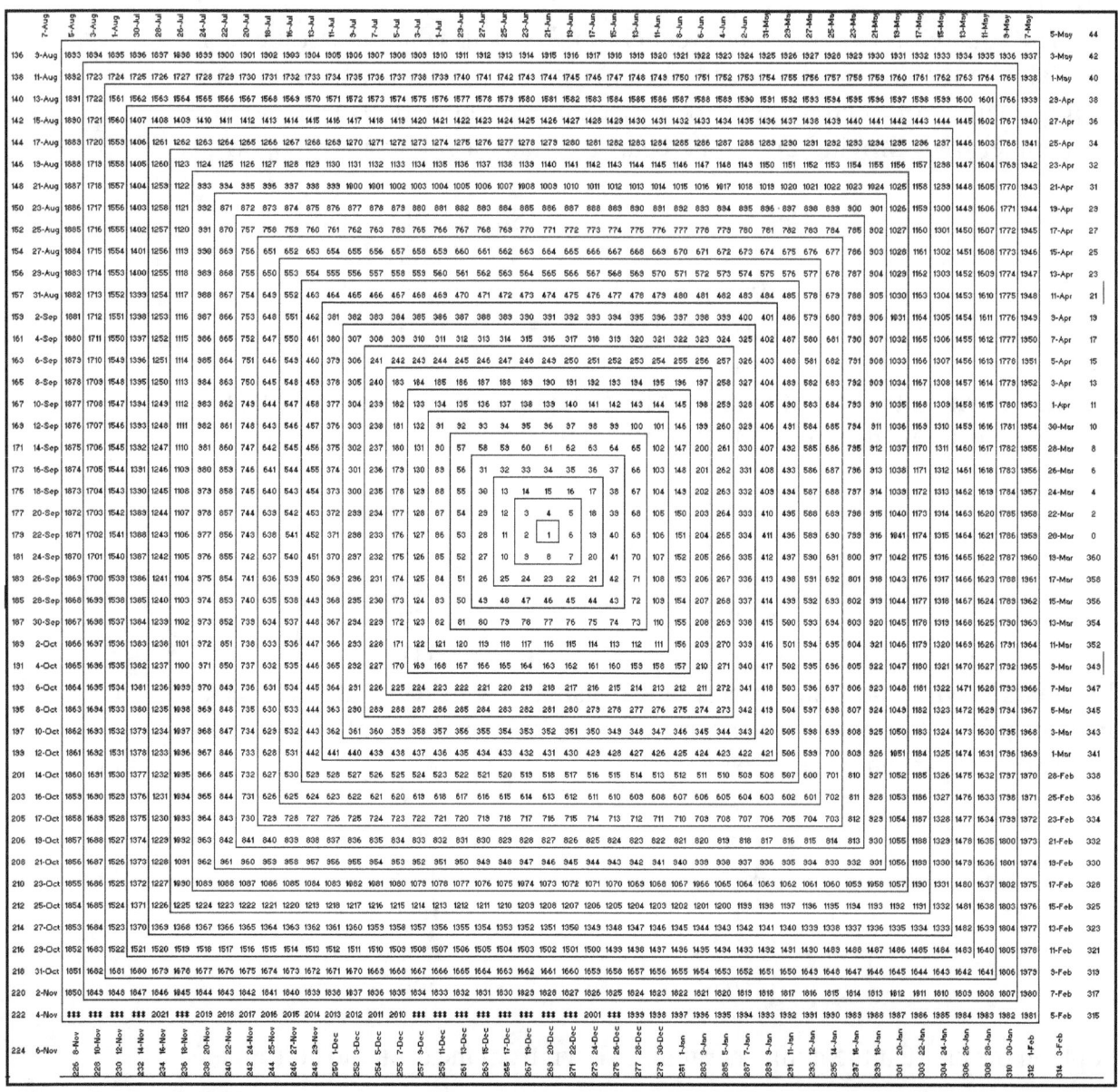

EXHIBIT 12.1 - Square of Nine Chart

Trend	Rates as to Importance
45 day	2
90 day	1
120 day	6
135 day	4
180 day	3
225 day	8
270 day	5
315 day	7
144 day	9
216 day	10

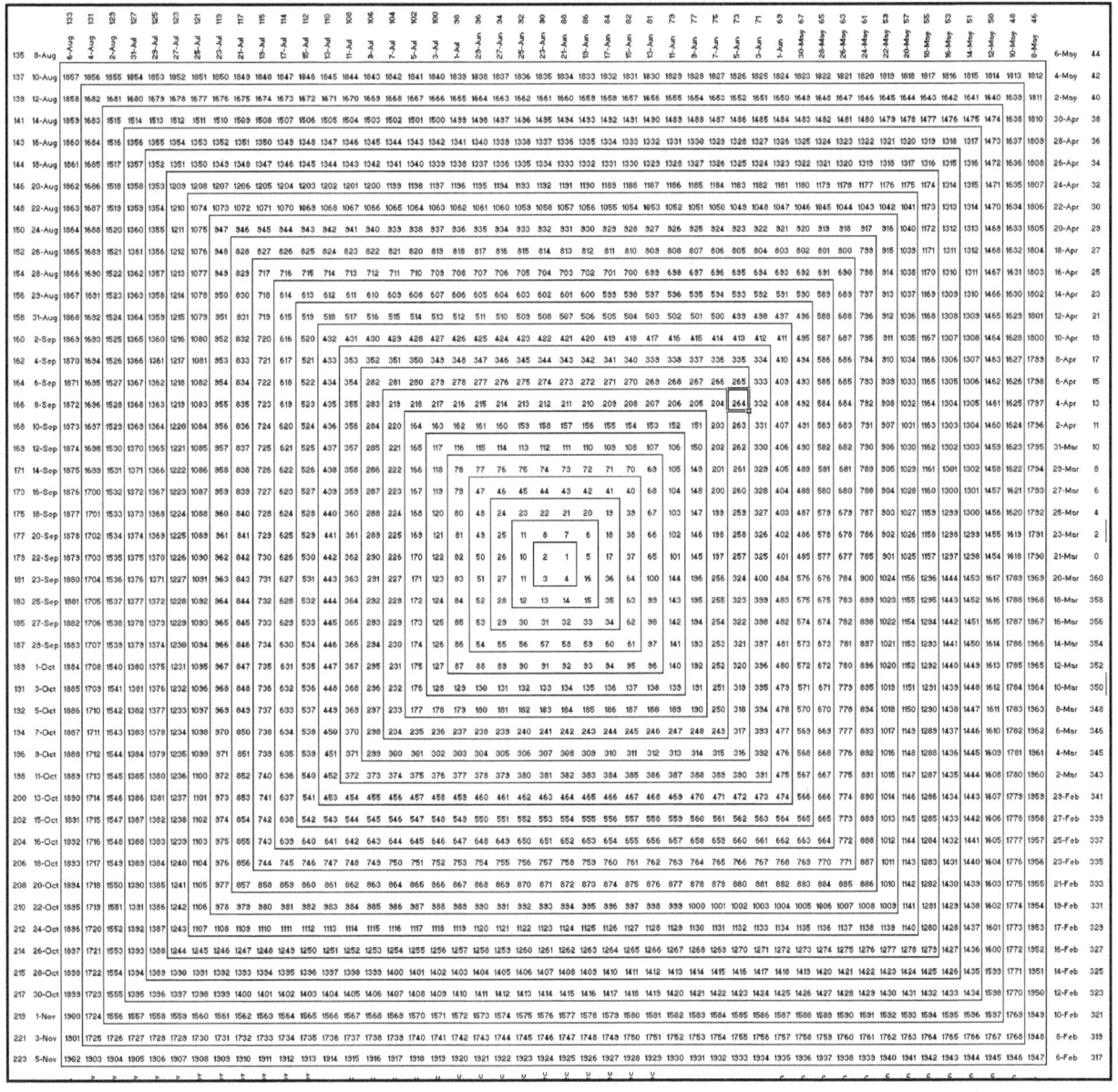

EXHIBIT 12.2 - Square of Four Chart

MAJOR YEAR CHANGES OF TREND

The major yearly long term trends usually terminate on their anniversary dates. They are confirmed by the minor trend directions. For example after a major trend has topped, the minor trend may have a 45 day bottom to high and a 90 day bottom to high trend reversing the market down. See the following rules concerning vibrations of trend direction.

RULES OF VIBRATIONS OF TREND DIRECTION

When the trend ends at the high it is assumed the market will turn down. When the trend ends on the low it is assumed the market will turn up. Follow

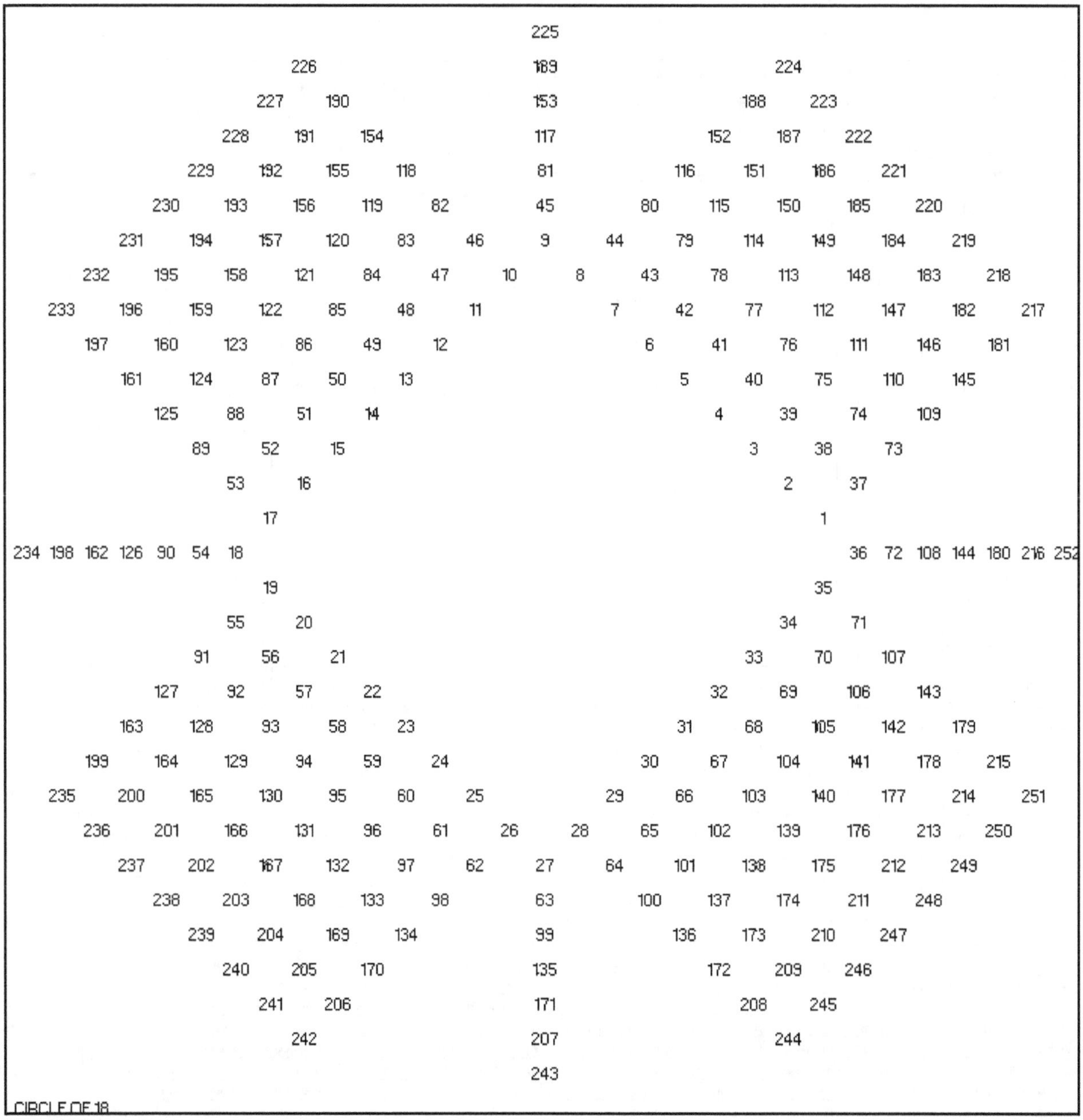

EXHIBIT 12.3 Circle of 18

the next 4 rules concerning this. Study the historical market of each commodity or stock to determine which particular trend from 45 - 315 day has turned its trend in the past.

1) When the vibrations of trend start moving from low to high the trend is turning down.

2) When the vibrations of trend start moving from high to lower high the trend is turning down.

3) When the vibrations of trend start moving from high to low the trend is turning up.

4) When the vibrations of trend start moving from low to higher low the trend is turning up.

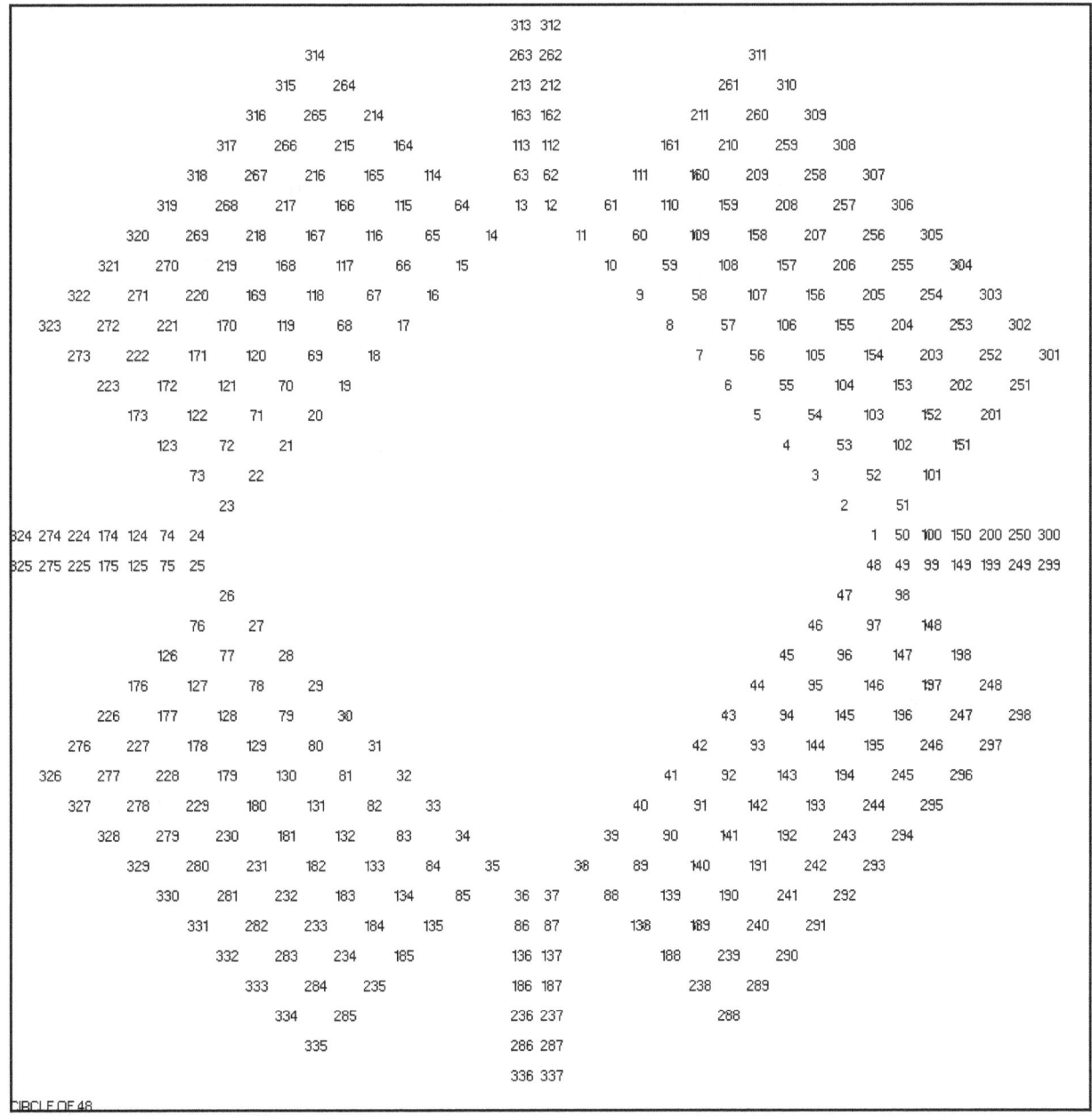

EXHIBIT 12.4 Circle of 48

USING THE SQUARE OF 9 FOR FORECASTING

The square of 9 has become very popular for forecasting time and price. Many expensive Gann wheels have been sold in the last few years. The Gann square of 9 in the Excel template program is an electronic version of one of those expensive wheels. In fact it is much better, because it is precisely accurate. It's based on formulas. For ease of use you may want to create a simple plastic overlay which fits over your computer screen. The advantage of this overlay is that it can be rotated over the square of 9. This is something that the Excel spreadsheet program can't do yet. If you want to, of course, you can figure the points out on the screen without the overlay using the drawing lines in the program. Exhibit 12.8 is an example of the overlay to draw on your screen. Remember, it must be to the scale of your screen. The angles on the overlay

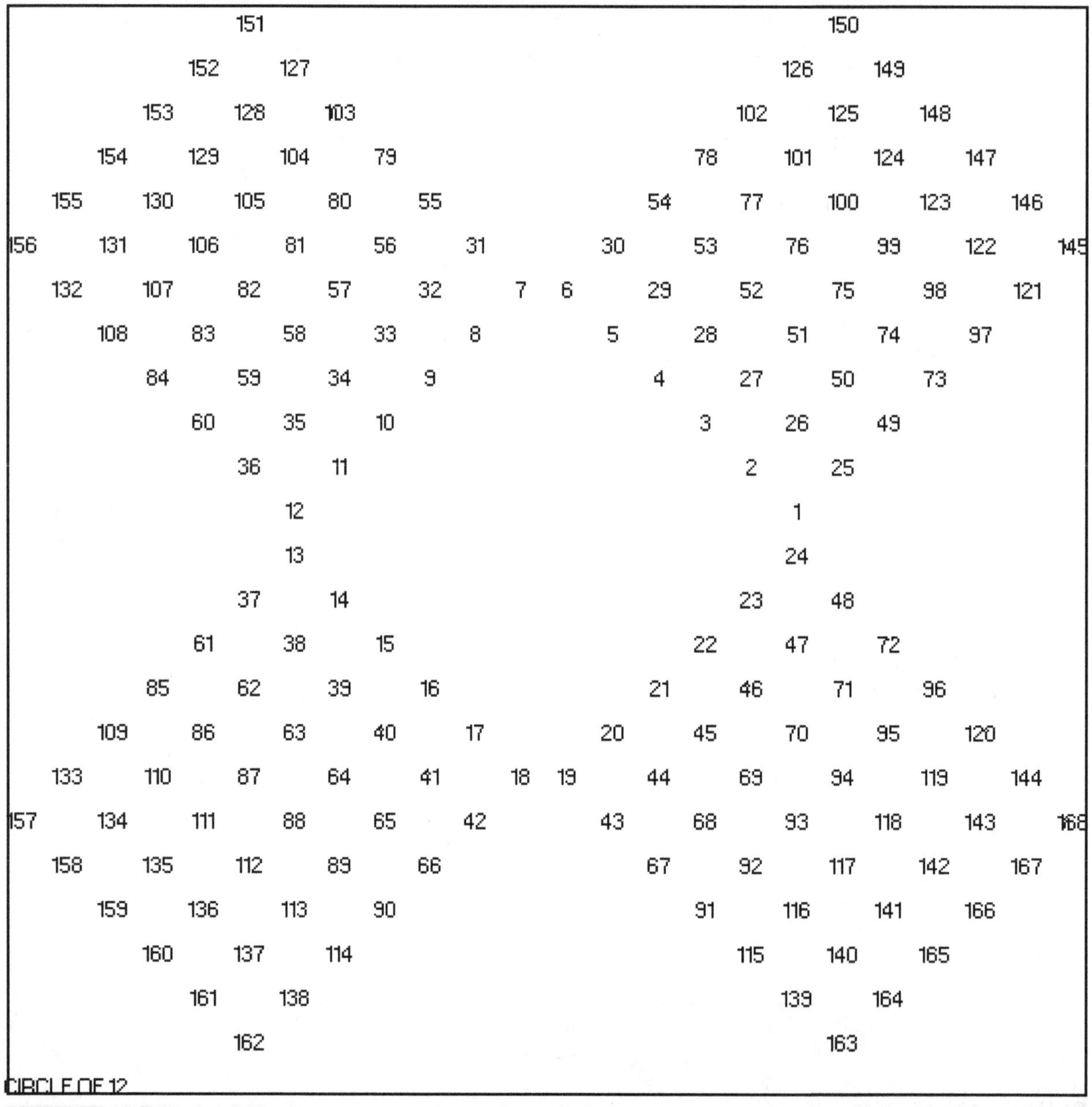

EXHIBIT 12.5 Circle of 12

must be checked carefully with the degrees on the square of 9 for accuracy. We recommend a 17" flat computer screen with adjustable sizing controls so you can get the overlay to fit precisely. With these controls you can adjust the horizontal and vertical size of the screen so it is perfectly square.

The square of 9 is important, because it is based on the number nine. The number nine is the basis of our entire number system. The square of 9 is actually known as the Pythagorean Cube. It starts with a small number in the center and then it spirals outward in ever increasing numbers. The first square ends with the number 9, the second square ends with the number 25. All of these numbers can be exactly squared (3 x 3 = 9, 5 x 5 = 25 and so on). The outside of the square of 9 has both the 360 degrees of the circle and calendar dates of the year on it. This is programmed into the Excel template. The dates

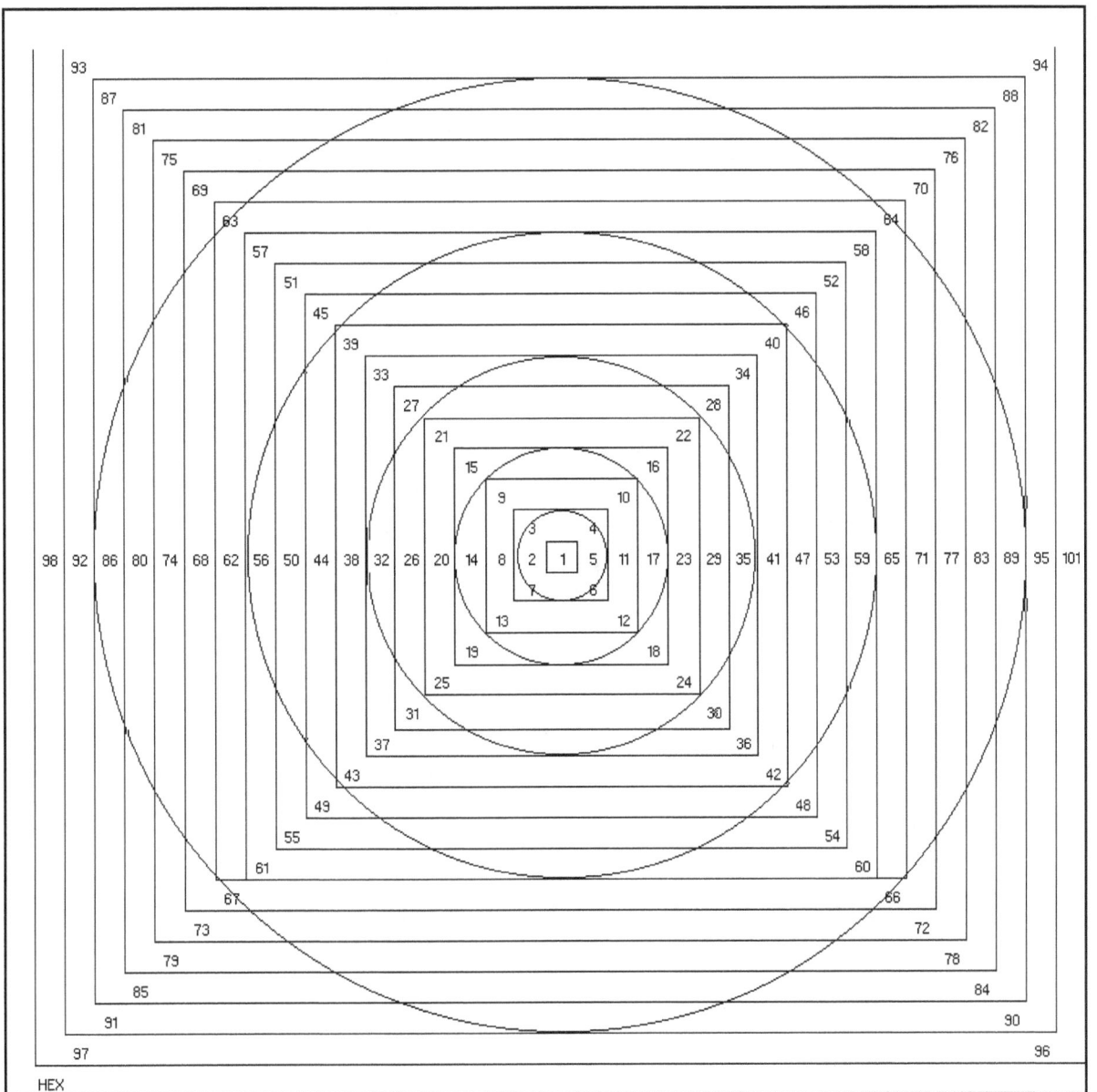

EXHIBIT 12.6 Hexigon chart

include the four quarters of the year starting with the Spring Equinox (March 21st) on the right. The Summer Solstice (June 21st) at the top. The Fall Equinox (September 23rd) at the left and the Winter Solstice (December 21st) at the bottom. These dates run counter clockwise.

The overlay that you can make to overlay on your computer screen can divide the square of 9 into 45 degree sections, 120 degree sections and 144 degree sections. Also on the overlay can be indicated important timing dates such as Fibonacci numbers of 1, 2, 3, 5, 8, 13, 21, 34 55 and so on and lunar 30 day cycles. Also weekly numbers of 5 can be placed around the circle of 5, 10, 15, etc. Also good to put on the overlay is the important death zone of Gann which is the 42 to 55 calendar days.

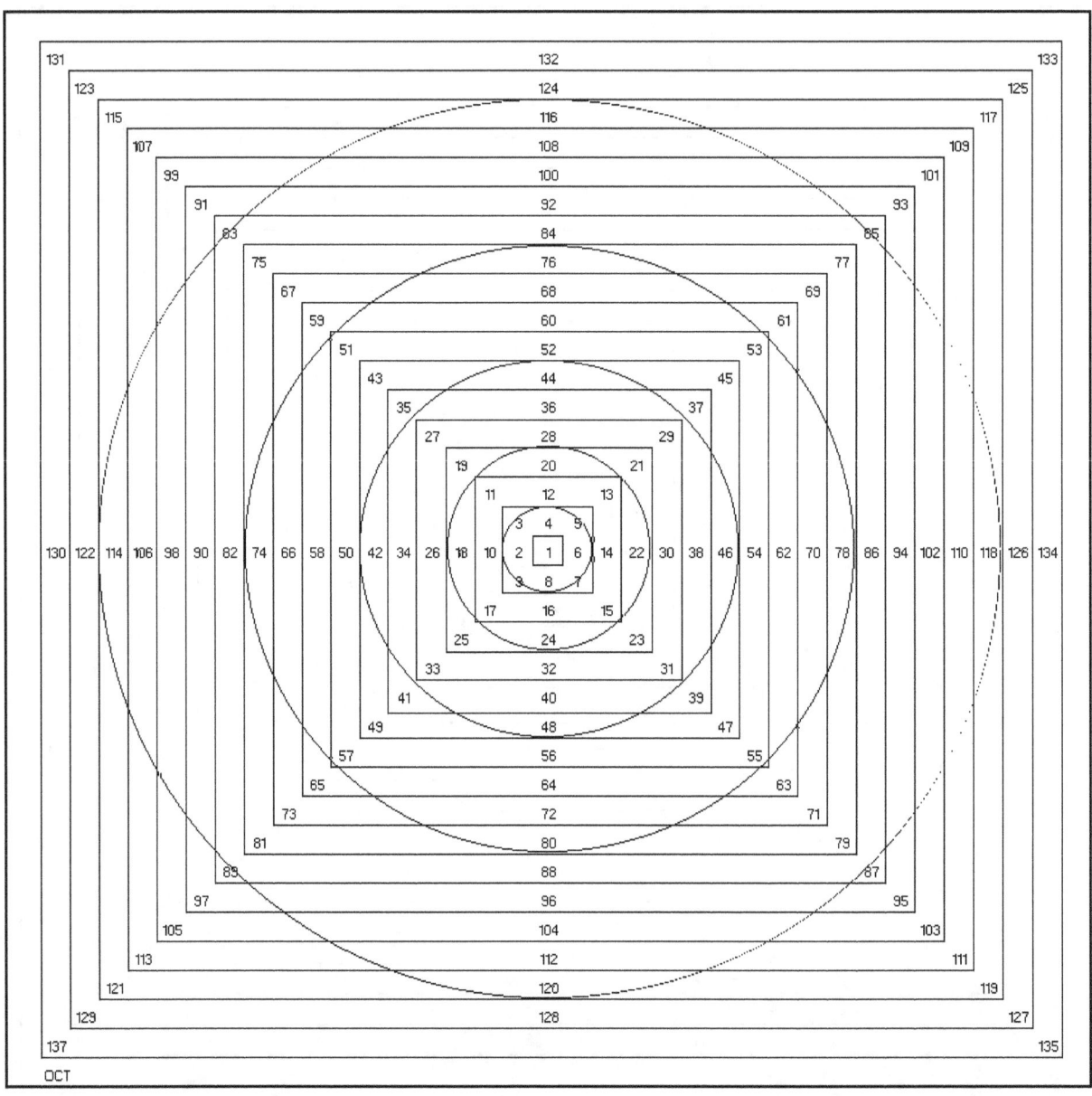

EXHIBIT 12.7 Hexigon Chart

HERE IS HOW TO USE THE OVERLAY

When the market makes an important low or high on a particular date, you should place the overlay on top of the square of 9 on your computer screen. Rotate the overlay so that the 0 point is on that date. Now look on the overlay over 45 days to get the important date of a possible change of trend. The 45 degree line is actually minor resistance. The next 45 degree line over is the next resistance which is 2 x 45 or 90 degrees. This represents major resistance. The market almost always goes through to the 90 degree point in time. The 0 line on the overlay should be placed on the price of the market low. 45 and 90 degrees over in price represent resistance in price. When the time arrives for the possible change in trend, watch were the price is. If it's at one of the angle lines, it's probably major resistance and a major change of trend will usually occur. Sometimes when the market is very strong in one direction it can continue its trend through to the next resistance levels in both time and price. It will go to the 120, 144, 216, 270, 315 and 360 levels in both time and price. Watch all the points carefully for changes in trend. Also watch the Cardinal Square and Fixed Cross points for resistance in price. Also watch the area of square numbers at the end of each circle for resistance points. Using the square of 9 is an art rather than a science.

THE SQUARE OF 4

This chart works exactly as the square of 9. It works in some markets where the square of 9 doesn't. You can find resistance numbers on both the fixed cross and the cardinal square the same way as the square of 9. To determine if you should use this square over the square of 9, count the contract days of the entire contract.

THE HEXAGON CHART

In Exhibit 12.6 the hexagon chart is very important as it shows how angles affect the markets at both low and high levels to different degrees and why markets move faster at high levels than low levels. In the chart:

The second circle ends at 7
The third circle ends at 19 - which is 12 over the second
The fourth circle ends at 37 - which is 18 over the third.
The fifth circle ends at 61 - which is 24 over the fourth.
The six circle (not shown) ends at 91 - which is 30 over the fifth circle.
The seventh circle (not shown) ends at 127 - which is 36 over the sixth.
The eight circle (not shown) ends at 169 - which is 42 over the last circle
The ninth circle (not shown) ends at 217 which is 48 over the last circle.
The tenth is completed at 271 which is a gain of 54 over the last circle.
The eleventh is completed at 331 which is 60 over the last circle
The twelfth is completed at 397 which completes the hexagon which is a gain of 66 over the last circle.

THE OCTAGON CHART

The octagon chart is also very important to show how the markets move from one level to another.

In this chart the second circle ends at 25
The third circle ends at 49 - which is 24 over the second
The fourth circle ends at 81 - which is 32 over the third
The fifth circle ends at 121 - which is 40 over the third and so on.

THE CIRCLE CHARTS OF 12, 18 AND 48

These charts were composed with the Excel spread sheet program. The charts begin with 1 and run around the circle in a counter clockwise motion. The 12 chart expands outward with the multiplier number of 24 and the 18 chart expands outward with the multiplier number of 36, the 48 chart expands outwardly with a multiplier of 50. Gann used these charts by circling recurring prices or dates on the same diagonal level. Go back on the chart that you are following and circle the important highs and lows of the market on the circle charts. Notice how they seem to land on the same diagonal. The Excel spread sheet template can also be changed to dates using these circle charts. If set up in such a manner the important dates of highs and lows will also land on the same diagonals.

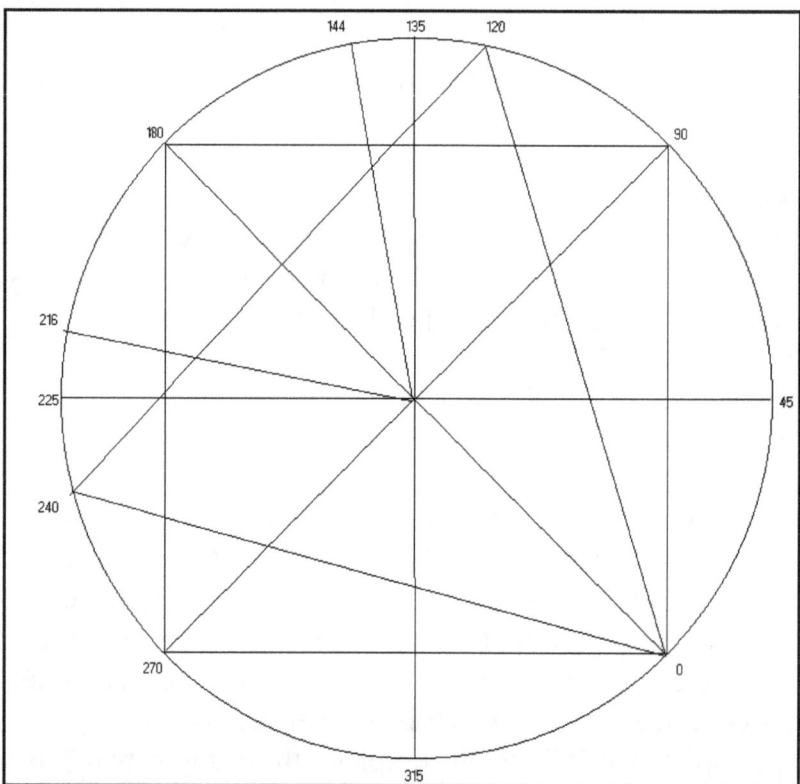

EXHIBIT 12.8 Overlay for the Square of 9

CHAPTER 13

FORECASTING TIME

"Time is the most important factor"

One trader once told me that you can not trade a market unless you know where it is going. W.D. Gann was able to forecast time cycles with amazing accuracy. This chapter tells you how he did most of it. W.D. Gann believed that the future is but a repetition of the past. There are no new things under the sun. By studying the past one can forecast future cycles of the market.

THE 120 YEAR MAJOR CYCLE
This is a very important cycle which is 6 times the 20 year cycle, 4 times the 30 year cycle and 2 times the important 60 year cycle.

THE 100 YEAR MAJOR CYCLE
This is one of the largest cycles which you need to watch closely for comparison to the current time period. Watch for price trends that are similar in their direction with current direction.

THE 90 YEAR MAJOR CYCLE
This is a very important cycle which is 3 times the 30 year cycle and 1 1/2 times the important 60 year cycle.

THE 80 YEAR CYCLE
This is an important cycle which repeats over and over again in the trading history of the markets.

THE 60 YEAR MASTER CYCLE
This the master cycle that repeats over and over again. You should go back and find past 60 year cycles and compare them to the current cycle. To be very accurate in forecasting time you must know this cycle.

THE 49 - 50 YEAR CYCLE
You should also find the 49 - 50 year cycles in the market. This is a very

important cycle. There are seven 7 year cycles in the 49 - 50 year cycle. Watch each 7 year cycle, many times they act the same as prior cycles. For example, the last 7 year cycle in the 49 year cycle is usually down. This knowledge is very important to have.

THE 40 YEAR CYCLE
The 40 year cycle is most important as it is 1/2 of the 80 year cycle. Watch to see how it closely.

THE 30 YEAR CYCLE
Watch the 30 year cycle which is 1/2 of the 60 year master cycle. Each of these 30 year cycles inside of the big 60 year cycles is important.

THE 20 YEAR CYCLE
This cycle is important as their are 3 of these in each 60 year cycle. Watch for similar action to determine the trend of this cycle.

THE 15 YEAR CYCLE
This cycle is also important as it is 1/2 of the 30 year cycle. Watch it closely in conjuction with the 30 year cycle.

THE 10 YEAR CYCLE
This is a very important cycle as their are 6 of these in the 60 year cycle, 5 of these in the 50 year cycle, 3 of these in the 30 year cycle and 2 of these in the 20 year cycle.

THE 8 YEAR CYCLE
This is a very important cycle that often shows up which is 1 year above the 7 year cycle.

THE 7 YEAR CYCLE
This cycle is also important to watch as their are 7 of these in the 49 year cycle and 14 of these in the 98 year cycle.

THE 5 YEAR CYCLE
This is a very important cycle to watch as it is part of every other cycle above. This is the smallest cycle that we look at for comparison purposes.

THE 2 /12 - 3 1/2 YEAR CYCLE
This cycle is most important as most counter trends react against the main trend with one of these small cycles.

HARMOMICS OF THESE CYCLES

All of these cycles have harmonic years. To get these harmonics just divide the cycle into 10. For example the important 60 year cycle divided by 10 is 6. Therefore every 6 years there will be a harmonic of of the major cycle. The 90 and 60 year cycles are the major ones and are very important. It is impossible in most cases to get data going back 60 - 90 years. You have to scan the NY Times for even sometimes cash data to interpolate. The harmonic years give you an idea of what the major cycle is even if you don't have the data. For the 60 year cycle if you go back for example every 6 years for 20-30 years you will have a good idea of what the major 60 year cycle was. This is especially true if every 6 years back the market did exactly the same thing.

THE 1 YEAR AND UNDER CYCLE

The cycles under one year are all based on the circle. The cycles inside of the year are the 45, 90, 120, 135, 144, 216, 240, 244, and 270. The 45 day cycle can be broken down even further into 22 1/2, 11 1/4 day cycles. The 120 day cycle can be broken down into 60, 30, 15 and 7 1/2 day cycles. The 144 day cycle can be broken down into 72, 36, 18, and 9 day cycles. It is important to understand that all cycles must fit within each other. The smallest cycle of 11 1/4 is a part of even the 100 year cycle. The cycles in this paragraph make up all the important cycles in the world. Everything is based on these cycles. If you find an important cycle that is not one of these, then it must be a Fibonnaci ratio of one of these cycles.

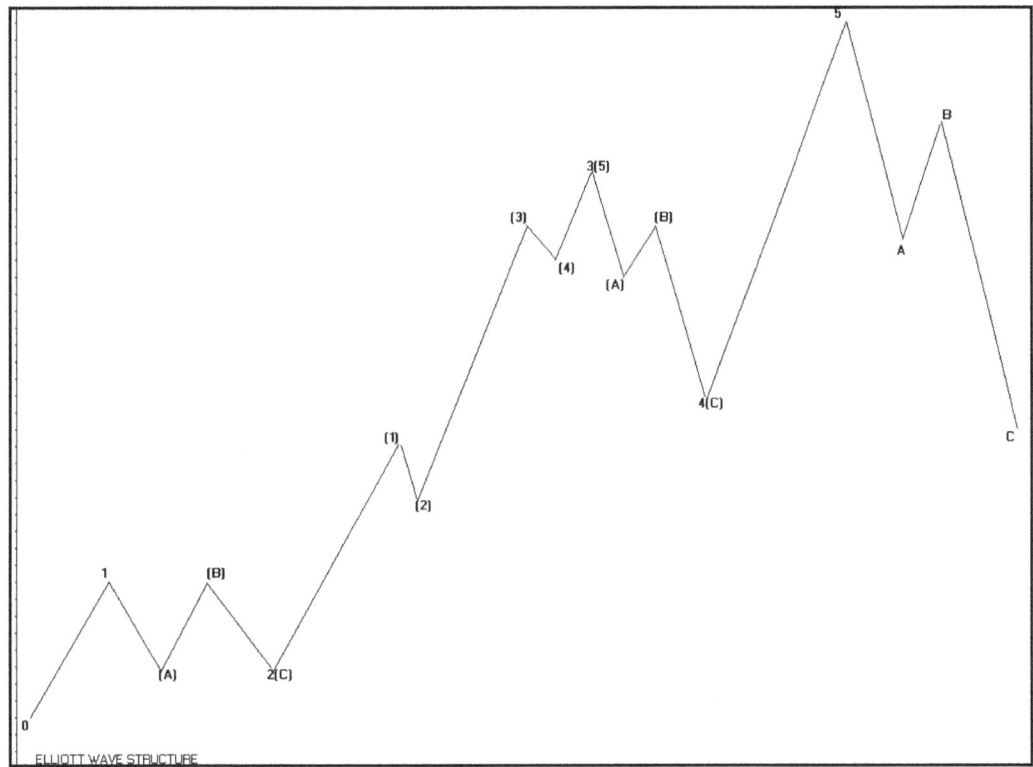

EXHIBIT 13.1 Elliott wave structure of the market

HOW TO USE THE CYCLES

The most important thing you can do is to watch how the cycles are working. Compare the current cycles with those of the past. Go back to each of the cycle years and compare them to the current ones. You should print out all past harmonic cycle years on translucent paper and overlay them on top of each other. When most of the harmonic cycles are in the same direction then the probability of that direction in the market today is pretty sure. Sometimes when only half of all the cycles are in one direction, you must wait for all cycles to turn in that same direction. All of the major cycles can be divided by 10 or 5 to get harmonics of the big cycles. Watch those 10 and 5 divisions of prior cycles to determine how the market might move in each future division. Many times each division will have the same exact movement as prior divisions. Watch the major 90 and 60 year cycles as these represent the dominate cycles of the market. If both of these change in one direction, it is almost a sure thing that the market will move in that direction.

USING DAILY CHARTS FOR FORECASTING

Daily price movements give the first change of trend in the markets. Watch for the 10 week time period. Also watch for the 7 1/2, 11 1/4, 15, 22.5, 30,

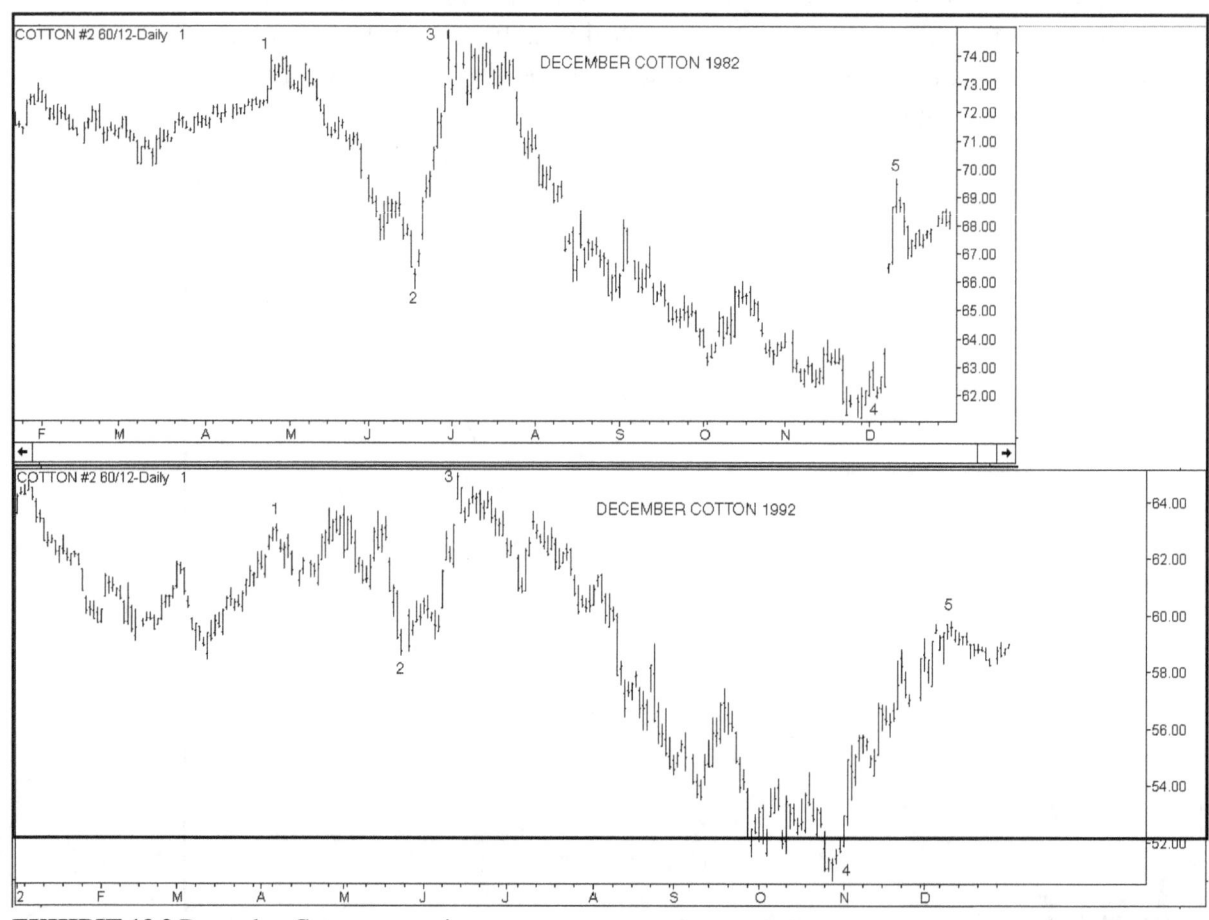

EXHIBIT 13.2 December Cotton comparison

45,60, 72, 90, 100 day cycles. This works the same as using the major cycles. For example if 10 weeks ago the market started to move up then watch the current time period. If it starts to move up exactly 10 weeks from its last low then it is important.

SHIFTS IN CYCLES

There are sometimes shifts in the major cycles several days from anniversary high or low days. This is caused by progression of time. That means that time has gotten out of sink or has shifted several days. You can find that shift and make allowences for it by looking at the pattern of today and comparing it the pattern of a past cycle. You should use transparent chart paper and overlay them on top of each other and slide the paper to the right or left to allow for that shift of time. There are many cases the anniversary dates of past harmonic cycle years hit the exact date! In Exhibit 13.2 we show a comparison of December Cotton 1982 to December Cotton of 1992. We have shifted the 1982 contract to the left to allow for the change in progression of time. See how the swings of the market are almost identical.

BEGINNINGS OF TIME PERIODS (CHANGING OF TRENDS)

Watch the first and third week of the beginnings of these important times of the year. Usually a range of days will set up with a high and a low. When prices break out one way or another the other side of the range becomes resistance or support. In order of importance these are the periods to watch for:

January 21 - Watch the first 5 days
March 21- Watch the first 5 days
June 21- Watch the first 5 days
September 21- Watch the first 5 days

Yearly - Watch the first and third week of January
Semi-Annual - Watch the first and third week of July
Quarterly - Watch the first and third of week of April and October.

You should also divide the year into divisions and watch the first 5 days of each division for a change of trend.

Divide the year into 2 to get 6 months
Divide the year into 4 to get 3 months
Divide the year into 3 to get 4 months
Divide the year into 8 to get 1/2 months
Divide the year into 16 to get 22 1/2 days
Divide the year into 32 to get 11 1/4 days

COMPARISONS OF YEARS ENDING WITH SAME DIGIT

Go back over the years and overlay all years that end in the same digit. For example for the current year of 1995, you should compare 1985, 1975, 1965, 1955 etc. This can be done easily with a program such as SuperCharts or Trade Station. The program is windows based and allows windows of the different years to be overlaid vertically on top of each other. In Exhibit 13.3 December Wheat tends to have highs in years ending with 9 and lows with years ending in 7.

REOCCURRING CYCLES

The market normally makes the same amount of moves from it's peaks and troughs. You should go back and look at all past cycles carefully. Watch the following combinations to determine the probable cycle length. Write all prior counts down and keep tract of them for future reference. List all of the following in the market:

High to Low
Low to High
Top to Top
Bottom to Bottom

EXHIBIT 13.3 Comparison of years with same digit

Those moves can be in both calendar days and market days. To calculate the differences you can use the Excel spread sheet for the calendar days and the master plastic overlays for market days. The two projections will create a time windows for you to trade on.

RATIOS

It is also a good idea to use ratios between the following:

High to Low
Low to High
Top to Top
Bottom to Bottom

The following Fibonacci ratios work very nicely. These are the ratios that we have programmed into the Excel spreadsheet See Exhibit 13.4. This is a picture of the Excel spread sheet module for wave forecasting based on those ratios. By inputting three dates in this spread sheet you can get the top to top or bottom to bottom time calculations. By inputing 2 dates in the spreadsheet you can get bottom to top and top to bottom calculations of timing points. See exhibit 13.4 and 13.5.

.382
.500
.618
1.00
1.382
1.500
1.618
2.000
2.382
2.500
2.618

WAVE STRUCTURE

To be able to understand major cycles of the market, it is necessary to use wave structure of the market. Exhibit 13.1 is basic Elliott wave pattern which must be understood to do proper cycle analysis. All wave patterns are based on this diagram. The distance between wave bottoms and tops are based on Gann numbers and Fibonacci ratios of these numbers. You must understand there are different degrees of wave patterns. A lot has to do with what picture you are looking at. Are you looking at a daily (short term) chart, a weekly (intermediate term) chart or a monthly (long term) chart. Each of these time frames is working in its own wave structure. All wave structures must mesh with each other from the smallest all the way up to the monthly. It is best to do a wave analysis of the three important time frames of the market. These time frames are as follows:

1) Major - use a 15 - 30 year monthly chart.
2) Intermediate - use a 5 - 10 year weekly chart
3) Minor - use a 5 year daily chart.

TIMING BASED ON RATIOS OF WAVE STUCTURE

Future timing points are based on ratios of prior tops and bottoms in the market. The Excel spread sheet is set up to calculate many of these ratios which will save you a lot of time. These ratios of couse will be based on calendar days, not on market days. You will find that you might get away with just using the Excel spread sheet for these calculations because we have found that in many cases they both come up with close to the same dates. Now lets go into some of the time ratios caluclations with some examples.

DATES						Diff	1st Date Projections								
No	1st date	No	2nd date	No	2rd date	Diff	45.00	90.00	120.00	135.00	144.00	180.00	216.00	225.00	240.00	270.00
1	10/8/91	1	10/22/91	1	12/11/91	64.0000	11/22/91	1/6/92	2/5/92	2/20/92	2/29/92	4/5/92	5/11/92	5/20/92	6/4/92	7/4/92
2	8/19/82	2	8/20/82	2	10/4/82	46.0000	10/3/82	11/17/82	12/17/82	1/1/83	1/10/83	2/15/83	3/23/83	4/1/83	4/16/83	5/16/83
3	10/12/82	3	10/12/82	3	11/1/82	20.0000	11/26/82	1/10/83	2/9/83	2/24/83	3/5/83	4/10/83	5/16/83	5/25/83	6/9/83	7/9/83
4	5/18/82	4	5/18/82	4	6/17/82	30.0000	7/2/82	8/16/82	9/15/82	9/30/82	10/9/82	11/14/82	12/20/82	12/29/82	1/13/83	2/12/83
5	5/6/92	5	5/6/92	5	5/1/94	725.0000	6/20/92	8/4/92	9/3/92	9/18/92	9/27/92	11/2/92	12/8/92	12/17/92	1/1/93	1/31/93
6	5/19/92	6	5/19/92	6	5/1/94	712.0000	7/3/92	8/17/92	9/16/92	10/1/92	10/10/92	11/15/92	12/21/92	12/30/92	1/14/93	2/13/93
7	5/1/94	7	5/1/94	7	9/1/94	123.0000	6/15/94	7/30/94	8/29/94	9/13/94	9/22/94	10/28/94	12/3/94	12/12/94	12/27/94	1/26/95
8	5/1/94	8	5/1/94	8	6/1/94	31.0000	6/15/94	7/30/94	8/29/94	9/13/94	9/22/94	10/28/94	12/3/94	12/12/94	12/27/94	1/26/95

2nd Date Projections										3rd Date Projections								
45.00	90.00	120.00	135.00	144.00	180.00	216.00	225.00	240.00	270.00	45.00	90.00	120.00	135.00	144.00	180.00	216.00	225.00	240.00	270.00
12/6/91	1/20/92	2/19/92	3/5/92	3/14/92	4/19/92	5/25/92	6/3/92	6/18/92	7/18/92	1/25/92	3/10/92	4/9/92	4/24/92	5/3/92	6/8/92	7/14/92	7/23/92	8/7/92	9/6/92
10/4/82	11/18/82	12/18/82	1/2/83	1/11/83	2/16/83	3/24/83	4/2/83	4/17/83	5/17/83	11/18/82	1/2/83	2/1/83	2/16/83	2/25/83	4/2/83	5/8/83	5/17/83	6/1/83	9/6/82
11/26/82	1/10/83	2/9/83	2/24/83	3/5/83	4/10/83	5/16/83	5/25/83	6/9/83	7/9/83	12/16/82	1/30/83	3/1/83	3/16/83	3/25/83	4/30/83	6/5/83	6/14/83	6/29/83	7/29/83
7/2/82	8/16/82	9/15/82	9/30/82	10/9/82	11/14/82	12/20/82	12/29/82	1/13/83	2/12/83	8/1/82	9/15/82	10/15/82	10/30/82	11/8/82	12/14/82	1/19/83	1/29/83	2/12/83	3/14/83
6/20/92	8/4/92	9/3/92	9/18/92	9/27/92	11/2/92	12/8/92	12/17/92	1/1/93	1/31/93	6/15/94	7/30/94	8/29/94	9/13/94	9/22/94	10/28/94	12/3/94	12/12/94	12/27/94	1/26/95
7/3/92	8/17/92	9/16/92	10/1/92	10/10/92	11/15/92	12/21/92	12/30/92	1/14/93	2/13/93	6/15/94	7/30/94	8/29/94	9/13/94	9/22/94	10/28/94	12/3/94	12/12/94	12/27/94	1/26/95
6/15/94	7/30/94	8/29/94	9/13/94	9/22/94	10/28/94	12/3/94	12/12/94	12/27/94	1/26/95	10/16/94	11/30/94	12/30/94	1/14/95	1/23/95	2/28/95	4/5/95	4/14/95	4/29/95	5/29/95
6/15/94	7/30/94	8/29/94	9/13/94	9/22/94	10/28/94	12/3/94	12/12/94	12/27/94	1/26/95	7/16/94	8/30/94	9/29/94	10/14/94	10/23/94	11/28/94	1/3/95	1/12/95	1/27/95	2/26/95

Fib Projections																	
0.3820	Diff	0.5000	Diff	0.6180	Diff	1.0000	Diff	1.3820	Diff	1.5000	Diff	1.6180	Diff	2.0000	Diff	2.3820	Diff	2.5000	Diff	2.6180	Diff
1/4/92	24	1/12/92	32	1/19/92	40	2/13/92	64	3/8/92	88	3/16/92	96	3/23/92	104	4/17/92	128	5/11/92	152	5/19/92	160	5/26/92	173
10/21/82	18	10/27/82	23	11/1/82	28	1/26/92	3401	12/6/82	64	12/12/82	69	12/17/82	74	1/4/83	92	1/21/83	110	1/27/83	115	2/1/83	120
11/8/82	8	11/11/82	10	11/13/82	12	12/3/91	3347	11/28/82	28	12/1/82	30	12/3/82	32	12/11/82	40	12/19/82	48	12/21/82	50	12/23/82	27
6/28/82	11	7/2/82	15	7/5/82	19	7/10/92	3494	7/28/82	41	8/1/82	45	8/4/82	49	8/16/82	60	8/27/82	71	8/31/82	75	9/3/82	64
2/1/95	277	4/28/95	363	7/23/95	448	12/5/93	-147	1/26/97	1002	4/22/97	1088	7/17/97	1173	4/20/98	1450	1/21/99	1727	4/17/99	1813	7/12/99	2578
1/27/95	272	4/22/95	356	7/15/95	440	11/22/93	-160	1/8/97	984	4/3/97	1068	6/26/97	1152	3/25/98	1424	12/21/98	1696	3/16/99	1780	6/8/99	2531
10/17/94	47	11/1/94	62	11/16/94	76	4/12/92	-872	2/17/95	170	3/4/95	185	3/19/95	199	5/5/95	246	6/20/95	293	7/5/95	308	7/20/95	400
7/10/94	39	6/16/94	16	6/20/94	19	1/1/92	-872	7/13/94	43	7/17/94	47	7/22/94	50	8/2/94	62	8/13/94	74	8/17/94	78	8/21/94	67

EXHIBIT 13.4 Date and Fibonacci projections

HIGHS TO LOWS

In the Elliott wave model take all highs to lows and plug them into the program. For the Elliott wave model from Exhibit 13.1 use the following waves:

Wave 1 - 2(c)
Wave 3(5) - 4(c)
Wave 5 to C

LOWS TO HIGHS

In the Elliott wave model take all lows to highs and plug them into the program. For the Elliott wave model from Exhibit 13.1 use the following waves:

Wave 0 - 1
Wave 2(c) - 3(5)
Wave 4(c) - 5
Wave 0 - 5

TOP TO TOP

In the Elliott wave model take all high to highs and plug them into the program. For the Elliott wave model from Exhibit 13.1 use the following waves:

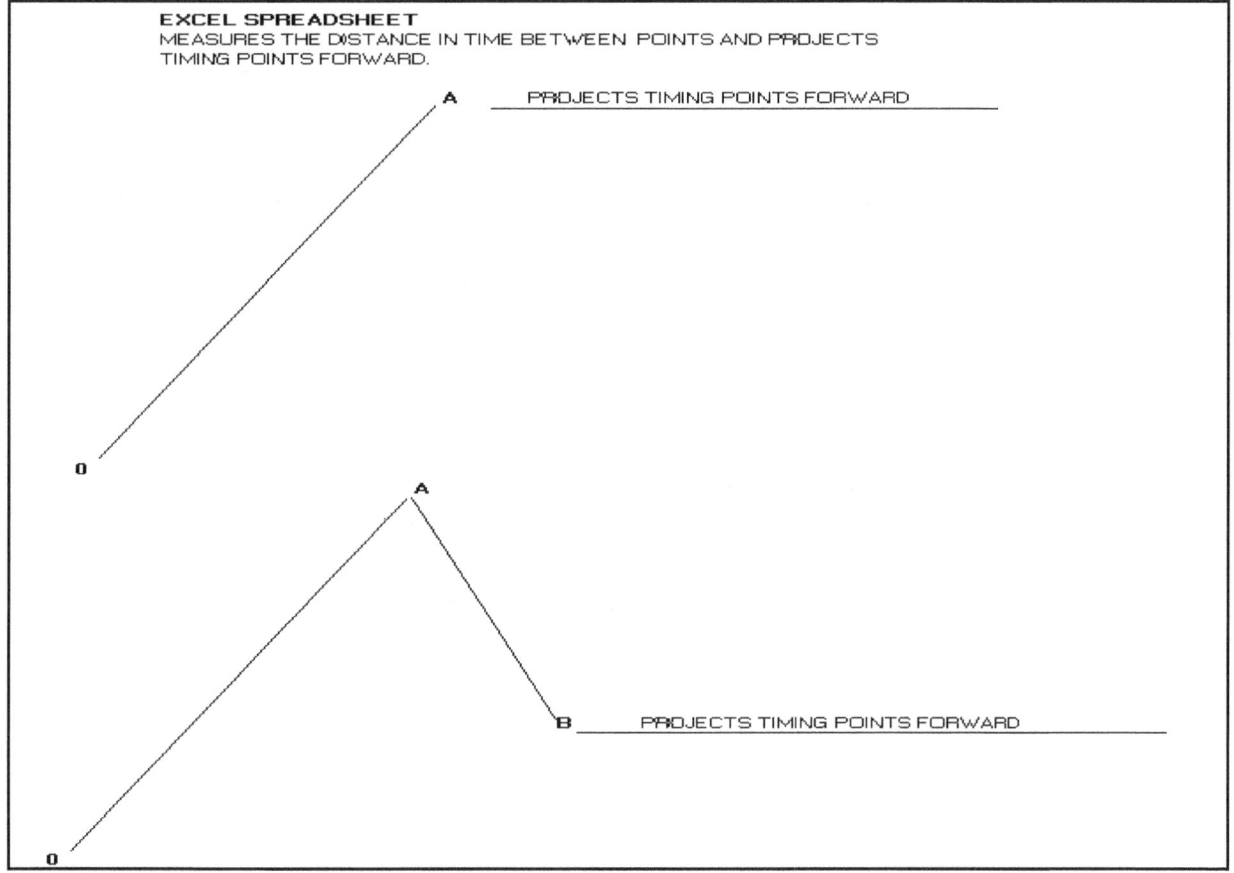

EXHIBIT 13.5 Excel spread sheet projects timing points forward.

Wave 1 - 3(5)
Wave 3(5) - 5
Wave 1 - 5

BOTTOM TO BOTTOM

In the Elliott wave model take all lows to lows and plug them into the program. For the Elliott wave model from Exhibit 13.1 use the following waves:

Wave 0 - 2(c)
Wave 2(c) - 4(c)
Wave 4(c) - C
Wave 0 - C

USING MINOR TO MAJOR CYCLES

All of these calculations are based on the minor degree of daily chart data. These will give you only minor calculations of important pivot points. You should also calculate the same ratios based on intermediate (weekly data) and major (monthly data). These are much more important and signal major changes of trend from major pivot points. All three degrees - minor, intermediate and major must work together. That means if you are expecting a major top based on the monthly charts, then the intermediate (weekly charts) and the minor (daily charts) should all concide without conflict.

SAME WAVE PATTERN

The program will calculate future timing points based on Fibonacci ratios from these tops and bottom. When three or more dates come together it should be an important pivot timing point. In comparing past major time cycles with current time cycles it is necessary to understand that if you are comparing a major time cycle pattern that happened 30 years ago with one today, it is very important that both patterns have the same wave pattern.

PROGRAMMED RATIOS

From the number of days between the 1st, 2nd and 3rd or the 2nd and 3rd, the time sheet calculates ratios forward from the 3rd date. The ratios programmed in are as follows: (See Exhibit 13.4)

1) .382
2) .500
3) .618
4) 1.00
5) 1.318

6) 1.500
7) 1.618
8) 2.000
9) 2.382
10) 2.50

From these ratios the time sheet projects forward the time in days between the 1st, 2nd and 3rd or the 2nd and 3rd dates forward in those Fibonacci ratios. Every wave is a ratio of a prior wave. When you get several dates that are exactly the same projected forward by both the Gann and Fibonacci numbers, you have a significant timing point in the future. When you get 3 projection dates close to each other, it is significant. The market will usually change direction when it hits these significant cluster of dates. The ratios in the Excel time sheet are variable, so that you can change them to fit the market. Some markets work better with some ratios than others.

NUMBER OF DAYS

The Fibonacci ratios have the difference in days beside the date, so you can determine if the number of days is significant. This gives you the measure of the wave in time. If the numbers are close to the Gann circle numbers (45, 90, 120 etc.) they are significant and you should put more importance on them. You will also notice that the distance between the 1st, 2nd and 3rd dates are totalled in a column in days.

INTRADAY TIMING POINTS

This time sheet can also be adjusted to project intraday timing points down to the very minute. It has been tested with 1 minute tick charts and many times it will project the intraday turns of the market within 5 minutes! The Fibonacci ratios of the swings projected forward are very important again when they are a Gann circle number. For example 45, 90, 120 hours etc.

USING BEGINNING NUMBERS FOR FORECASTING

When a major bottom is formed the market will start up and go up the amount of the beginning number of its bottom. When it makes a major top the market will go down the amount beginning number of it's top. For example, it Wheat made a bottom at 43, it will move up as follows:

43 minutes
43 hours
43 days
43 months
43 years

When a major bottom is made it causes ripples in the market almost like throwing a rock in a pond. The bottom causes waves in the market. When the Wheat market makes a top at 395 that too creates market ripples that last through time. The market will move down:

395 minutes
395 hours
395 days
395 weeks
395 months
395 years

The time sheet can be used to forecast time from beginning numbers. Those beginning numbers can be put into the time sheet. Daily numbers should be used for the minor time frame. When using the intermediate and major time frame - that is weekly and monthly charts, you should use the bigger numbers. Those weekly and monthly numbers must be converted into daily numbers to be used in the Excel time sheet, as it will only work with daily numbers. For example, 395 weeks equals (395 x 7) or 2765 days. Remember when using the intermediate and major cycles that all trends end with the minor cycle. For example a cycle might end in 395 weeks and 395 days.

For example, if wheat just formed at major bottom at 43, you could set the time sheet to project out 43 days, 43 weeks, or 43 months. Remember it is necessary to convert the weekly and monthly numbers to daily as the time sheet won't understand weeks, or months.

USING CIRCLE NUMBERS FROM BEGINNING NUMBERS

The important circle number can also be used to forecast from important tops and bottoms. These can be put into the time sheet also. Remember the more clusters of timing point out in the future the more important is the projected pivot point. Using the circle numbers of:

45
72
90
120
144
216
240
270
360

HARMONICS OF BEGINNING NUMBERS

The time sheet can also be set to forecast harmonics of the beginning number. For a low of 43 days set the numbers to 43, 86, 129. 172 and so on. This would give you a turning point at every interval of 43.

SQUARE OF 9 AND 4 FOR TIME PROJECTION

We have also programmed into the Excel template the square of 9 and the square of 4 charts. These charts are an electronic marvel! They are 10 times better than any other Gann wheel, because you can change the center number to a beginning number or date for time and price projection. For time that number should be set a beginning date of a contract or of a minor, intermediate or major bottom. See Exhibit 13.6.

USING THE CENTER WITH BEGINNING NUMBERS

The square of 4 should be used with a contact with an even number of days and the square of 9 should be used with a contract with an odd number of days. Experiment of with both squares to see which one is hitting the numbers better. For time set the center number to the beginning date of the contract. You will find resistance to advance at the end of each circle and at the Cardinal and Fixed Cross points.

USING THE SQUARES WITH 1 AT THE CENTER

The squares can also be used effectively in their natural state with 1 at the center. This gives you the natural numbers from which to find time resistance points. If you locate the prior market tops and bottoms in the square you will

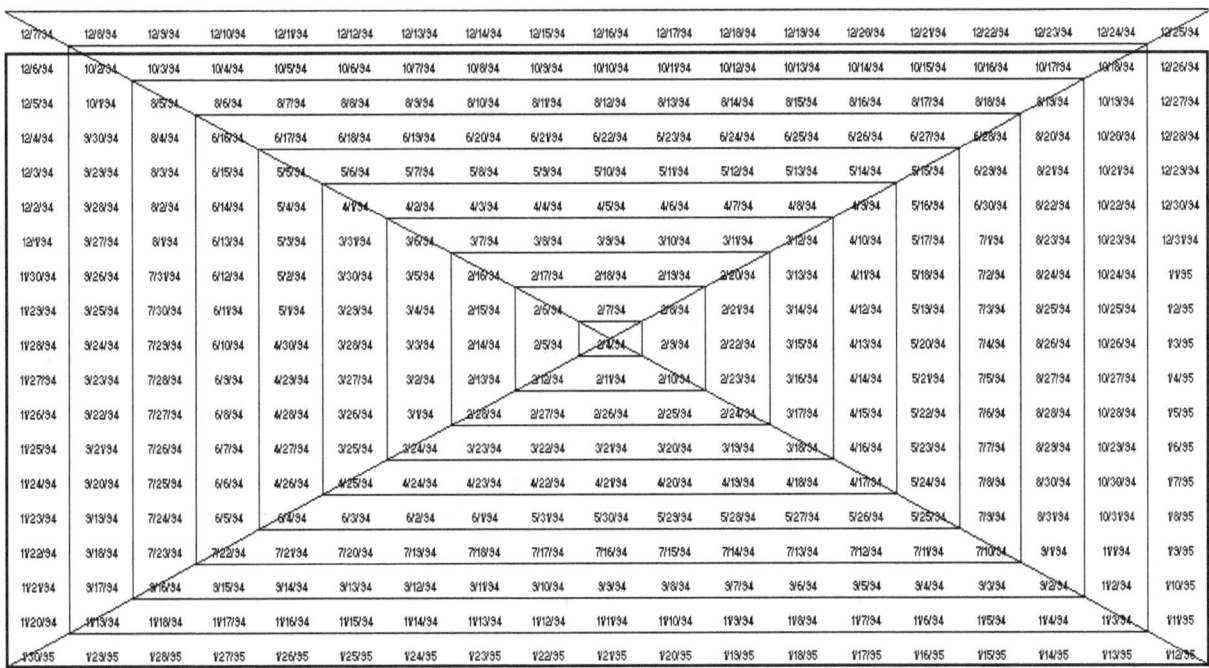

EXHIBIT 13.6 Square of 9 for dates

find that many of them are on natural Cardinal or Fixed Cross points. These are dates around the outside of the square. If you find the dates hit the same time as the price in the square this is a very significant. This means that the contract is locked in with natural time and resistance points. You will have to use the plastic overlay to match the date on the outside with the inner square numbers. See the overlay example in Exhibit 12.8. You will have to draw this on a plastic overlay sheet in the scale of your computer screen or print the square out on paper and use it over that.

The overlay divides the square of 9 or 4 up into proportions. Place the 0 point of the overlay on the date a market starts to move. Then watch for a turn in the market over 45, 90, 120, 144, 180, 216, 240, or 270 degrees using the plastic overlay. When you move the overlay to the projected date check to see if the price of the commodity it intersecting the line going through the center to the other side. It is important if the price of the commodity is at an some important angle to the date that it is on. For example, 90, 180, or 120 degrees over. This is called price aspecting. When the market starts to run up in price and intersects at numbers on the 45, 90, 120 degree lines then there will probable be a change of trend. In the opposite fashion if the price starts to decline into the 45, 90, 120 degree points and aspects with key prices then the market will then again have a change of trend.

TABLE CHART SHEETS FOR TIME PROJECTION

The Excel sheet has also been programmed to have all of the important Gann table charts.

1) Table of 3
2) Table of 6
3) Table of 9
4) Table of 12
5) Table of 19
6) Table of 20
7) Table of 24
8) Table of 27
9) Table of 36
10) Table of 52
11) Table of 90

These table charts can be used effectivelt to indicate resistance in time for markets. You must find what table the market is working to use them effectively. For example, Gann used the Table of 20 chart for the New York Stock Exchange. He called it his NY Stock Exchange Permanent Chart. These table charts can be used for both time and price forecasting. For time you would set the beginning 1 number to an important beginning date of a minor, intermediate or major low. It could also be set to the first trading day of a contract. Draw 45 degree angles off of the beginning of the bottom and top of the table and carry them through the table. Intersections of these angles as well as the top and bottom of the table charts are support and resistance to time. Therefore using the NYSE Permenent Table Chart major resistance is found every 20 calendar days from an important bottom. See Exhibit 13.7.

These table charts can be adjusted so that a prior market high date is on top. By trial and error keep changing the 1 position to a date that makes a high date on the top of the table.

USING THE MASTER OVERLAYS TO FORECAST TIME

The plastic overlays should be used to forecast important time points in the future as to market days. The master overlays can save significant time in projecting time based on market days. They are as effective with market days as the Excel spreadsheet is with calendar days.

You should make up all the imporant overlays to match your computer screen or the paper charts that you are following. The need to be adjusted to the proper scale of both price and time. If you use a computer screen, this can be done using a good program like SuperCharts which can lock the scale in. You will also need to have a horizontal and vertical adjustment on your computer screen to make sure the chart is square.

You will find that tops and bottom are formed based on the circle numbers and the circle numbers are where the overlays come from. Tops and bottoms occur every 45, 72, 90, 120, 144, 216, 240, 270 and 360 days from other tops and bottoms.

Another imporant feature the master overlays have is that markets will work in certain squares and will change directions when they cross from one square to the next. The market will usually work out 9 squares in one major direction. This takes a lot of trial and error to find the right square the market is working in. Using this method it is usually necessary to use either MAX:CHART or GannTrader to print out the charts for testing overlays.

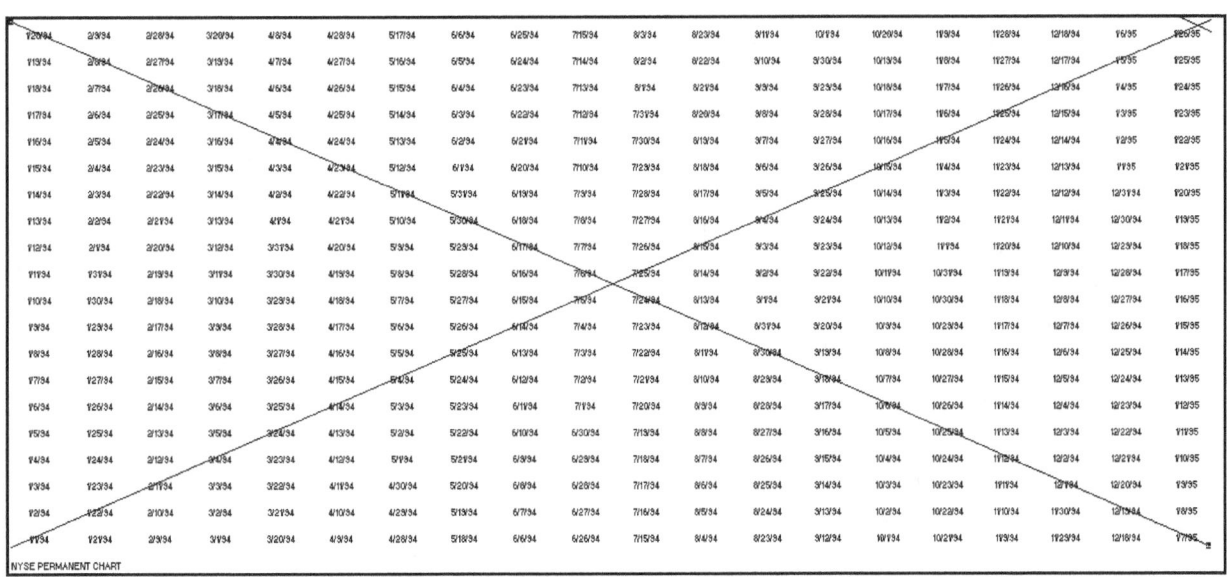

EXHIBIT 13.7 Table Chart for time analysis

CHAPTER 14

FORECASTING PRICE

•••

To be successful in trading you must know where price is going.

Price forecasting is one of the most difficult Gann techniques. In this chapter we will go into the techniques that are available. Many of the techniques are different, but in the end they come out to the same price projection. These techniques should be used in combination with the time forecasting techniques. Time must in the end square out with price. In many respects time and price are one and the same thing. Using our Excel template you will find that you can change the format of the squares in a sheet from numbers to time and the same sheet can be used for time forecasting. This includes every sheet in the Excel template that we have programmed for you.

TABLE CHARTS

One of the easiest ways of forecasting price is to the table chart. We have all the basic number formats programmed into the Excel template. These table charts work with the internal time structure of the market. This is the vibration rate of the market. This vibration rate is usually based upon the all time low or high of the contract. It may also be based on the beginning or opening price of the contract or stock. It's a matter of trial and error to find the right vibration rate. In many cases the vibration number is based on a key circle number. You can set the number 1 on the table chart to a major high or low

Prices						Diff	1st Price Projections										2nd Price Projections							
No	1st price	No	2nd price	No	3rd price	Diff	45	90	120	135	144	180	216	225	240	270	45	90	120	135	144	180	216	225
1	465.000	1	469.000	1	478.000	13.00	510.000	555.000	585.000	600.000	609.000	645.000	681.000	690.000	705.000	735.000	514.000	559.000	589.000	604.000	613.000	649.000	685.000	694.000
2	#######	2	######	2	######	46.00	######	######	######	######	######	######	######	######	######	######	######	######	######	######	######	######	######	######
3	#######	3	######	3	######	20.00	######	######	######	######	######	######	######	######	######	######	######	######	######	######	######	######	######	######
4	#######	4	######	4	######	30.00	######	######	######	######	######	######	######	######	######	######	######	######	######	######	######	######	######	######
5	#######	5	######	5	######	725.00	######	######	######	######	######	######	######	######	######	######	######	######	######	######	######	######	######	######
6	#######	6	######	6	######	712.00	######	######	######	######	######	######	######	######	######	######	######	######	######	######	######	######	######	######
7	#######	7	######	7	######	123.00	######	######	######	######	######	######	######	######	######	######	######	######	######	######	######	######	######	######
8	#######	8	######	8	######	31.00	######	######	######	######	######	######	######	######	######	######	######	######	######	######	######	######	######	######

EXHIBIT 14.1 Price projecting

and watch the top and bottom numbers on the square. These numbers are quite often the highs and lows of the swings of the market when the table is set correctly. Table charts are programmed so you change the 1 number and every number in the entire table chart changes. Each square has it's own formula except for square 1. Square 2 is based on the formula of square 1 plus 1. Square 3 has a formula of square 2 plus 1 and so on. In the table charts, never change any number but the base number of 1 otherwise, you will ruin the entire table chart. Always keep a backup of your Excel spread sheet so if one of the other squares gets changed by accident, you can replace the entire template with your backup. See Exhibits 11.1, 11.2, 11.3, 11.4, 11.5, 11.6, 11.7, 11.8, 11.9, 11.10 and 11.11.

Besides changing the number 1 position of the table chart to a bottom of a contract it can be left at 1. The resulting top, bottom and midpoints of the table chart are natural resistance points. For example using the table chart of 20 which is Gann's NYSE Permanent Table Chart every 20 points up is a natural resistance and support point of price. This is the number vibration the NYSE moves in.

CIRCLE CHARTS

The circle charts programmed into the Excel template have an amazing ability to forecast price. They work in the same way the square table charts do, except that instead of price going up and down, price spirals around a circle. The charts work in the same way as table charts do. You can change the beginning number 1 to a contract low, high or starting price to get important resistance and support prices. In the circle charts you will find the support and resistance numbers all on the same line going out from the center. Remember you can also leave the center at 1 for natural resistance and support prices going out from the center. See Exhibits 12.3, 12.4 and 12.5.

Fib Price Projections

0.3820	Diff	0.5000	Diff	0.6180	Diff	1.0000	Diff	1.3820	Diff	1.5000	Diff	1.6180	Diff	2.0000	Diff	2.3820	Diff	2.5000	Diff	2.6180	Diff
482.966	5	484.500	7	486.034	8	491.000	13	495.966	18	497.500	20	499.034	21	504.000	26	508.966	31	510.500	33	512.034	-2
######	18	######	23	######	28	524.000	-29704	######	64	######	69	######	74	######	92	######	110	######	115	######	120
######	8	######	10	######	12	498.000	-29758	######	28	######	30	######	32	######	40	######	48	######	50	######	27
######	11	######	15	######	19	508.000	-29611	######	41	######	45	######	49	######	60	######	71	######	75	######	64
######	277	######	363	######	448	1203.000	-33252	######	1002	######	1088	######	1173	######	1450	######	1727	######	1813	######	2578
######	272	######	356	######	440	1190.000	-33265	######	984	######	1068	######	1152	######	1424	######	1696	######	1780	######	2531
######	47	######	62	######	76	601.000	-33977	######	170	######	185	######	199	######	246	######	293	######	308	######	400
######	39	######	16	######	19	509.000	-33977	######	43	######	47	######	50	######	62	######	74	######	78	######	67

EXHIBIT 14.2 Fib price projecting

HEXAGON CHART
The hexagon spiral is based on the same principals of the square of nine. The charts start with the number 1 at the center and spirals around. The hexagon chart has six points extending outward. You can change the number 1 to a low or beginning price of the contract and all numbers will change accordingly around the chart. Gann used these charts to show how the further out you get in spirals the wider the price fluctuations will be. See Exhibit 12.6.

OCTAGON CHART
The Octagon spiral is also based on the same principal of the square of nine. The chart starts with the number 1 at the center and spirals around the higher numbers. The chart has 8 points extending outward instead of the 6 points of the hexagon chart. Support and resistance points can be seen at different levels out on the spiral. In this chart you can also change the number 1 to a low or beginning price of the contract and all numbers will change accordingly around the chart. See Exhibit 12.7.

TRITABLE 1 & 2 CHARTS
The tritable charts 1 and 2 are another form of table chart which can be used to forecast price resistance and support levels. The tritable 1 chart has the number 1 at the bottom - this is the odd chart. The triable chart 2 has the numbers 1 and 2 at the bottom this is the even chart. Again when you change the number 1 in either of these charts to a low or beginning price all the numbers in the chart will change accordingly. Resistance and support levels will show up on both sides of the triangles going up and also at the top and midpoints of the triangle. See Exhibits 12.12 and 12.13.

SQUARE OF 9
The square of nine has become a very popular chart. It can be used in many different ways to forecast price. See Exhibit 12.1.

BEGINNING PRICE OR CONTRACT LOW
The first way this chart can be used is the set the center number 1 at either the beginning price of the contract or a the contact low. Use the square of 9 on contracts that have an odd number of total contract days. Use the square of 4 for contracts that have an even number of contract days. So if wheat had a low at 43, you would change the number 1 to 43. Every time the square of 9 completes a circle there is resistance at that level. Price meets the square of its own starting price at the end of each circle. When the price exceeds that resistance, it then becomes support. The further the price gets out on the square the wider is the distance between the different resistance and support levels and the wider range of the fluctuations.

NATURAL NUMBERS

The second way to use this chart is to leave the center number as 1 and use the numbers at the end of each circle as natural resistance numbers. The other numbers of importance are the numbers at the Fixed Cross (those are the numbers that are vertical and horizontal from the center) and the Cardinal Square (those are the numbers that are X from the center). When price hits the natural resistance numbers there is opposition to advance.

GANN WHEEL

The third way to use this chart is to use the 360 degrees and dates around the outside and a plastic overlay (see Exhibit 12.8) divided into the angles of 90, 120, 144, 180, 214, 240 and 270 degrees. When the price of a contract or stock makes a low, you move the plastic overlay 0 point to that price and line it up with the price found inside the wheel. Now continue counter clockwise using the overlay till you get to the 90 degree line. The 90 degree line intersects with the next level of price inside the square. This is resistance. If price gets through this resistance it will go to the next level. The prior resistance then becomes support. Watch for a change of trend at every angle line. Sometimes price will be at an adjacent angle or an opposition angle. Watch the rallies and declines into these angles.

If rallies stop exactly on 90 degree lines and go back down, the main trend is down. If declines stop exactly on 90 degree lines and go back up the main trend is up. The secret is the wheel tells you that all counter trends against the main trend will end up on a key angle line. Resumptions of the main trend do not usually end on an exact angle line. They usually go through it. However, when you do notice that the main thrust of a trend does land on a key angle line, then the trend is reversing.

If you keep the 0 point of the overlay on March 21 and look at the prices the angles of the plastic overlay hit, you will find that sometimes the dates on the outside of the wheel hits the same price that an angle is on at the same time. This is called time aspecting price. This is natural time and price resistance. You always check this particular use of the wheel, as it happens too many times to be coincidence. These are very strong points of support and resistance.

SQUARE OF 4

The square of 4 can be used exactly as the square of 9. In all aspects it is identical except that it is an even square instead of an odd square. It should be used for contracts that have an even number of days in the contract. It has all the same functions as the square of 9. It can work with the beginning contract price or with the lows in the contract. It is a mystery why square of 4 is not as popular as the square of 9. Perhaps it was because it was too expensive to print it on plastic as was done with the square of 9 in the making of the expensive Gann wheels that cost as much as $900 in the past few years. Now with the Excel electronic spreadsheet you can use both of these squares.

MULTIPLE PRICE PROJECTIONS

While the square of 9 and 4 are excellent for giving resistance at the ends of natural circles which represent squares of the center, it is difficult to use these square with very many past lows and highs. One disadvantage also of the square of 9 and 4 is that they are designed for expanding waves and not for contracting waves. Contracting waves are when prices are coming down. Both the square of 9 and 4 are like a shell starting small at the center and getting bigger as prices get higher. To overcome these problems a sheet was designed to give multiple price projections and to allow for both expanding and contracting waves. This sheet also allows for Fibonacci price projections with counts of actual days. This is one of the most valuable sheets in the Excel template. Here is how the sheet works.

It allows for three prices to be placed in the spreadsheet on each row: 1st price, 2nd price and 3rd price. There are 8 rows down so it gives you a potential of 24 points to use for forecasting forward. It is very easy to add rows to this spreadsheet using the copy and paste routine, so you could actually add as many points as you wished. In each of these slots, you place past highs and lows of historical data. We have found it an excellent tool to place all the highs and lows of Elliott wave in this spreadsheet. Try to keep the same degree. For example make up one 8 row for the major degree which is a monthly chart going back 15-30 years. Make up another 8 rows for the intermediate degree which is weekly chart going back for 5 - 10 years. Then you should make up another 8 rows for the minor degree which is a daily chart going back 3 - 5 years. In this module also allows for variable lengths in projections. We have it programmed for the wheel numbers of 45, 90, 120, 144, 180, 216,

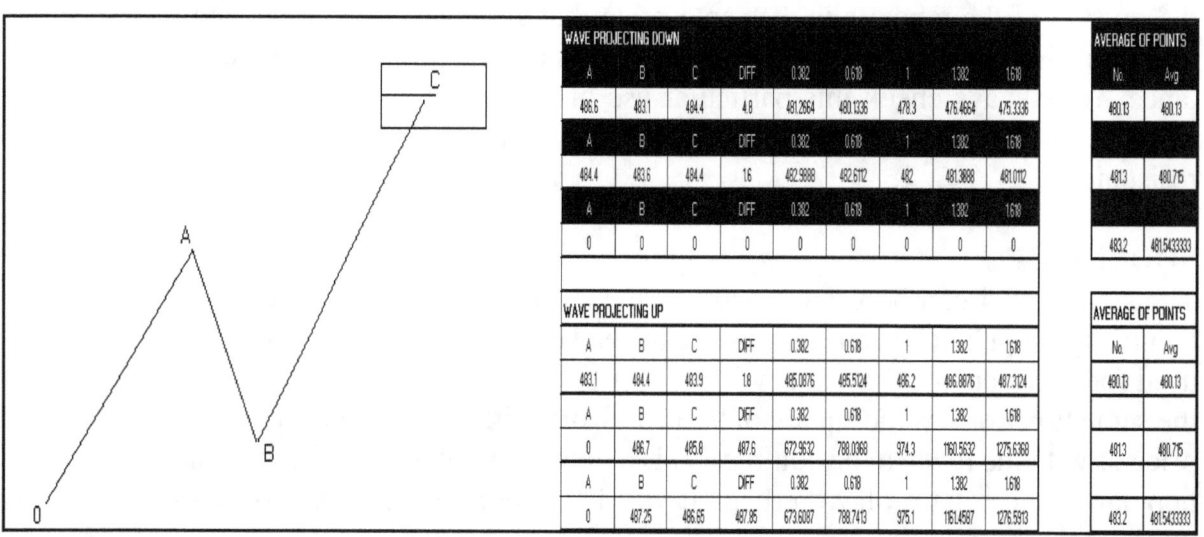

EXHIBIT 14.3 Wave projecting down and up

240 and 270. These can be changed to other counts. Excel will only do daily price projections, so for weekly and monthly, you will have to change these settings to multiples of the daily counts. For weekly projections you might put in much larger counts for example put in the following 45 x 5 = 225 days, 90 x 5 = 450 days, 120 x 5 = 600 and so on. For monthly counts you would put in 45 x 30 = 1350 days, 90 x 30 = 1800 days, 120 x 30 = 3600 days and so on.

The counts forward give you important probably future cycle points. The bigger the degree, the more important the cycle is. The biggest advantage of this module is that you can match up several futures dates that are within 3 days of each other. The more match ups you get the more important the cycle is. When you get a major, intermediate and a minor degree to match up to the exact date, you have a very important cycle.

This module can also be used to forecast forward price and time of a bottom or top. You set the 1st price to a major bottom, for example 225 in March 95 Corn. Now set the module to forecast forward the following: 225 hours, 225 days, 225 weeks, 225 months. Therefore you would set it to the following days: 225/24 = 9.375, 225 x 1 = 225, 225 x 5 = 1125, 225 x 30 = 6750 days. When the points in time are reached check the price and if it is a multiple, harmonic or Fibonacci ratio of the bottom price, then it is a significant point. If the difference from that price and the bottom is a Gann circle number, then it is significant.

FIBONACCI PRICE FORECASTING

This module also has an important function of forecasting Fibonacci price points. This is how it works. If you want to forecast out the Fibonacci ratio in price of an A, B, C wave you would put in A as the 1st price, B as the 2nd price and C as the 3rd price. From the 3rd price the module will forecast forward a predetermine ratio of the C and (B - A). The Fibonacci ratios are

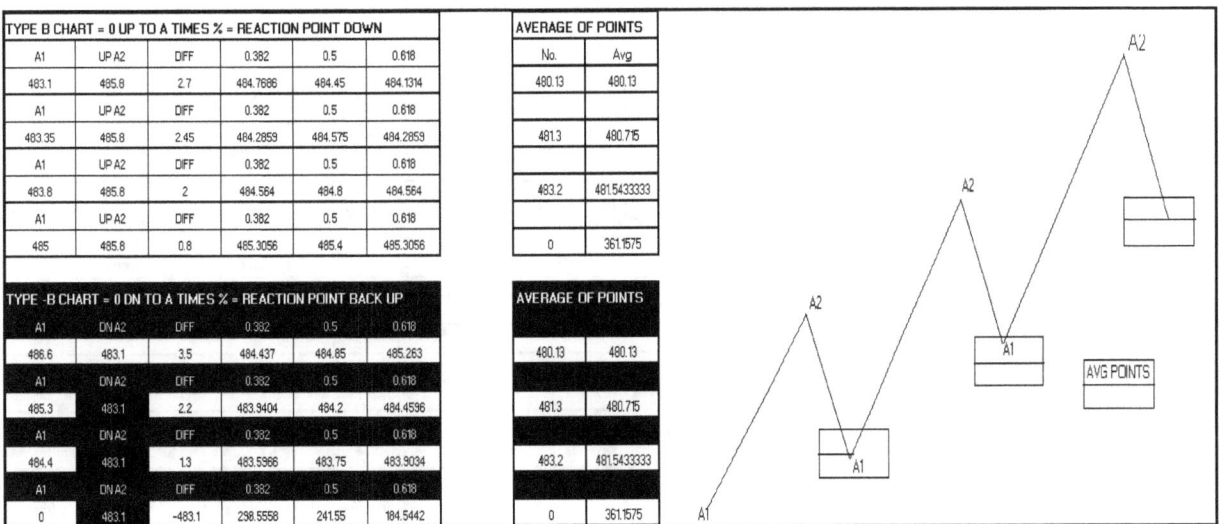

EXHIBIT 14.4 ABC wave projecting

.382, .500. .618, 1.000, 1.382, 1.5000, 1.618, 2.000, 2.382, 2.50 and 2.618. The module will also give you the difference in price between (B - A) and C. If it is a perfect circle number for example 45, 90. 120, 144 etc., then it price has more validity. If you make the 1st price equal to the 2nd price then you would be getting ratios between only the 2nd and 3rd prices. You would also be getting yhe difference in price between them. The more cluster of prices that match up in the 3 price projections the more it is a confirmation of an important future pivot point. These Fibonacci ratio numbers are variable, so you can change them to specialized numbers. See Exhibit 14.1 and 14.2.

PATTERN

One of the secrets of price forecasting is pattern formation. Knowing where you are in the pattern formation. The secret is that virtually all markets continually form the same price patterns If you know where you are in this pattern formation then you know everything you need to know to make big money in the markets. What you are really doing in this situation is making a predetermined model of the market. At certain points in this pattern, you can check to see if in fact your are where you think you are. The formulas in the Excel template can tell you where you are most of the time. Now we are going to give you the exact pattern all market trade. It is in fact the Elliott wave pattern. The difference is that we have the formulas that tell you were you are in the wave at all times. Here are the formulas used with Exhibit 14.6

$$c = (a - b) + c$$

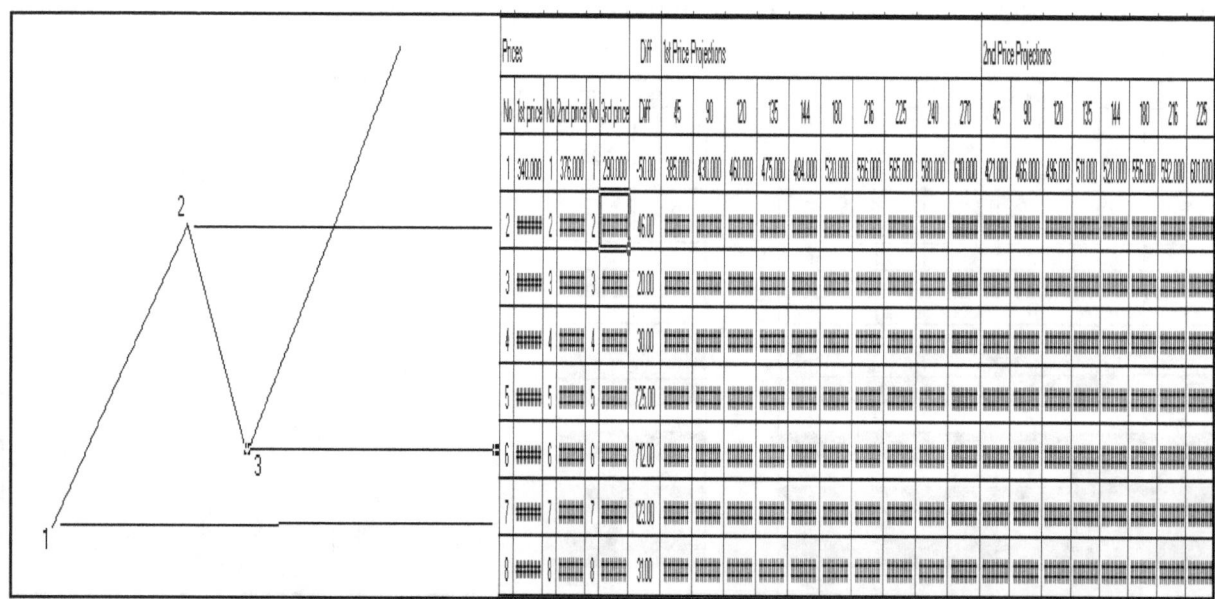

EXHIBIT 14.5 Projecting from several single points

$d = c - (c - b)$
$m = (l - 0) + 1$
$d = c - (c - 0) \times .618$
$l = i - (i - d) \times .382$
$f = e - (e - d) \times .236$
$h = g - (g - h) \times .146$
$g = f + (e - d) \times 1.618$
$g = d + (a - 0) \times 2.618$
$i = d + (c - d) \times 4.236$
$h = g - (g - f) \times .1459$
$m = l + 1 \times (a - 0)$
$m = l + .618 \times (a - 0)$
$m = l + 1.618 \times (a - 0)$
$m = l + 1.618 \times (i - o)$ extended
$l = k - (i - j + k - j \times .618)$
$p = o - (m - n + o - n \times .618)$

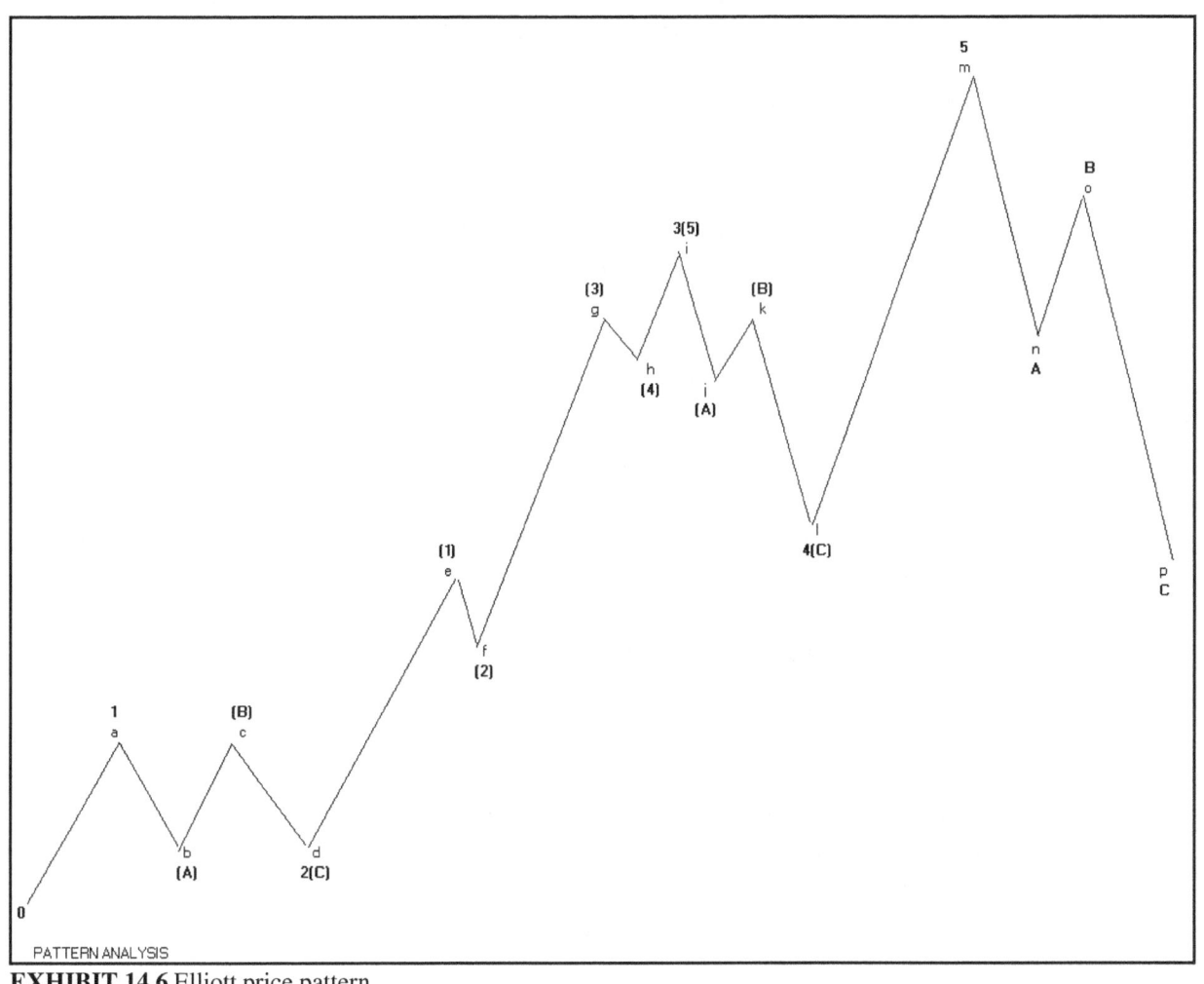

EXHIBIT 14.6 Elliott price pattern

These formulas give you the probable price of almost every wave on the chart before the price gets there. If when the price gets to what looks like a 5 and the estimated price is not there, then there is a good chance that there is something wrong with your wave count. (See Exhibit 14.6)

The square of 9 and 4 chart can also help you get an idea of the end of every wave. By placing the beginning number of the wave at the 1 position in the center of the square you will find that most waves will end at the end of each circle in these squares. Sometimes the wave also might end at the one of the Fixed Cross and Cardinal Square numbers. (See Exhibit 12.1 and 12.2)

ABC FIBONACCI PRICE PROJECTING

If you want to know how strong the market is and where a wave is going and where to take profits use the ABC ratio method. We have set up such a module in the Excel spread sheet for this purpose. (See Exhibit 14.3) Every wave is a function of its two prior waves. 0 to A and A-B x ratio + B = Projection. Ratios = .382, 6.18, 1.000, 1.382. The prior 2 waves tells you where the current wave is going. The strength or weakness of the market can be determined from how strong each wave is. You can average several ABC waves together and tell where the average of the ABC's project.

A1 TO A2 RETRACEMENTS

The market will retract .382, 5.00 or .618 of the prior move. We have set up a module in the Excel spreadsheet to calculate that and average it out. See Exhibit 14.4. Initially you put in the bottom of the up move at A1 then you put in the price of the upmove at A2. Every time the market moves up to a new high you put in a new value for A2. One every bottom of a new wave you put that in another A2. The module will calculate the retracements for each A1 to A2. You can put them in and average the retracements to a common figure.

PROJECTING FROM SEVERAL SINGLE POINTS

One of the best methods of forecasting is to forecast time from a set of single points such as highs and lows. The Excel spread sheet can be used for this also. See Exhibit 14.5.

TIMING FROM DOUBLE OR TRIPLE POINTS

The Excel Spread sheet can also be used to check timing from double or triple points. Simply by putting in prices in the 1st, 2nd and 3rd price slots, it will project ratios from between the 1st + 2nd and the 3rd. It you only want ratios between the 2nd and 3rd make the 1st and 2nd prices the same. The ratios in the spread sheet are .382, .500, .618, 1.000, 1.382, 1.500, 1.618., 2.000. 2.382, 2.618. The ratios are variable so you could also change these to 1.00, 2.00, 3.00 etc. This would project equal time distances from those points.

USING THE MASTER OVERLAYS

The master overlays should be used to forecast price based on market days. You should create the following overlays on clear plastic in the scale of your charts. 45, 52, 72, 90, 120, 144, 216, 240, 270, and 360. They should be used in two different ways. One is to place them on highs and low. This is using it the variable way. From every top or bottom the market will move 45, 52, 72, 90, 120, 144, 216, 240, 270 and 360 points. You can take multiples of the squares also for price projecting. For example the market may move three squares of 144 from a price point. So if for example May Soybeans bottomed at 460 you would place the overlay left bottom on that point and project up 3 squares of 144. (460 + 144 + 144 + 144 = 892)

The squares can also be used the fixed way in that on every major bottom you could place the square at 0 point and project upward for price projections. For example with the previous example of Soybeans at 460 the fixed price resistance points would be at (144, 288, 432, 576, 720, 864, 1008 et c.) remember the more price clusters you have at one point the more important the price point is. You should also check back on all prior tops and bottoms for other indications of support and resistance.

The market will usually work in one of the natural squares of 45, 52, 90, 120, 144, 216, 240, 270 and 360. You must experiment to see which square it is working it. On daily charts in most cases it will be either the square of 90 or 144. In some cases it will work in the square of 120 or 52. You will also find that some of the square work better with the weekly and monthly charts better than the daily charts. It is just a big process of experimentation and trial and error until you find the right square or combination thereof.

Also the market will also work in the square which is usually based on the all time low of the market. For example in May Soybeans the market works in the square of 67 which is the all time low of that contract. You must make up a master plastic square of 67 for use with that contract. Use this in combination with the fixed square that you use.

Remember the more price clusters you have at one point the more important that point is. Use all the techniques presented in this course to arrive at those clusters. Use both market and calendar days. You will be suprised at the results.

CHAPTER 15

EXCEL SPREAD SHEET

A necessity for time and price analysis

The Excel Spreadsheet is an excellent piece of software, necessary for the forecasting of both time and price using Gann analysis. This chapter explains how to use the program and the template that we have included in this course. Exhibit 15.1 is the picture of the Excel spread sheet that you get on your screen.

INSTALLING THE PROGRAM
It is necessary that you have at least a 486 IBM compatible computer with at least 4 MB of RAM and at least a 200 MB hard disk drive to use this program. You also need Microsoft Windows 3.0 or higher. It is suggested that the video card you use should be accelerated for windows programs with a resolution of at least 1024 x 768. It is also suggested that you use a 17" flat screen computer monitor with horizontal and vertical controls.

To install the program just insert the number 1 program disk into your disk drive. From the windows run menu access drive a and run setup. Follow the instructions and it will lead you through the setup of 5 installation disks.

When installation is complete you are now ready to install the Gann template into the program. Insert the Gann template disk in drive a. Pull up the Excel file menu. On it you will see 1 A:\GANN.XLS. Click this with the mouse and it will load the template into the Excel spreadsheet. Exhibit 15.1 will appear on your screen.

The Excel spread sheet is multi-tasking capable. That means you can run your windows chart program such as SuperCharts and the Excel spread sheet at the same time. To switch between the two programs you just press CTRL and ESC at the same time. This takes you to a task list. From this you will see Excel and SuperCharts. You can switch between the programs with the click of the mouse. This allows you to use both programs at the same time which is desirable for Multi-tasking runs quicker if you have at least 8 MB of RAM in your computer.

The spread sheet is graphically intensive. That is what makes it such a nice program for Gann time and price analysis. At the bottom of the screen, you can see OCT, HEX, NYSE PERM, TBL3, TBL 6, TBL 9, TBL12, TBL19, TBL20, TBL24, TBL27. These are the sheets that are programmed into the template. You can scroll back and forth as there are even more sheets programmed than you can't see. In addition to those in view, there are the TBL36, TBL 52, TBL 43, TBL 67, TBL 90, PRICE PROJ, TIME PROJ, OVERLAYS, SQ9, SQ4, FIB PROJ, CIR18, CIR24, CIR12, TRI-1 AND TRI-2 charts. You can instantly bring up any of the charts with a click of the mouse.

TABLE CHART BASE CELL NUMBER 1

All of the table charts have a base of 1 which can be changed to any number. All other cells in the spread sheet have a formula in their squares which changes automatically when you change the number 1 cell. The number 1 cell can be changed to the contract beginning price or a low contact price. All the other cells then increase by a factor of 1.

PROJECTION CHARTS WHITE SQUARES

The three projection charts which includes the PRICE PROJ, TIME PROJ AND FIB PROJ have programmed cells which should not be disturbed. The colored cells are programmed and the white cells are the only ones you can input numbers into.

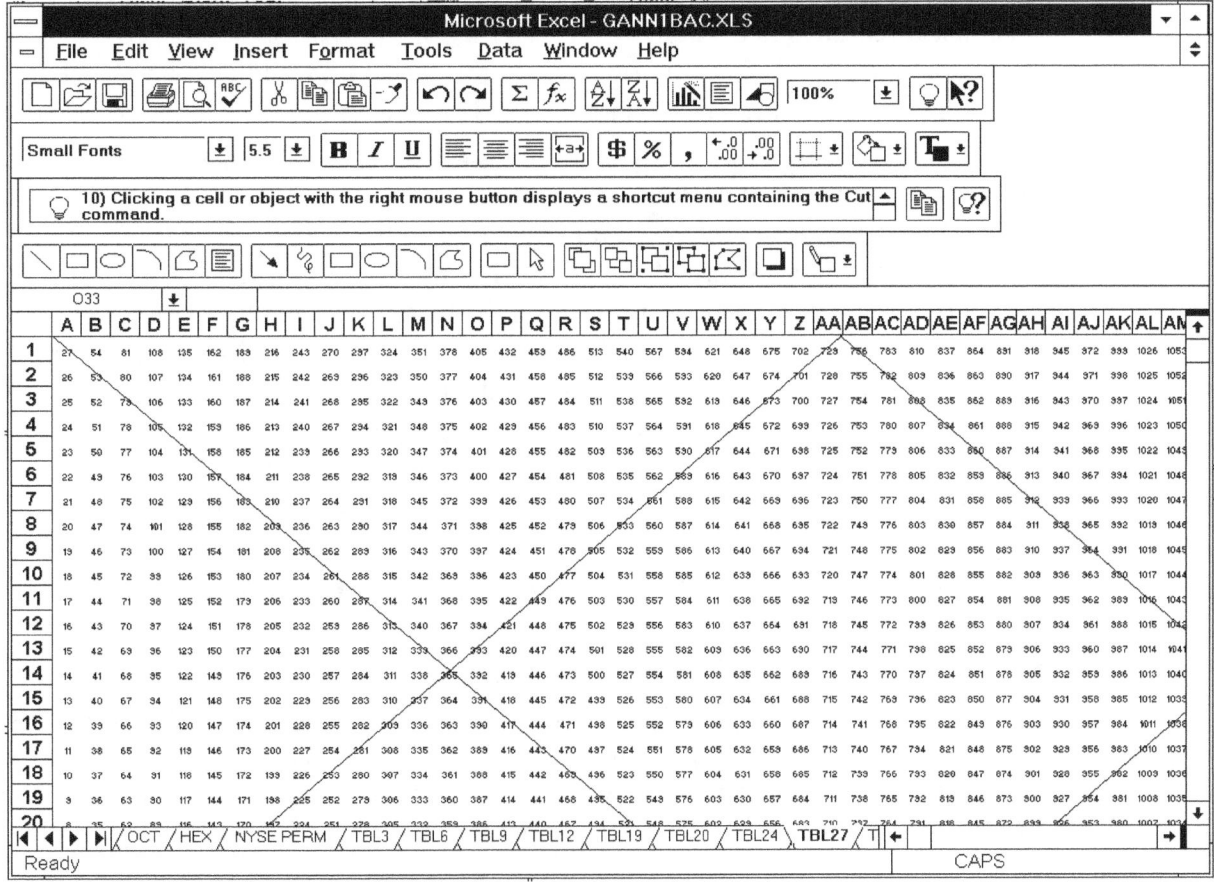

EXHIBIT 15.1 Program display

CHAPTER 16

% SWING CHARTS

....

Swings charts tell you the direction of the market.

One of Gann's favorite tools was his swing charts. The rules for trading his swing charts are very simple. You can use swing charts to give you the trend of the market in the different degrees such as daily, weekly and monthly.

Gann's trend line indicator was a 1 day swing chart. In a rising market he keep moving his trend line up until the low of the prior day was broken. When that point was broken, he moved his trend line down until the high of the prior day was broken. The principal of his 3 day swing chart is the same. Keep moving the trend line up on a rising market until the low of the last 3 days is broken. When that low is broken move the trend line down until the high of the last three days is broken.

Gann used the 3 day swing chart to tell the main trend of the market and the 1 day swing chart for the short term. The two can be combined to make a good trading system, in that when the 3 day swing chart goes long use the 1 day swing chart to enter the market.

Swing charts can be based on any amount of days, weeks, months, quarters or even years. Many traders experiment and try to find the best swing chart that best fits a particular market. It is difficult to beat the combination of the 1 day and 3 day swing chart. The same combination works well on weekly, monthly and quarterly charts. For example, use a combination 1 week and a 3 week swing chart. One of Gann's favorite swing charts for the main trend was based on quarterly prices.

Swing charts can also be based on price instead of time. When the low of the prior day is broken by say 2 cents in corn the trend line turns down. The trend line stays down until the market reverses up over the prior days high by 2 cents.

To increase the effectiveness of swing charts you can also use both time and price in the formula. By that, I mean that if on a 3 day swing chart the price declines below the prior day's low it must also decline a certain amount of cents also to confirm the down turn. For example in Corn the price must break the prior 3 day's low and also break the low by 2 cents to confirm the change of trend. If doesn't break both the time and price point, then the trend line indicator remains up.

Swing charts are effective for seeing a change of price trend both on the short term and the main trend. The swing chart is a good place for you to know where to place stops. Stops can be placed below or above the last important swing points.

Swing charts are excellent for entering the market after a correction has occurred. For example, when a main uptrend has turned down, use the 1 day uptrend chart to enter the market when the prior days low is broken by 2 cents.

Swing charts should be watched very carefully with the concept of overbalancing prior time and price points. For example, if in the last three corrections in a major uptrend, corn retraced no more than 10 days and 20 cents, do not consider that the main trend turning down until the current correction exceeds the 10 days and 20 cents of the last biggest correction.

Time and price swing charts have many problems. They often give bad signals to the trader. Using past historical data our research has found that using price correction is not as effective as time calculation. Time, as Gann said is the most important factor.

Percentage retracements of the last swing has proven to be more effective than price retracements. In a bull market the percentage retracements should be less and less as you go up. If the percentage retracements start to get bigger, then it is an indication that the trend is changing. Once a prior swing percentage retracement is exceeded there is a loss of momentum and it is possible that the market is topping.

Another way to check the market's strength is to do a check of the markets price and time swings in the direction of the main trend of the market. When they are less than the prior advancements the market is losing momentum.

To check the strength of the market's strength, you can also figure the market's percentage swing of the last two moves. When this percentage starts declining, there is a possible change of trend coming.

Many times when a swing chart is broken, it also gives another indication of a change of trend, such as a reversal day. This was one of Gann's favorite signals. There are three basic reversal days: A gap up and reverse day, a hook reversal and a key reversal.

So you can monitor both retracements and advances for their swing properties we have programmed a spread sheet module for this purpose. (See Exhibit 16.1)

With this spread sheet template you can put in the high and low of swings as the market is moving up. The spread sheet will automatically calculate the points of the reaction. If the points come up close to a Gann number then more importance is put on it. The spread sheet also calculates the % retracement for each swing.

When the market advances to a new high, the spread sheet will calculate the points move and the percentage of the move. This gives you an indication of the strength of the market. From this you can tell the strength of the market. This tells you that momentum is increasing or declining.

A swing chart can be set up based on the information coming from our spread sheet module. For example, if the price breaks under the prior 3 day low by 2 cents, if the market exceeds a 3 day reaction, if the market reacts more than 20% of the last move up, then start moving the trend line down.

This spread sheet can also be used effectively to spot when there is an overbalance of time, price and percent. When all three confirm an overbalance of time, price and percentage there is a major change of direction.

UP SWING CHART

NO.	TYPE	BEGIN	A	-B	A UP	B DN	% REACTION	+C	C UP	% ADVANCE
1	PRICE	0	1000	500	1000	500	50.00%	1000	500	100.00%
1	TIME	3/7/95	3/14/95	3/15/95	7	1	14.29%	3/18/95	3	300.00%
2	PRICE	0	1000	500	1000	500	50.00%	1000	500	100.00%
2	TIME	3/7/95	3/14/95	3/15/95	7	1	14.29%	3/18/95	3	300.00%
3	PRICE	0	1000	500	1000	500	50.00%	1000	500	100.00%
3	TIME	3/7/95	3/14/95	3/15/95	7	1	14.29%	3/18/95	3	300.00%
4	PRICE	0	1000	500	1000	500	50.00%	1000	500	100.00%
4	TIME	3/7/95	3/14/95	3/15/95	7	1	14.29%	3/18/95	3	300.00%
5	PRICE	0	1000	500	1000	500	50.00%	1000	500	100.00%
5	TIME	3/7/95	3/14/95	3/15/95	7	1	14.29%	3/18/95	3	300.00%
6	PRICE	0	1000	500	1000	500	50.00%	1000	500	100.00%
6	TIME	3/7/95	3/14/95	3/15/95	7	1	14.29%	3/18/95	3	300.00%
7	PRICE	0	1000	500	1000	500	50.00%	1000	500	100.00%
7	TIME	3/7/95	3/14/95	3/15/95	7	1	14.29%	3/18/95	3	300.00%
8	PRICE	0	1000	500	1000	500	50.00%	1000	500	100.00%
8	TIME	3/7/95	3/14/95	3/15/95	7	1	14.29%	3/18/95	3	300.00%

DN SWING CHART

NO.	TYPE	BEGIN	A	+B	A DN	B UP	% REACTION	-C	C DN	% DECLINE
1	PRICE	494.7	487.8	493.05	6.9	5.25	1.08%	483.1	9.95	189.52%
1	TIME	3/7/95	3/14/95	3/15/95	7	1	14.29%	3/21/95	6	600.00%
2	PRICE	494.7	487.8	493.05	6.9	5.25	1.08%	483.1	9.95	189.52%
2	TIME	3/7/95	3/14/95	3/15/95	7	1	14.29%	3/21/95	6	600.00%
3	PRICE	494.7	487.8	493.05	6.9	5.25	1.08%	483.1	9.95	189.52%
3	TIME	3/7/95	3/14/95	3/15/95	7	1	14.29%	3/21/95	6	600.00%
4	PRICE	494.7	487.8	493.05	6.9	5.25	1.08%	483.1	9.95	189.52%
4	TIME	3/7/95	3/14/95	3/15/95	7	1	14.29%	3/21/95	6	600.00%
5	PRICE	494.7	487.8	493.05	6.9	5.25	1.08%	483.1	9.95	189.52%
5	TIME	3/7/95	3/14/95	3/15/95	7	1	14.29%	3/21/95	6	600.00%
6	PRICE	494.7	487.8	493.05	6.9	5.25	1.08%	483.1	9.95	189.52%
6	TIME	3/7/95	3/14/95	3/15/95	7	1	14.29%	3/21/95	6	600.00%
7	PRICE	494.7	487.8	493.05	6.9	5.25	1.08%	483.1	9.95	189.52%
7	TIME	3/7/95	3/14/95	3/15/95	7	1	14.29%	3/21/95	6	600.00%
8	PRICE	494.7	487.8	493.05	6.9	5.25	1.08%	483.1	9.95	189.52%
8	TIME	3/7/95	3/14/95	3/15/95	7	1	14.29%	3/21/95	6	600.00%

Exhibit 16.1 Excel swing chart spread sheet

CHAPTER 17

GAPS

Gaps help to tell the future of market activity

Gaps are the result of activity which causes prices to jump beyond the past days activity (the high or low of the last day) leaving an open gap. The open gap is usually caused by big buy or sell orders that result from a prior days government report on the market. It could also be caused by other factors such as overnight news from the overseas markets, weather reports and so on. Gaps were one of Gann's most important tools for reading the market.

Most gaps are ordinary in that they have no particular significance. They usually occur in the regular trading range of the market and are usually closed within a brief period of time.

Breakaway gaps are the gaps that breakout from a sideways trading range. These gaps are never filled and usually result in a fast move in the main trend of the market. If they are filled, then in most cases it is a failure and the move will not occur. These gaps usually are on big volume.

Measuring gaps usually occur in an accelerated trend of the market. The market is usually moving up or down with high volume. When these gaps occur, the market is very powerful and reactions against the main trend are almost nil. These gaps often occur in the fast third or fifth waves of the market. They many times become support or resistance areas. Most of the time these gaps can measure where the market is going. They are usually midway gaps. See Exhibit 17.1.

Exhaustion gaps usually occur in the last stage of a fast moving market. They happen before the major high or low is put in. They are the result of the last and final panic buying or selling by the public convinced that the move will never end. These gaps usually occur after a market has been moving for a long period of time. After the exhaustion gap occurs watch the market very carefully. If a reversal day occurs within a few days it usually confirms that it is a valid signal.

Gaps are important to the experienced trader who can match them to the pattern of the market. In the Elliott wave pattern for example, the breakaway gaps would occur out of consolidation ranges such as 2nd and 4th waves which are ABC corrections. Measuring gaps usually occur in the fast moves of the 3rd and 5th waves. Exhaustion gaps usually occur in the 5th and final wave of the market.

As you can see gaps can be very revealing as to where the market is going. To recognize gaps properly you must know what phase of the market you are in.

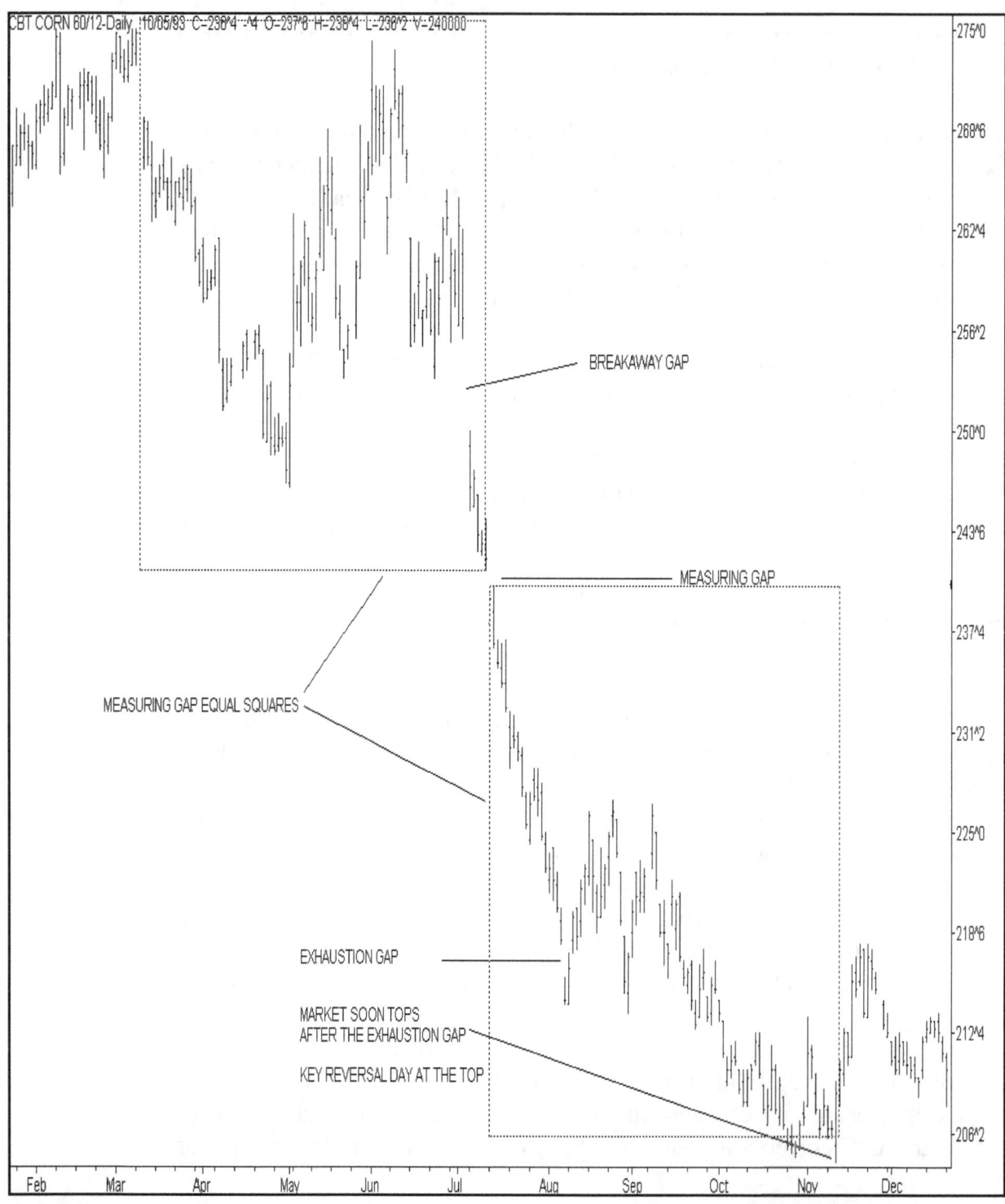

EXHIBIT 18.1 Chart illustrating gapping action.

CHAPTER 18

TOPS AND BOTTOMS

Tops and bottoms of the market can be defined.

One of Gann's most important rules was to sell double and triple tops with a stop above the market and buy double bottoms and triple tops with a stop below the market.

The bigger the amount of time involved in the double or triple top, the more important the resultant move will be. The breakout of a weekly double or triple top is more important than the breakout of a daily double or triple top. The breakout of a monthly double or triple top is more important than a weekly breakout.

In our research we have found that double and triple bottoms are more common than double or triple tops. That is because it is easier to build a base at a bottom than at a top. Tops are usually formed under high volume with many traders in the market and volume is much higher. Bottoms are usually formed with light volume and few traders.

With a double or triple bottom, rising bottoms are stronger than just flat bottoms. With rising bottoms, the market is showing that there is not enough weakness for the second or third bottom to get down to the bottom. Therefore the market is much stronger.

Buying the breakouts of a double or triple tops or selling breakdowns of double and triple bottoms is usually a very safe play as you are going with the direction and momentum of the market.

There is a method that works very well with Gann double and triple tops and bottoms. The method uses a displaced moving average. This method actually defines a double or triple top or bottom. In Exhibit 18.1 we show an example of December Cotton using a very tight 2 day moving average, the solid line, displaced to the right 2 days. The closing price line is dotted. In Exhibit 18.2 there is a blowup of the top of the market. It shows that the market made three tops at 1, 3, 5. Each time before it made the tops it had closed under the displaced moving average. Finally at point 6 the market closed under the low at 2. This broke the market down. This chart produced incredible profit in a very short period of time.

It's necessary to do back testing of prior tops and bottoms of the same commodity or stock to get the best working combination of moving average and displacement unit. What works in the past with a market, will usually work with a present market.

When the market makes a fourth attempt that results in a failure it will usually result to a fast move the other direction. Watch the fourth attempt closely. When the market brakes below the moving average three times and the closing low point and then reverses and goes through the 4th top reverse and go the direction of the market.

Know where you are in the pattern of the market. A triple bottom is much more important in the beginning phase of a major 5 wave move up. It must know the Elliott wave patterns of the market. Many markets have a particular pattern of their own that develops at important tops and bottoms.

If a breakout occurs from a double or triple bottom, it is important that any reactions must not be over three weeks. If this occurs watch the fourth

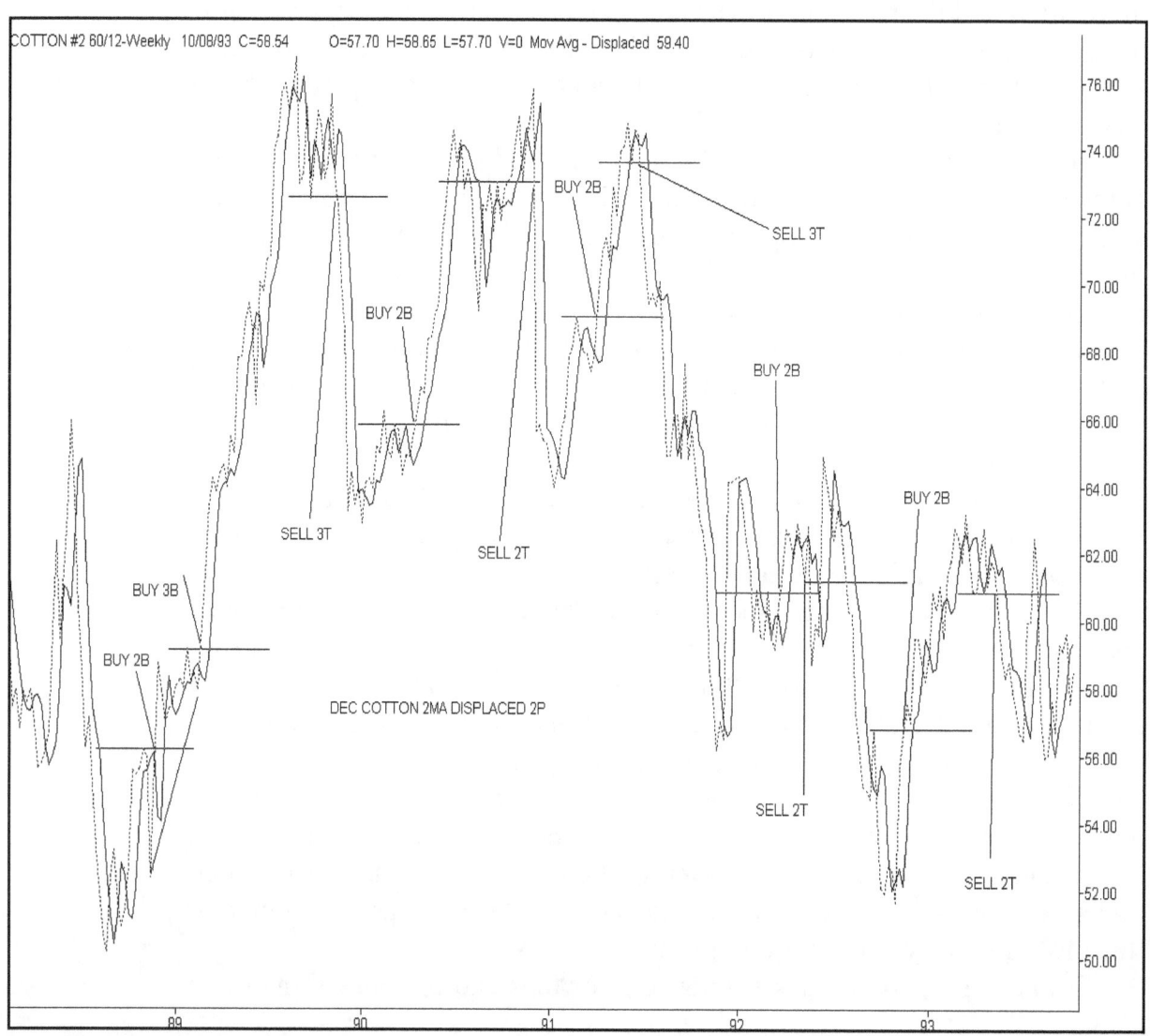

EXHIBIT 18.1 Displaced MA chart

week closely for the direction of the market. If that fourth week in a major uptrend has a lower high and then falls under the third week's low the uptrend is probably over.

If the market makes three tops and then breaks down and then makes a fourth and fifth attempt which are lower lows, then the market is very weak and should break sharply. These tops must be defined by the displaced moving average method. If the market makes three bottoms and then breaks up and then makes a fourth and fifth bottom which are higher then the market is very strong. These bottoms also must be defined by the displaced moving average.

This displaced moving average method of defining double and triple tops and bottoms gets you in the market safer than if you took your trade at the exact double or triple tops or bottoms.

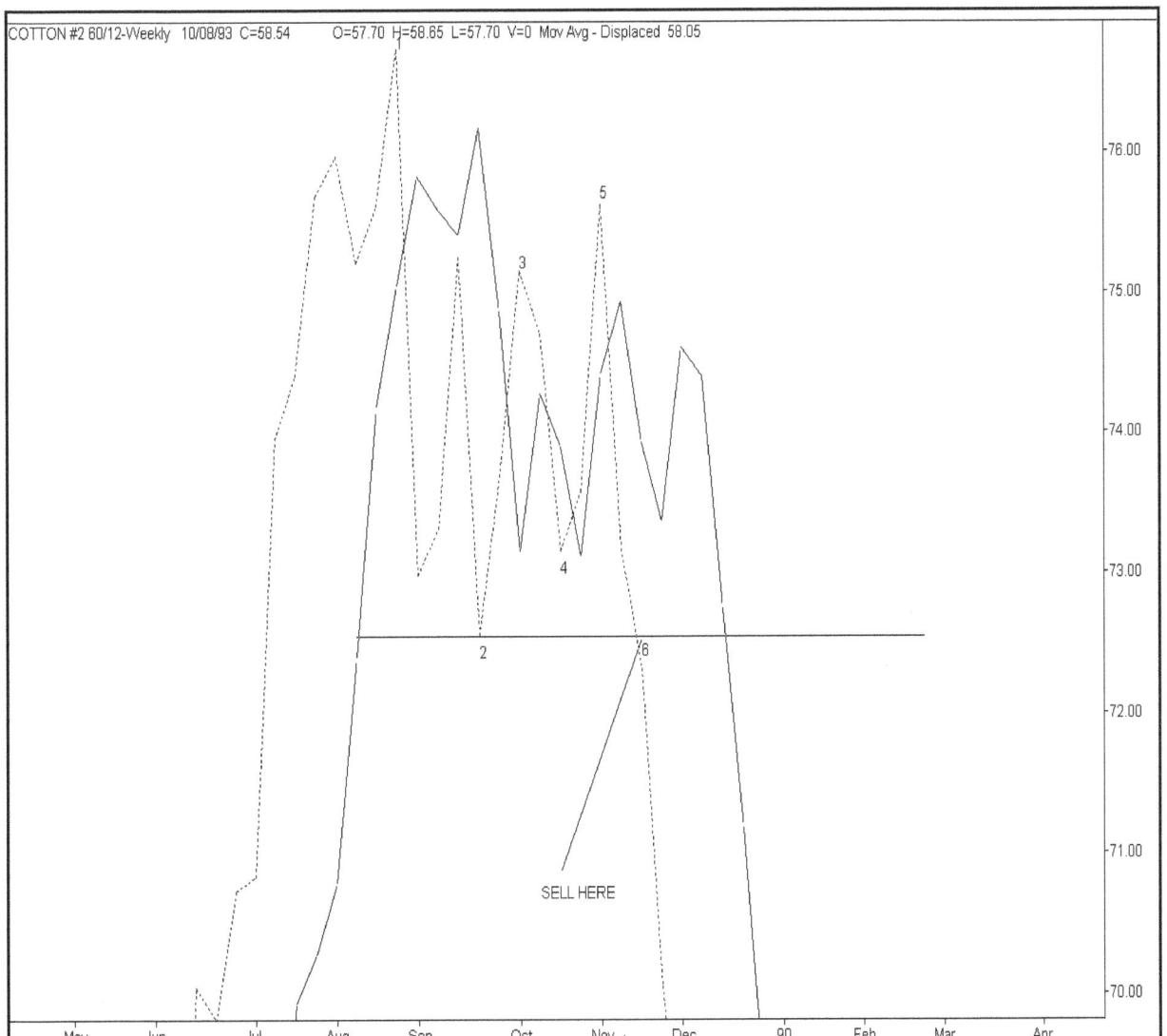

EXHIBIT 18.2 Blowup of displaced MA chart

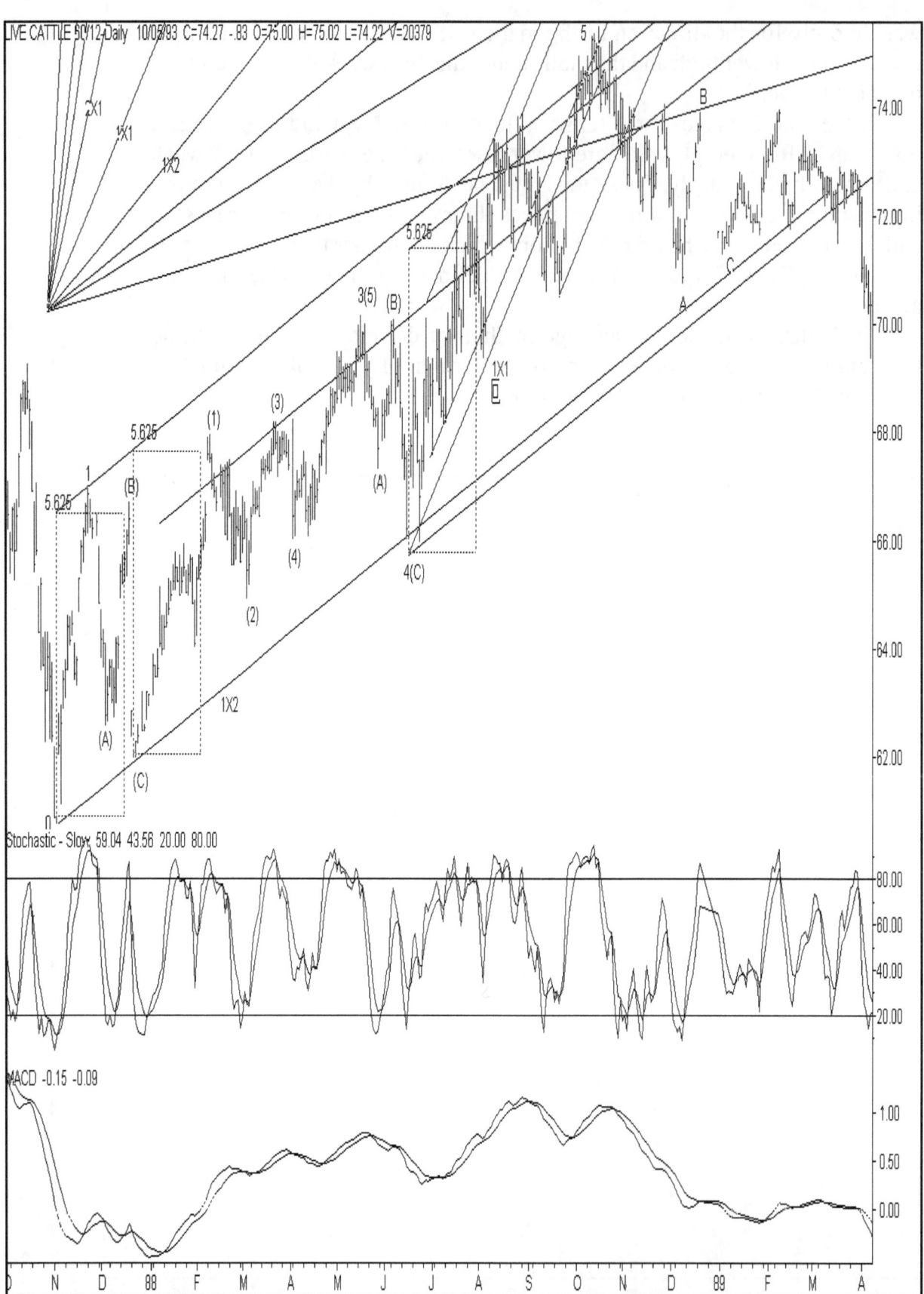

EXHIBIT 18.3 Stochastic, MACD Chart with Channel Lines

CHAPTER 19

VOLUME & OPEN INTEREST

Volume and open interest is what drives the market.

Gann felt that volume and open interest was very important to indicate market direction. This chapter will explain how to use these tools for indications of direction of trend.

Volume is what drives the market. This indicates if there is increasing demand for the supply in the market. Look closely at the trend of the volume. This will help you determine if trend of the market will continue.

Volume is the number of contracts that traded during the day. It represents either the purchases or sales, but not both. The more activity on the floor the more volume there is. This can increase due to day trading or overnight trading.

If volume does not increase or decrease then speculators feel the market will remain steady. Volume usually remains steady in consolidation areas, usually at low price levels.

If price moves out of a consolidation area with increased volume, then there is a good chance that the price move will be the beginning of a good move. If price moves out of a consolidation area and volume does not increase, then there is a good chance that it is a false breakout and the price will fall back into the consolidation area.

If prices start to fall out of a consolidation area with increase volume it is significant. If prices start to rise out of a consolidation area with increased volume then it is significant.

If when price falls the volume starts to fall, then the market may be ready for a turn back up.

If the volume increases when price falls back to a base, it means that traders are buying it as they think it is a bargain. If volume increase when prices run up to a resistance area, it means traders are unloading it thinking price is too high.

Volume also increases when the market runs into stops. The floor traders often times run the market into these areas when they can. If the market has run up into stops and does not continue, then these is a good chance prices will fall back as it just got the weak shorts who had to put in close stops.

For a big trend to continue, the volume must continue to rise. Watch the volume closely as it will give you the clue to the market direction. Without increasing volume, prices will not continue to increase.

After a long advance in prices many times the volume increases dramatically because small speculators are jumping into the market near the top thinking that prices will continue up forever.

After a long decline in the market many times volume will dramatically increase because the public who have been long the market and loosing lots of money are finally giving up and throwing in the towel. In this case the market will soon reverse as professional traders are buying the contracts from the small speculators.

When prices break out of a consolidation area and make their first advance and then decline, if the volume runs up and then declines it is bullish.

When prices break down out of a consolidation area and makes their first decline and then makes the first correction back up, if it decline is on heavy volume and the retracement back up is on declining volume then this is a good indication for a good move down.

Open interest is when there is a new buyer of a contract and a new seller. These two parties cross. The buyer buys and the seller sells making a complete transaction. The open interest then increases by 1 contract.

When prices increase with rising volume and open interest increases this is a further indication that the market will rise. Having all three rise is very bullish.

If prices are rising, with rising volume and decreasing open interest, then it is a good indication that there is short covering in the market. These traders are liquidating their contracts to get out of the market. When this happens the market will not trend much further.

If prices are stable and open interest is rising there is a good indication that positions are being accumulated. This is especially true if you are in a level of support such as wave 2 or 4 in the Elliott wave pattern.

If prices are stable and open interest is stable, there is no indiction of any change of trend. Look for the market to break out of a consolidation range with rising open interest and volume to change this stable condition of the market.

If prices are stable and open interest is falling then there is a good indication that the market is loosing interest and the public is going elsewhere.

EXHIBIT 19.1 Volume and OI chart

CHAPTER 20

GANN CHANNELS

This little known technique is the best channeling method know.

Gann placed the geometric angles on important tops, bottoms to indicate the trend of the market. These geometric angles accurately measure space, time, volume and price. The angles to draw on these tops and bottoms are the 1x8, 1x4, 1x3, 1x2, 3x4, 2/3, 1x1, 4x3, 3x2, 2x1, 3x1, 4x1 and 8x1. See Exhibit 20.1. These angles determine all important tops and bottoms. These angles drawn on a chart divide time and price into proportionate parts.

The angles should be drawn off of the 0 point - 1 square up, 1, 2(C), 2(C)

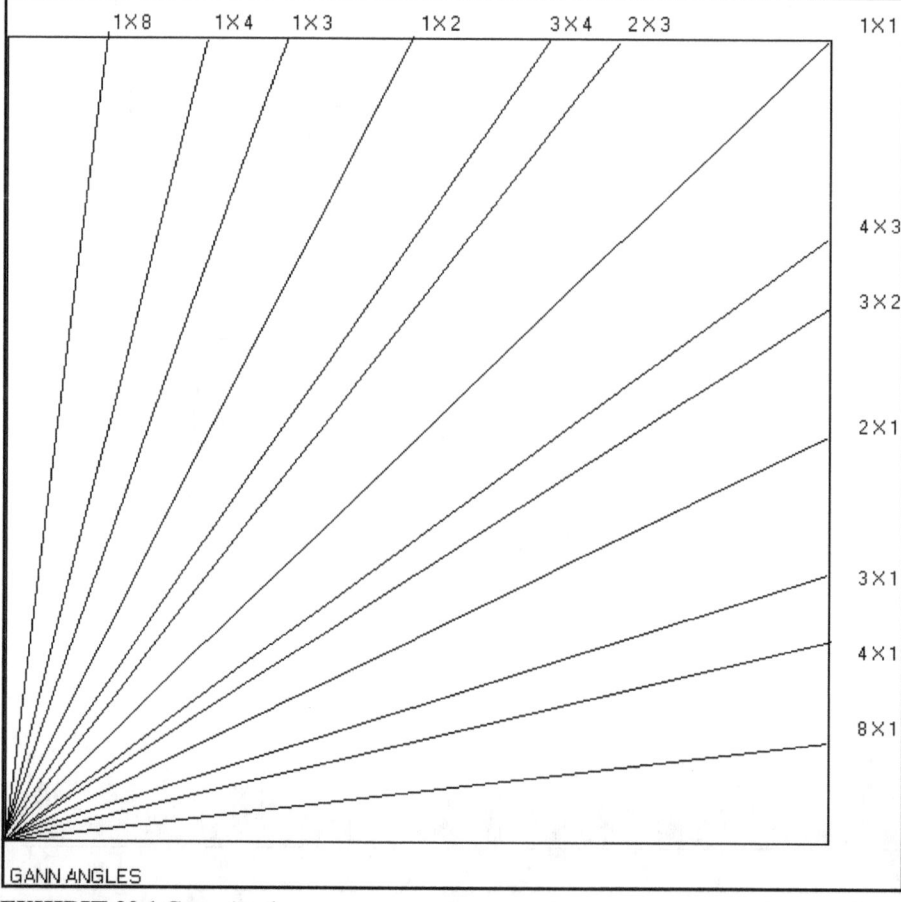

EXHIBIT 20.1 Gann Angles

one square up 3(5), and 4(C), 4(C) one square up. See Exhibit 20.2. To determine the angle you should draw you should look at the price it is moving off of. If the price is, for example, at a bottom of 72, then the market will move up 72 hours, days, weeks or months. Look first at those angles. They will be one of the angles in Exhibit 20.1. You may just want to use the best angle that fits initial price move best.

What I mean by one square up are the squares that are on the Gann overlays. For example the squares on the 144 overlay are 144/8 = 18 or multiples thereof. That is they are 2.25, 4.5, 9, 18, 36, 72. The square of 120/8 = 15 or multiples thereof. That is they are 7.5, 15, 30, 60. The square of 90/8 = 11.25. Those multiples are 5.625, 11.25, 22.50, 45, 90. The square of 52/8 = 6.5. Multiples are 13, 23, and 46. You must know the square overlay that the market is working in. Once the height of the channel is determined, prices will usually remain in the channel height until the market accelerates or direction the market changes trend. In Exhibit 20.3 you can see one point where the market accellerated and then it finally changed trend. If the volume of the market picks up the height of the channel may increase to the next multiple in the overlay. Where an angle starts off you can draw a square which is the same measurement high and wide. Timing and price projection should be

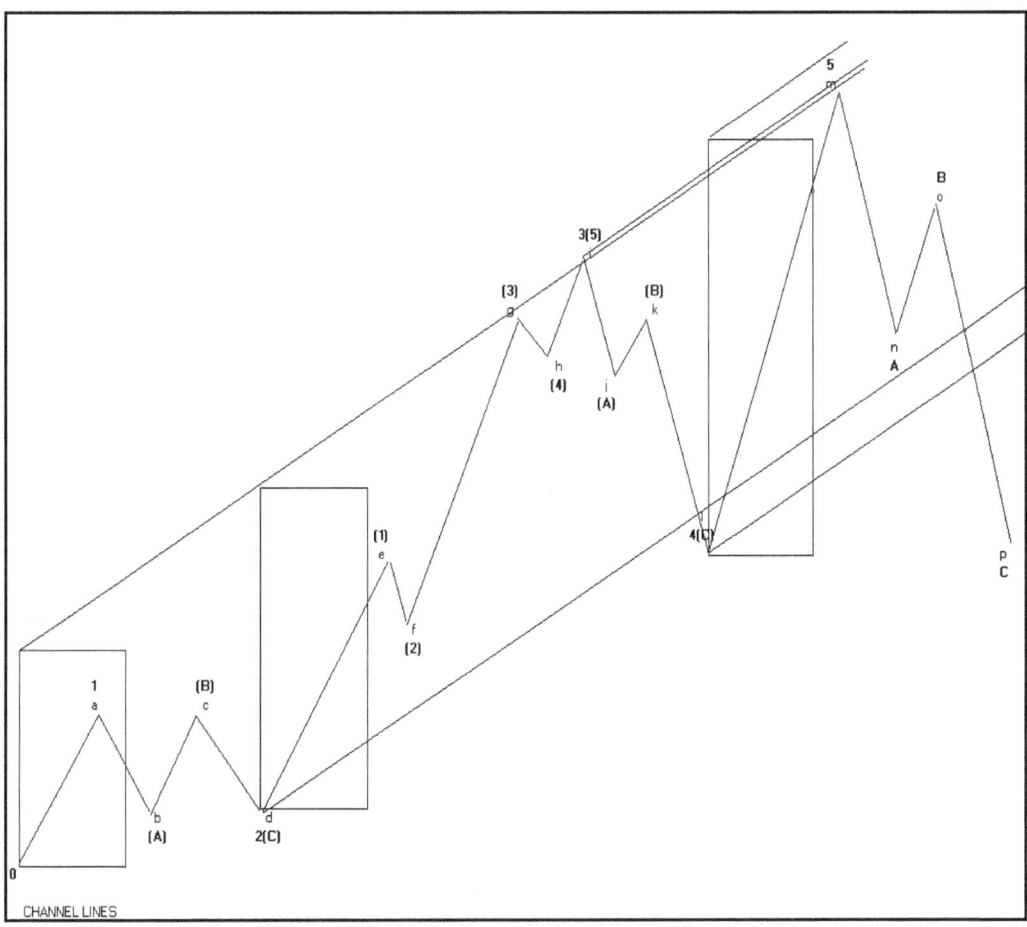

EXHIBIT 20.2 Channel lines on example chart

based on this square.

Using a fast MACD and a slow stochastic on your charts you can determine where to buy the bottom of 2(C) and 4(C). In most cases the MACD will get above the center point, putting the market in a strong position and the stochastic will drop down to the 20% line and give a double bottom with divergence. In buying watch the stochastic and the bars on the chart. When the market moves up and makes a new daily high after the turn up of stochastic, you should buy the market. It is also possible to use the stochastic to take profits when price gets to the top of the channel and divergence is occurring. Remember never go short the market based on stochastics in an up trend as the market can continue to advance.

After the 5th wave top is made and MACD gets under the center point, you can sell the first stochastic high B wave and go short the market. The procedure is just the reverse of buying the bottom. Watch the down wave C very carefully to determine in this is in fact a down wave beginning to start or just and ABC and resumption of the main trend up again.

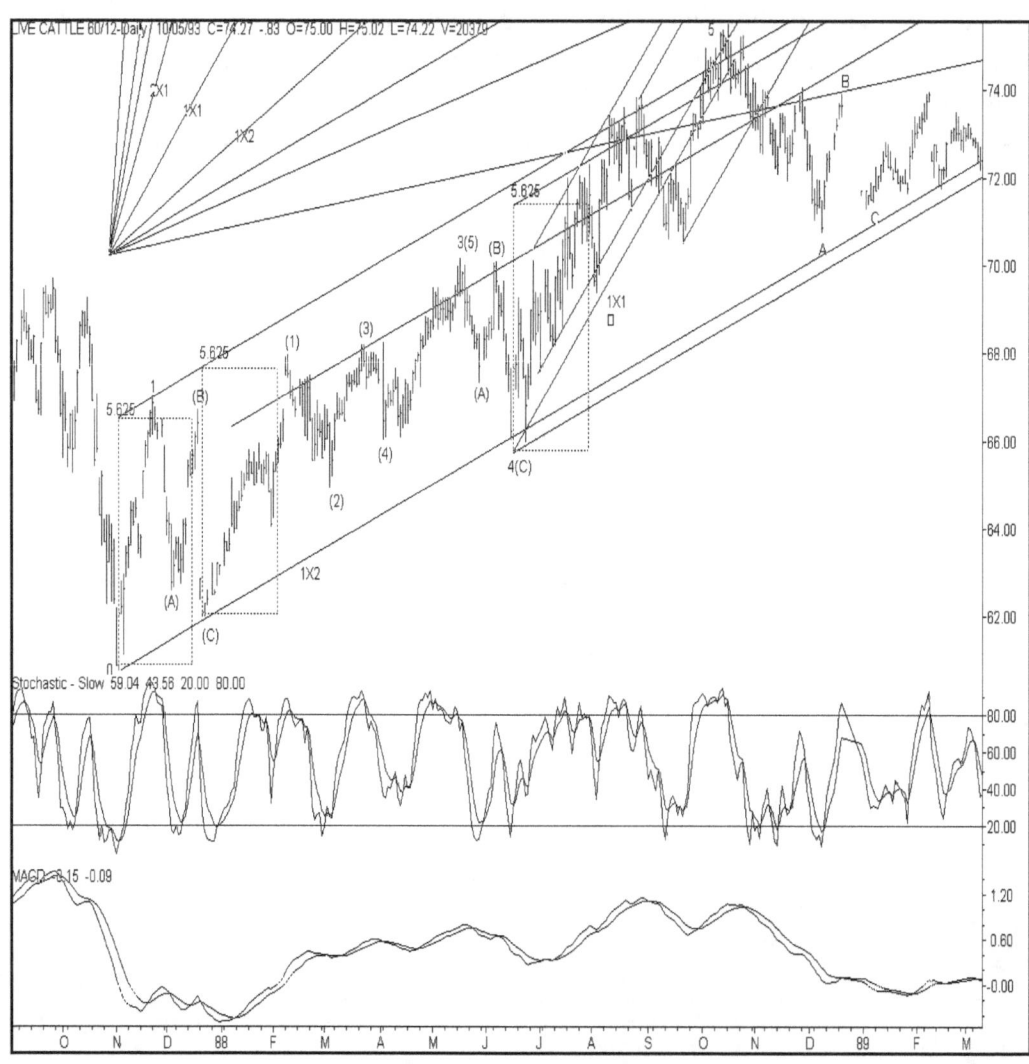

EXHIBIT 20.3 Channel lines on real chart

CHAPTER 21

TYPES OF ORDERS

The method of entering of the market can affect your profits.

You need to have a consistent plan for entering and exiting the market. There are different types of orders for entering the market. Most of the exchanges will accept any of the types of orders. The orders you place will be designed for two purposes. One to enter into a new position and to exit or stop out of your current position with a stop loss. The following are the types of orders you can use:

MARKET ORDER
When you use this type of order, you want the floor broker to fill your order immediately without any delay in time. It is used by traders who want to enter or exit the market as fast as they can without any regard to price. In most cases when this type of order is used you will loose a few points on the filled of the order by a floor scalper.

OR BETTER ORDERS
With this type of order, you want the floor broker to fill you at the price you put on the order or even better than you put. If this is an order to buy it is put above the market and if market price drops to your price or lower your order will be filled. You will rarely find that you get a better fill than you put as your price on the order. Sell or better orders are placed below the price put on the order. When the price rises and hits or goes high than the price put on the order it is filled. Again, rarely is the ordered filled at a price better than the one put on the order.
Some successful traders use this type of order to enter a trade based on a timing point. If they are not filled within a specified amount of time they change the order to market.

MARKET- IF -TOUCHED ORDERS
A market-if-touched sell order is placed below the indicated price on the order. If and when prices go up and hit that price, it is filled at the market.

Therefore it is possible that the fill could be below the price put on the ticket. In the case of market-if-touched buy orders if the market falls down and hits the price on the order it is filled at the market price. If order is good to use if you have calculated the exact price the market should go to and you want out if it hits that price.

MARKET-ON-CLOSE

This type of order is used if you want out at the market in the last closing minutes of the day. Your order becomes a market order and fills at any price at the close of the day. This type of order is used by day-traders who want out on the close of the day at any cost. Also many traders enter the market based of how it looks like it is going to close. In this situation market-on-close orders do the job. Market-on-close orders can also be a limit order. The price must not exceed the limit price on the order or it doesn't fill.

ONE-CANCELS-THE-OTHER

With this type of order you can put an order in at a certain price and another order in a price. If one of the orders is filled the other order is cancelled.

STOPS

Gann constantly said, always put a protective stop loss in the market as the market could turn against you anytime. Forecasting the market is all probabilities and therefore you need protection, just in case the market doesn't cooperate with you. This protection is necessary to preserve your capital. Gann felt that the stop should be placed as soon as your entered your buy order.

Stops can be placed on the basis of money using the rule of dividing your risk capital into 10 equal parts so no more than 10% is ever exposed to the market. This was explained in an earlier chapter.

Stops can be placed below the last swing bottom in the market. This swing bottom should be placed on the basis of time, price and percentage retracement swing charts. By using stops you will in many cases remain in the market for the entire market move.

TIME STOPS

Many traders use a time stop. The exchanges won't accept them, but they can save a lot of money. With this type of stop, if the market does not give you a profit within a certain time period, for example 3 days, you simply exit the position.

CHAPTER 22

MAKING IT WORK

Prove it to yourself and make a trading plan.

If you want to be successful, follow all the rules in this course. Everything that you read and learn in this course must be proved to yourself. Do not jump in and start trading until you are ready to trade. All the trading techniques must be programmed into your mind so you don't even think about them anymore. You must feel completely at ease and have no fear toward trading whatsoever. You must be ready to enter into the market when the public is being scared out. You must not enter into the market when the public feels that nothing can go wrong. 90% of the public looses money in the market.

The first thing you must do is get files of long term daily data that go back long enough to prove that Gann rules do work. Go back using the data and prove all rules that you have learned. You can use long term paper charts for this, or you can use long term computer files for this. If you are using computer files, make sure you have the equipment that makes these files look like long term paper charts on your computer screen. That is, you should have a program like SuperCharts or TradeStation that can display long term files. The program should be Windows compatible so you can take advantage of the virtual screen of an advanced video card like the Number Nine card. This card can act as a port with a mouse hardware pan on a screen 4 times larger than the screen you are looking at.

The Excel spread sheet program is a necessity for trading successfully. Gann Masters has programmed a template for this program that came with this course. The template has all the necessary table, circle and projection charts for trading successfully in the markets.

The biggest mistake that new traders make, is they don't spend the time to learn how to trade the successful rules of the market. They want to get into the action of trading the market immediately.

After you have learned the rules of Gann and have proved that they work, you are ready to trade. After you have successfully traded for sometime, it is necessary always to review the rules that you have learned. This constant reviewing keeps your mind alert and many times reviewing rules gives you even more insight on how to trade the markets.

Gann Masters has made a subliminal tape that can be used on regular intervals, usually before you go to sleep at night. This tape has many of the successful rules of trading on it. It helps your mind avoid the pitfalls of the market and strive to trade successfully.

Every trader is different and every trader that reads the same rules of trading will trade differently. The rules of successful trading that you pick up in this course for your own trading should be written down on a piece of paper and reviewed on a constant basis. Sometimes the rules need to be changed to accommodate the current market. Keep these rules refreshed in your mind constantly.

If you are going to be successful at trading, you must plan your way to profit. You must develop a complete trading plan for the entire bull or bear campaign from beginning to end. This plan must be followed to the letter with strict discipline. The following is a description of how one very successful

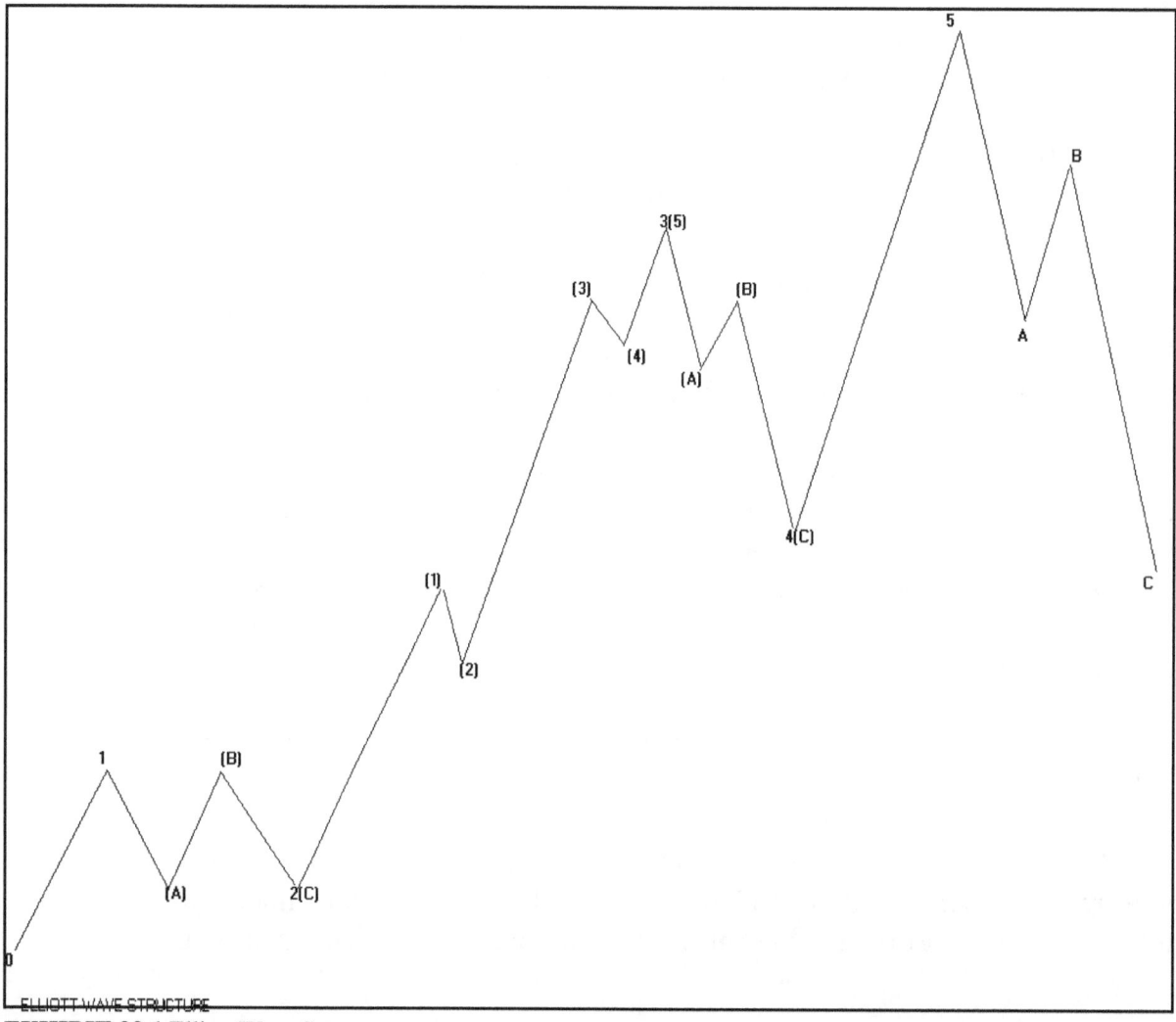

EXHIBIT 22.1 Elliott Wave Structure

Gann trader works his trading plan.

The first thing he does is scan his long term charts for past harmonic years in the future markets looking for similar trading patterns and exact anniversary dates to match today's market. The harmonic years are 5, 10, 15, 30, 45, 60, 90 and 100 years back. To do this he overlays these harmonic years on top of each other along with the current year. Many times he will find similiar trading patterns and anniversary dates hitting where they should. When he confirms the harmonic years that the current year is following, be continues the next phase of the plan.

Next, he uses all of the Gann cycle techniques for finding the next probable low if the next move is going to be up. He uses, for example, top to top, bottom to bottom and top to bottom time counts. If he is looking for a bull market, he will check the matching harmonic years to see where the major low should be basing this on both pattern and anniversary dates. Sometimes the low may be a double or triple higher bottom. He makes sure all the charts have turned to the upside overbalancing time, price and percentage moves, using quarterly, monthly, weekly and daily charts. He checks the market with cycle analysis finding out where the next cycle should be. This works best using the master time and price overlays of 90, 52 and 144. He checks retracements and resistance in the market and finds all important price numbers based on the square of 9 or the square of 4. He also uses either the square of 9 or the square of 4 for time counts from the beginning of the contract. He checks the market for its vibration rate, using the square table charts. When he knows the market has in fact bottomed at point 0 he uses pattern recognition and probable retracements to determine where he is and if the picture is coming together. (See exhibit 22.0) He waits for 1, (A), (B) and 2(C) to form. He then buys 3 contracts at 2(c) with a stop below 0. The market now continues up to (1) and he now liquidates 2 of his initial positions and moves his stop up on the remaining position to a breakeven, which includes commissions. When the market gets up to 3(5) he waits for the (A), (B), 4(C) correction to form. He then waits for the 1, (a), (b) and 2(c) to form (not shown) of the final 5th wave. He enters now 3 positions at 2(c) with a stop below 0. When the market rallies up to (1) he sells 2 positions and moves his stop up on his last purchase position to breakeven. When the market hits the top of wave 5 he sells his 2 positions and completes the trading program.

This method of trading works because it is based on proven Gann trading techniques which he has proven to himself. He has done the same trading plan over and over again. The routine of the plan is set in his mind and he has no reason or cause for fear of the market. He is always protected with stops and most of the time his stops are at breakeven, so he usually has no risk associated with his trading.

APPENDIX A
GANN MASTERS TEST APPLICATION

Besides proving it to yourself, you must prove it to us

We feel that it is very necessary for you to study this course over and over again and test out all Gann techniques before you trade in the real markets. We want to to be successful at trading the markets. We also feel that you need some incentive to study the contents of this course. We are therefore requesting that when you complete this course and feel you have learned the Gann techniques of trading that you take a final written test made up by Gann Masters. The test is free and is part of the couse.

If you pass the test, you will get an official certificate saying that you have successfully completed the Gann Masters Course and passed the final exam. You will at that time be entitled to receive the Gann Mind Tape which is a subliminal tape designed to help you remember many of the Gann principals of trading as well as handle the psychology of trading successfully. Please do not think the exam is easy. It is very difficult to pass. On the test, there will be true and false, multiple choice and essay questions. It will be an open book test as we have no way to enforce a closed book exam. If you pass the test, it will be an important credential to add to your others such as B.S. M.B.A. and PhD.

If you fail, you will have to retake the exam. There will be an additional charge of $10.00 to retake it. So it is in your best interest to pass the exam on the first try.

When you are ready to take the exam, please fill out the test application blank which is Exhibit A.1 on the next page. You must take the test within 4 months of receiving the last chapter of this course, after that you will be charged $10.00 to take the exam.

GANN MASTER'S TEST APPLICATION

Yes, please send me the Gann Masters test to prove that I have successfully studied and learned the Gann Masters Course. I understand that if I successfully pass the test, I will receive my Gann Mind Tape plus an official certificate providing that I have successful completed the Gann Masters Course and that I have passed the test.

If I fail to pass the test, I will have to retake the test at a charge of $10.00 per test. This is a very difficult test. Please be prepared. Study and know your material. It will be an open book exam.

You must take the test within 4 months of the time that you receive the last chapter of the course. After that you will be charged $10.00 to take the test.

Name..

Company..

Address..

City..

State..

Zip...

Telephone..

Fax..

Date..

Comment...

EXHIBIT A.1 Gann Masters test application

APPENDIX B
GANN MASTERS TRADING CERTIFICATION

Prove it to yourself and others with an official test.

One of the biggest mistakes you can make is to trade the markets while you are learning the Gann Masters Course. Please if you can help it, do not trade until you have completed the couse and have passed the Gann Masters test. You must prove with study and work that every technique that you learn in this couse works. You will need to spend many long hours of study doing this. It will pay off in benefits later on when you start to trade the real markets.

Proving trading techniques by going back and testing past data and trading for real is two different things. We recommend that you go one step further and take the Gann Masters Trading Certification. This is a real time test of your trading abilities. When you start this trading certification, you will receive trading order blanks. With these order blanks you must enter 10 trades within 6 months and trade an imaginary $50,000. The procedure is as follows:

1) You can use any of the types of orders explained in Chapter 21.

2) You must complete the order blanks and send them in at the close of the day to make the theoretical trade. These orders must be enclosed in an envelope that is cancelled by the U.S. Post Office that same day. Therefore you must put in in a Post Office Box that is picked up and cancelled the same day. The orders can also be faxed to us at 417-886-5180 on the same day.

3) The price of the entry or exit of the market will be the same as the close of that day. Stops and MIT orders will be filled at the exact price of the order intraday and no slippage will be assumed.

4) All U.S. Commodities and the 500 S&P stocks can be traded for this certification.

5) At the end of the 6 months a profit or loss statement will be generated from this trading test. The results of the test will be officially certified and will be official and can be used as reference by you to get new business if you are a CTA, trading advisor or broker. You can also use the results just to prove to yourself that you are ready to trade the real markets with real money profitably. In fact we think this certification should be requested by all clients wishing someone else to trade or advise them as to their trading.

TRADING CERTIFICATION

Yes, please enroll me the Gann Masters certification program. I understand that this is a real time trading trial period and is certified by U.S. Mail or via fax machine. I will receive necessary order blanks that must be mailed with postage stamp or faxed to Gann Masters by the end of the trading day. This will be trading with an imaginary $50,000. The trading must be completed at the end of 6 months and there must be 10 trades in the program. I will be given the certified results and the end of the test period. This trading certification will be official and I can use it to get new business if I am a CTA, trading advisior or broker. The results can also be used just to prove to yourself that you can trade the markets profitably.

I have enclosed $69.00 for the program's cost.

Name..

Company...

Address...

City...

State...

Zip..

Telephone...

Fax...

Date..

Comments...

....

EXHIBIT B.1 Gann Masters Certification Form

APPENDIX C

GANN MASTERS CATALOG LISTING

These are some of the products that we think you need to trade with.

1) Gann Masters Excel Template 3.5" Floppy (1.00)..........................FREE
2) SuperCharts(5.00)..$249.95
3a) MicroSoft Excel Spread Sheet 5.0 (Reg. Version)(5.00)....................$315.00
3b) Microsoft Excel Spread Sheet 5.0 (Competitive Upgrade)(5.00)......$119.00
You must have a old Excel or competitors program
3c) Microsoft Excel Spread Sheet 5.0 (Academic Version)(5.00).............$99.00
You must be a student in high school or college
4) MAX:CHART(3.00)..$79.95
5) GannTrader(10.00)..$1295
6) Windows 3.1(5.00)..$75.00
7) Parrallel Ruler(2.50)..$6.95
8) Ratio Compass Divider(2.50)..$69.95
9) Plastic Overlay Material (Roll)(5.00)..$19.95
10) SCUF Permanent Overlay Market(1.00)..$1.50
11) Ehrlich Cycle Finder(3.00)..$69.95
K&E Chart paper 11 x 16.5 (100 sheets)(5.00)..$25.00
12) 10 x10 to the inch - 5th line highlighted
13) 20 x 20 to the inch - 5th line highlighted
14) 16 x 16 to the inch. - 4th line highlighted
15) Big Paper Gann Charts ($3.50 each plus $3.00 shipping)
Please list order of charts.
Daily goes back 1 year
Weekly goes back 5 years
Monthly goes back up to 30 years
16) Please send me information and prices on the Number Nine virtual screen card.
17) Please send me information on your lastest trading computer setup.
We feature the latest Pentium Trading Computers and equipment.
18) Please send me information on obtaining real-time or delayed-time quotes on DBC Signal. (Gann Masters is a Signal dealer)
19) Please send me information on long term Gann data on disk.
Shipping is in ($000), Prices are subject to change.

GANN MASTERS
ORDER FORM

Name..

Company..

Address..

City..

State..

Zip...

Telephone..

Fax..

Please list items order or information requests and amount of order. Send check or use VISA, MC or AMAX number for order. Add shipping and also add sales tax if you live in the state of Missouri. Send, fax or call orders to Gann Masters, 2508 W. Grayrock Dr, Springfield, MO 65810 800-288-4266, 417-882-9697, Fax 417-886-5180.

....

....

....

....

....

....

....

....

EXHIBIT C.1 Gann Masters Order Form

APPENDIX D

GANN EXAMPLE CHARTS

One picture is worth a thousand words.

This a chapter giving visual charts of all the Gann techniques. Most people know the reason the Gann courses and books are so confusing, it is that there are so few charts the back up the text. Remember the Chinese proverb "one picuture is worth a 1000 words".

In this chapter we have gone through many of the Gann techniques found throughout the Gann courses and books and those recommended by the Gann traders that we know. We have illustrated them to show you how these techniques work.

You must go though each example chart and memorize the techniques. All of these charts were produced on either SuperCharts or Trade Station by permission of Omega Research. Some of the data goes back 40 years. W.D. Gann stressed having good data going back far enough to do proper research. He said if you have the right data going back far enough, you could easily trade any market profitably. Most people trade charts that are based on only 6 months of data. No wonder 90% of the people lose the money they put in the market.

We are working on our data files and taking them back even futher. To do high level research you need good data going back up to 100 years. Sometimes the 80, 90, and 100 year cycles are what the market is following. If you don't have those charts, you are out of luck. Sometime in the future, we plan on making this data to Gann Master students.

All of these charts were researched on our Trader's World computer designed for trading. It has the excellent #9GXE virtual screen video card which has a virtual screen 4 times the size of these example charts. This type of equipment really makes research and trading much simplier. If you are interested in one of these computers give us a call at 1-800-ATT-GANN.

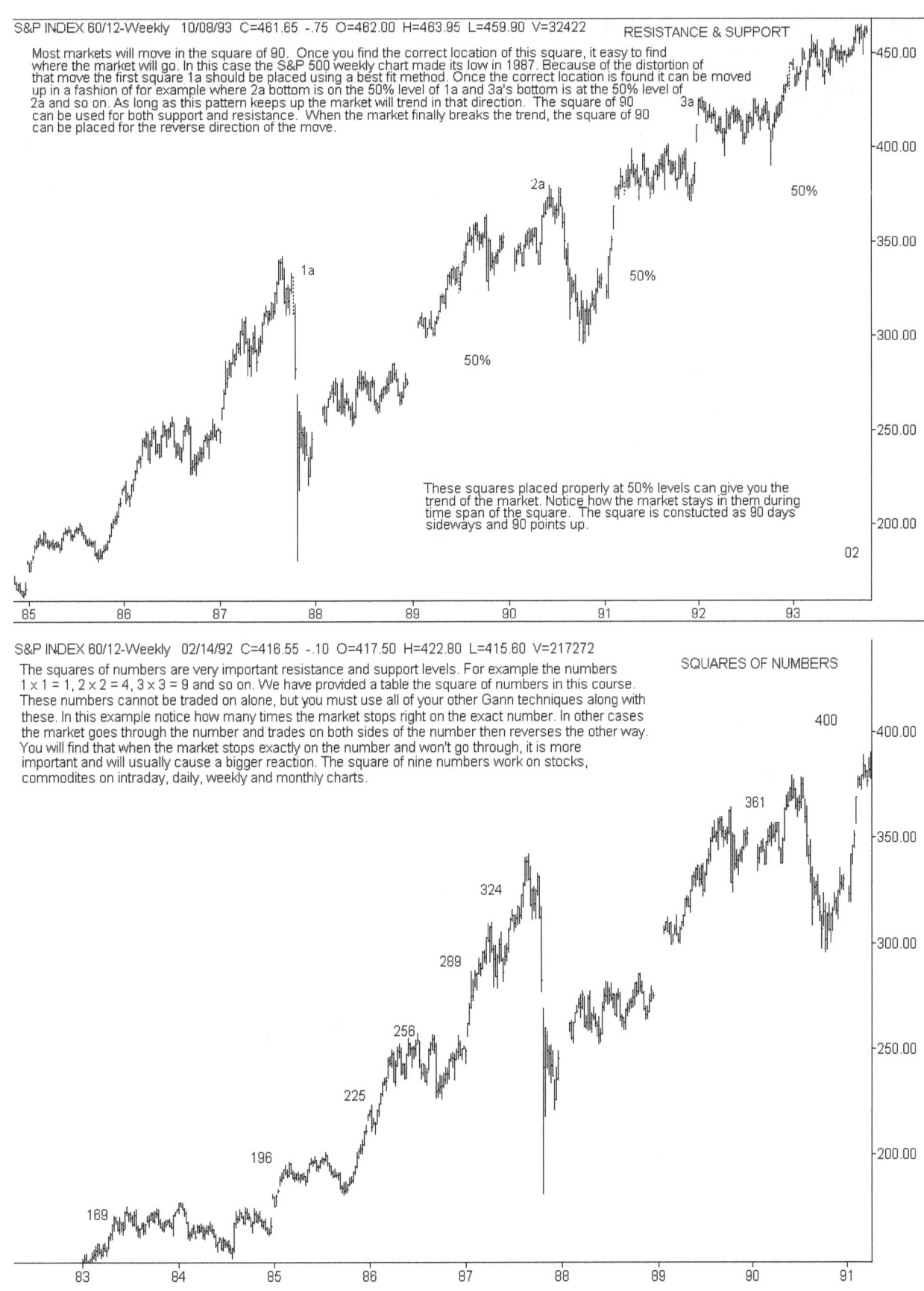

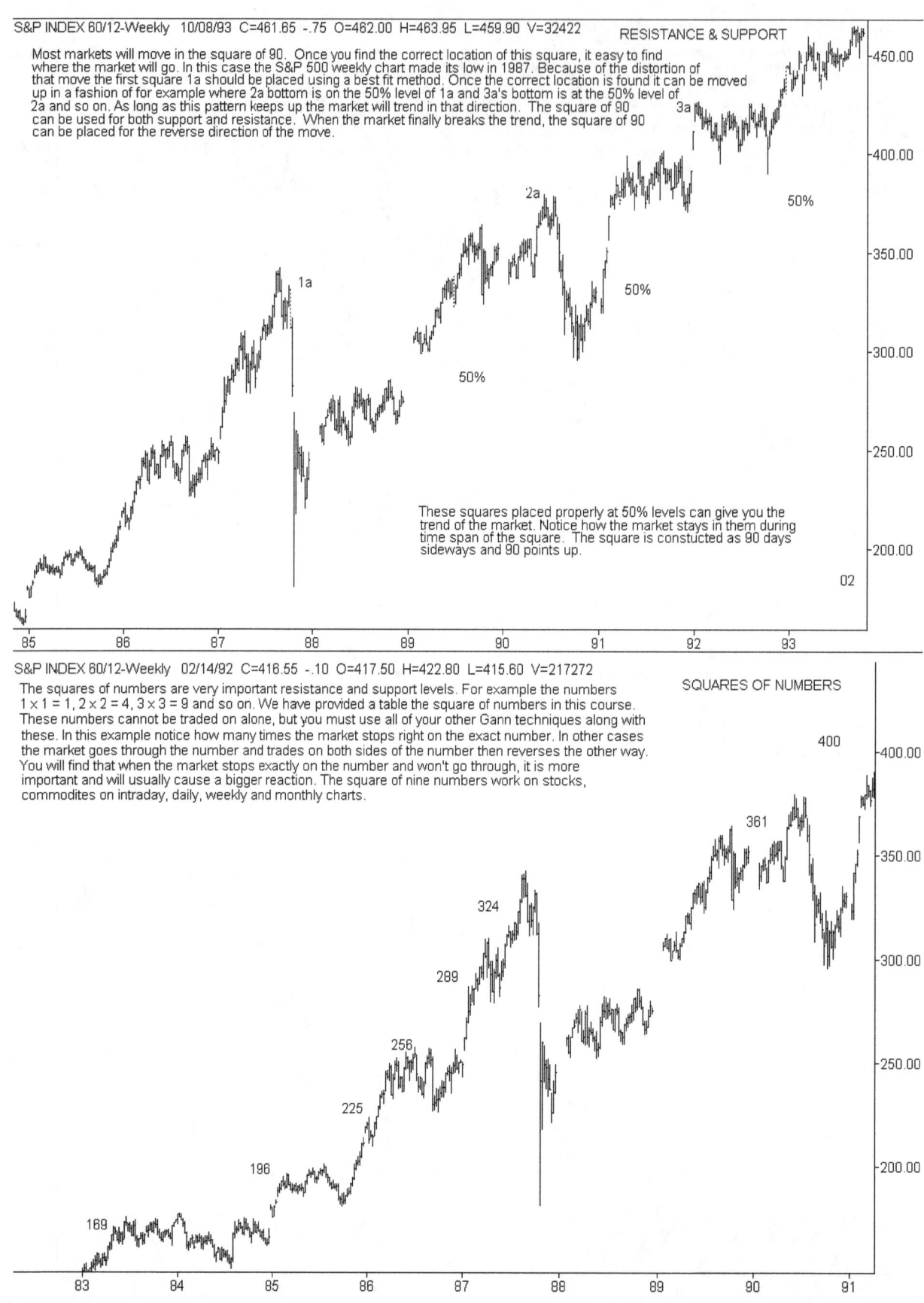

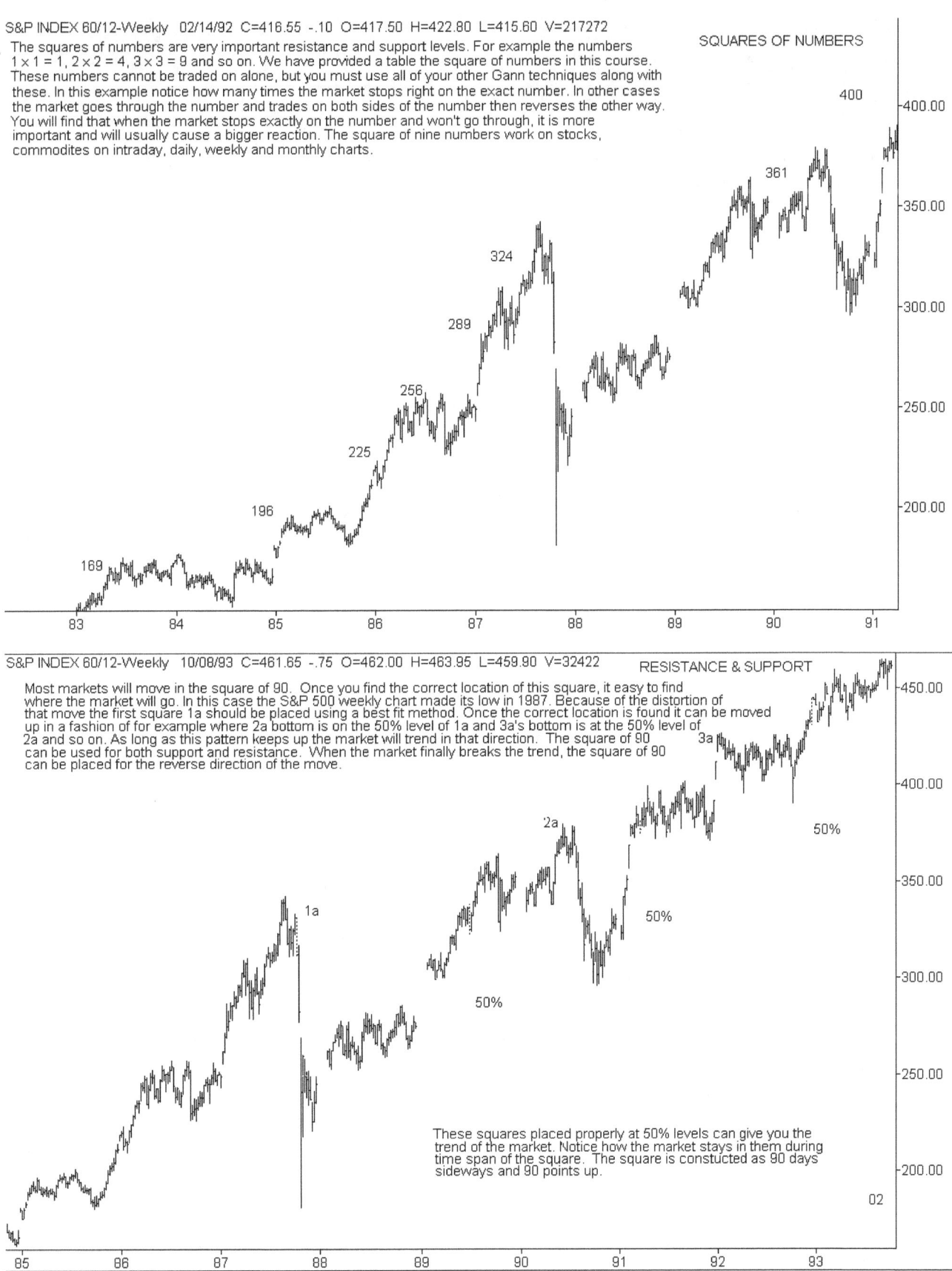

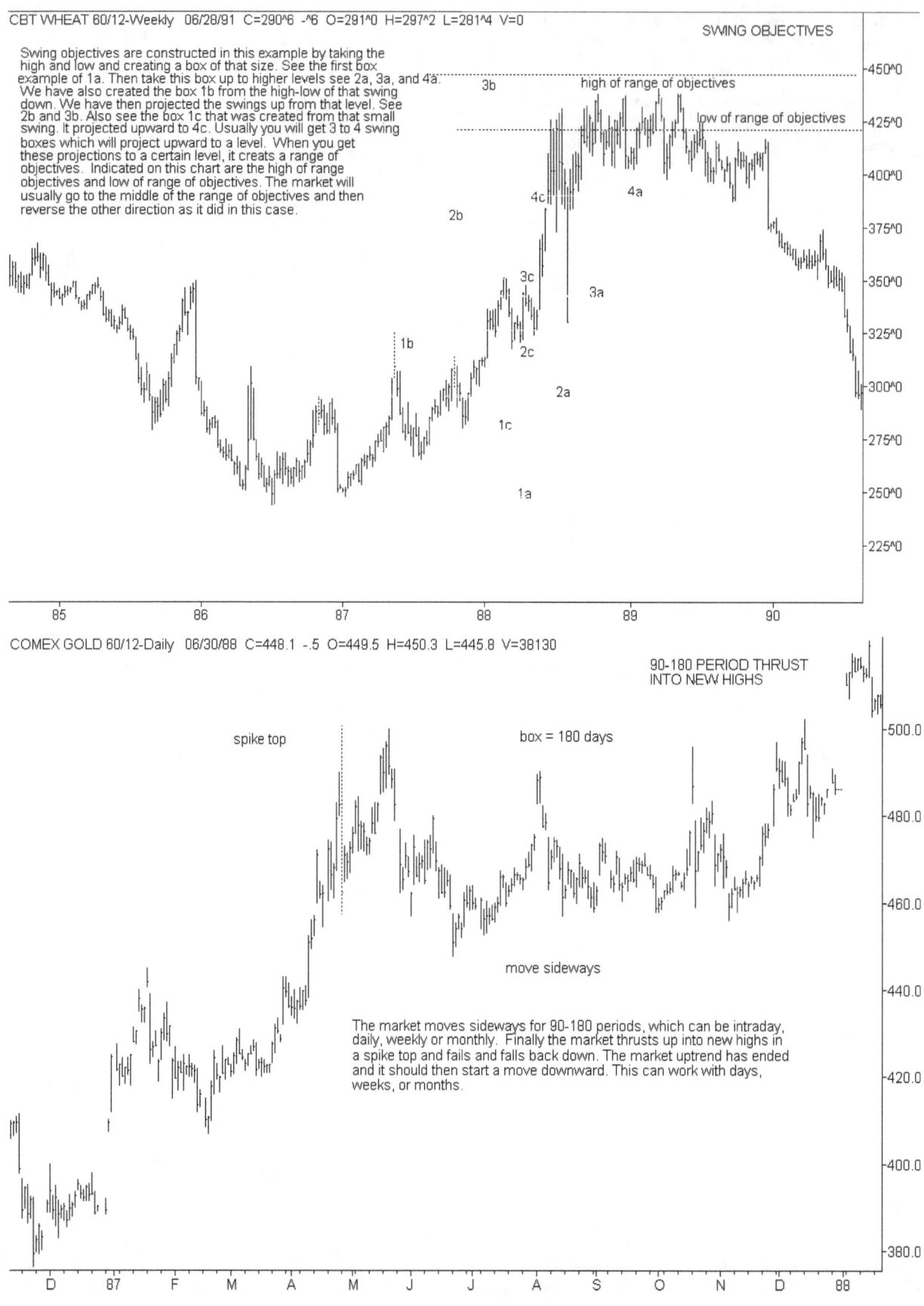

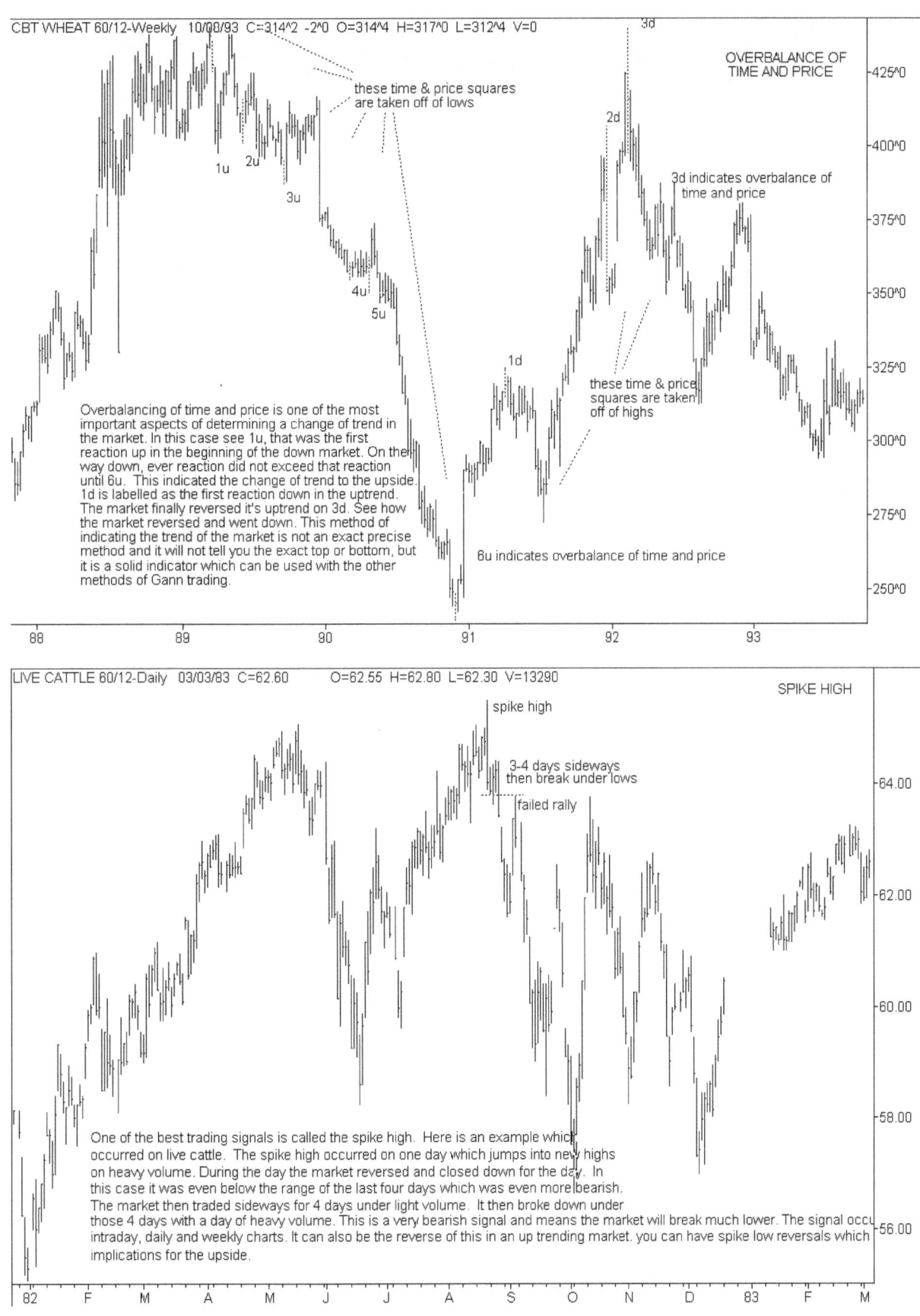

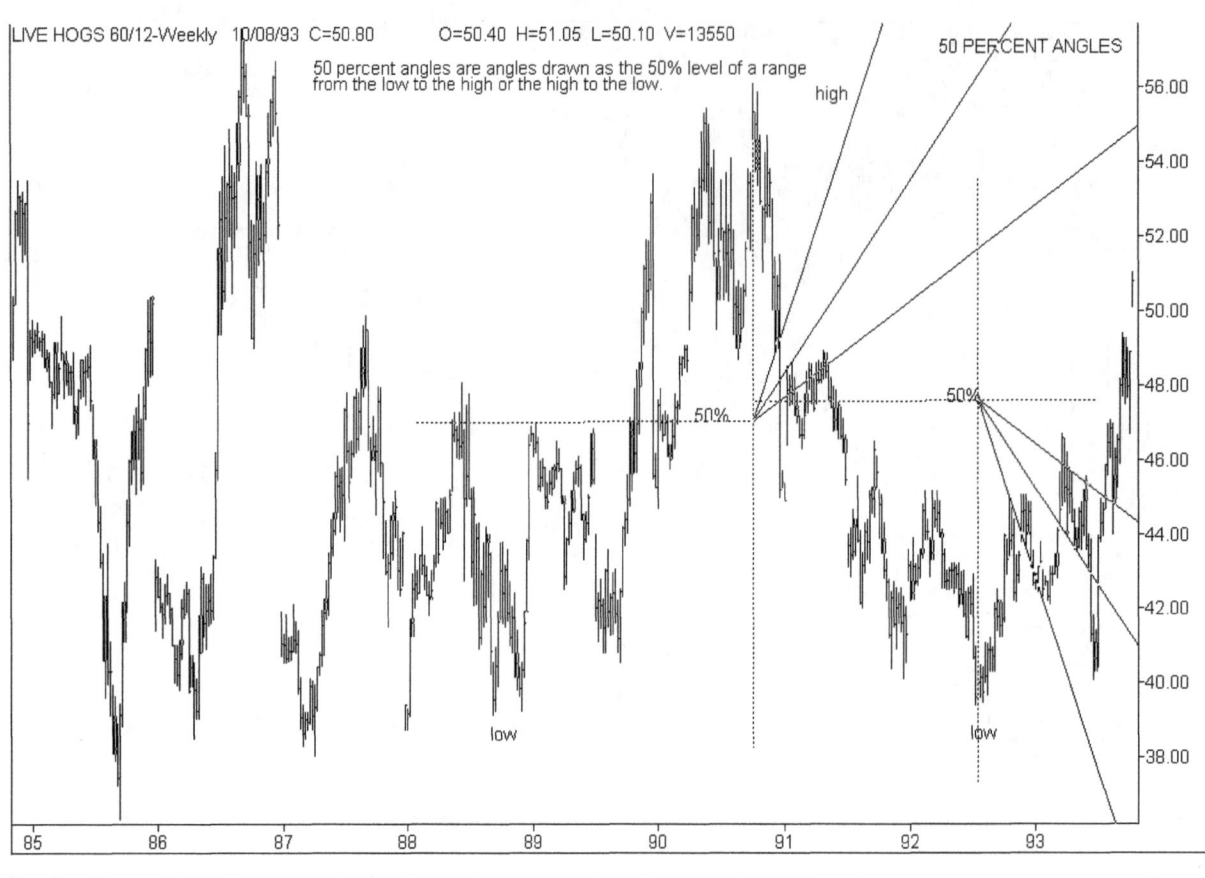

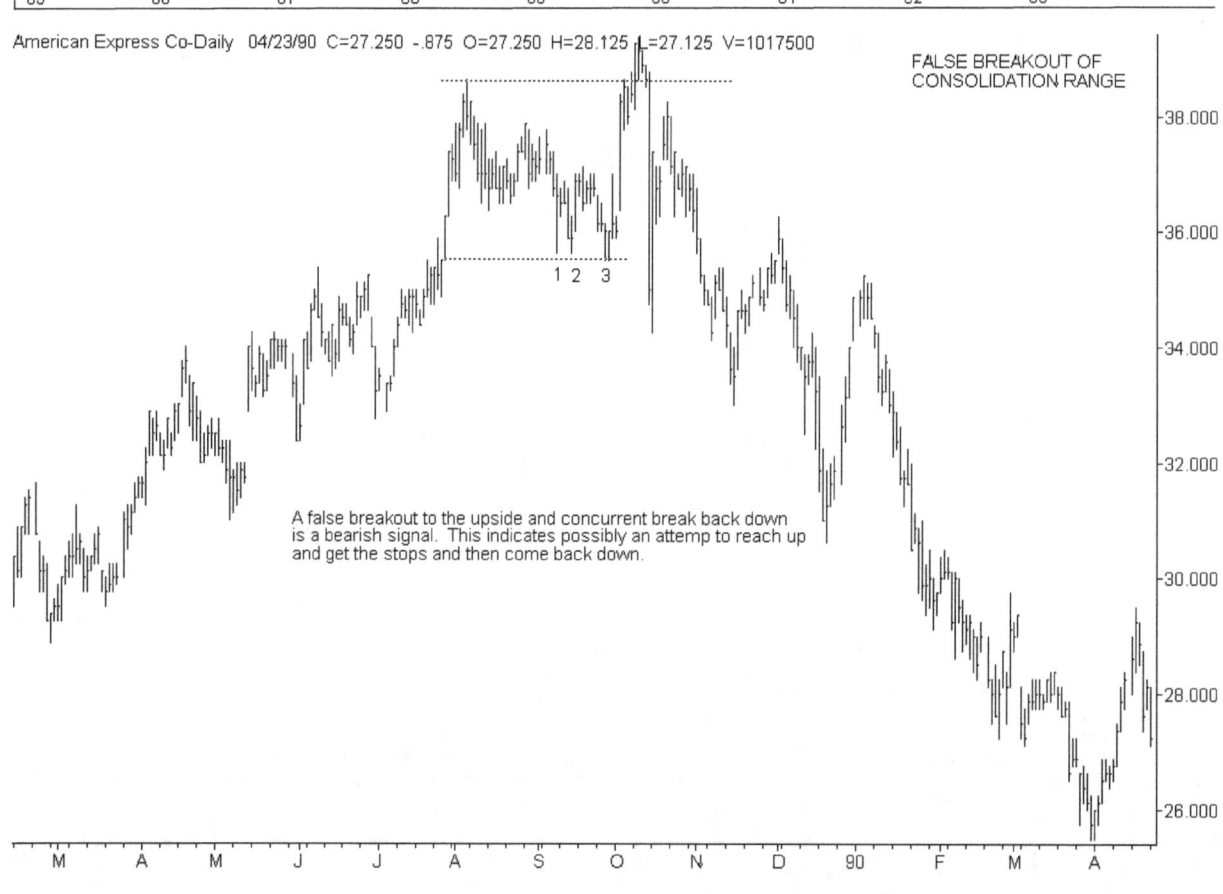

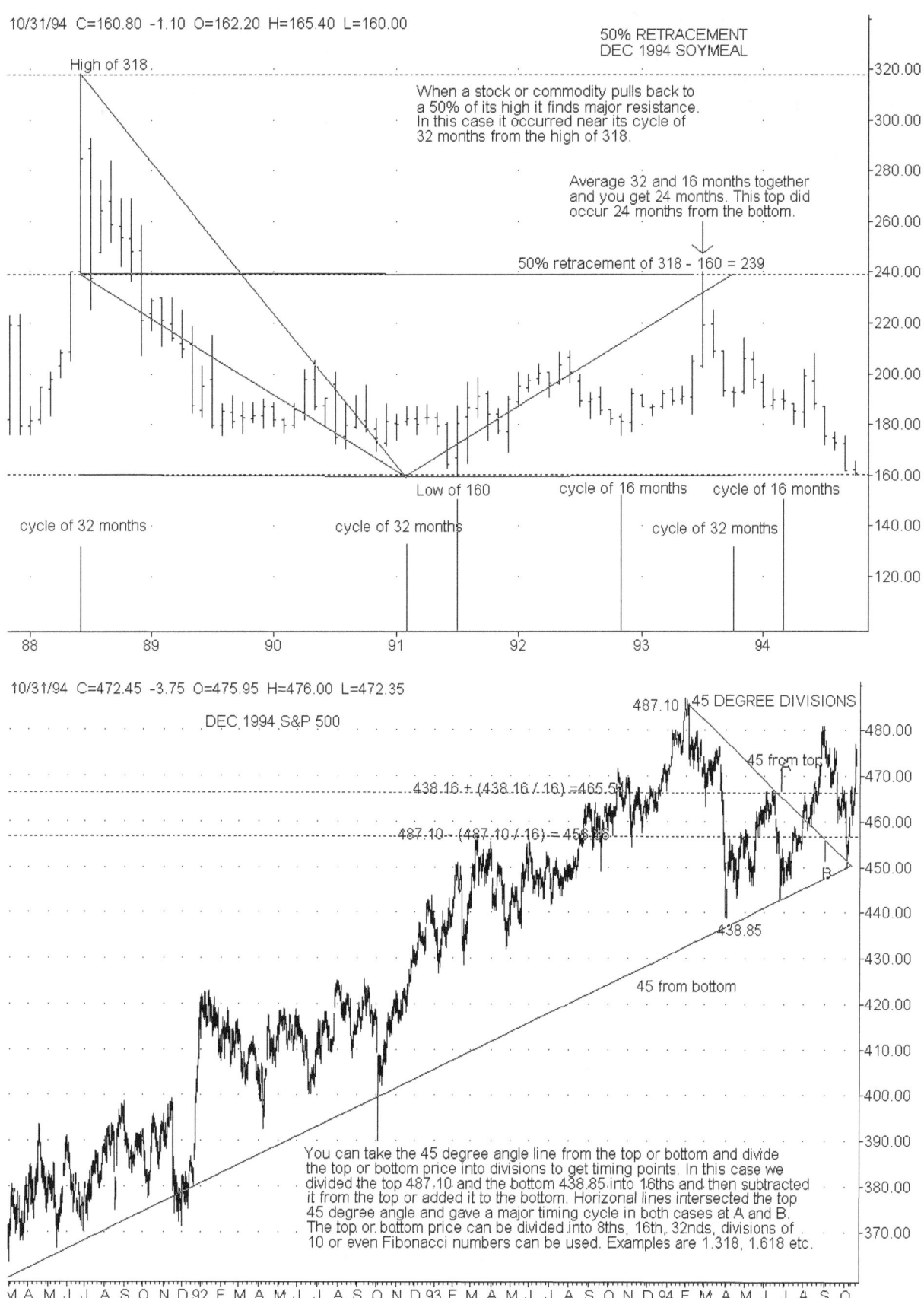

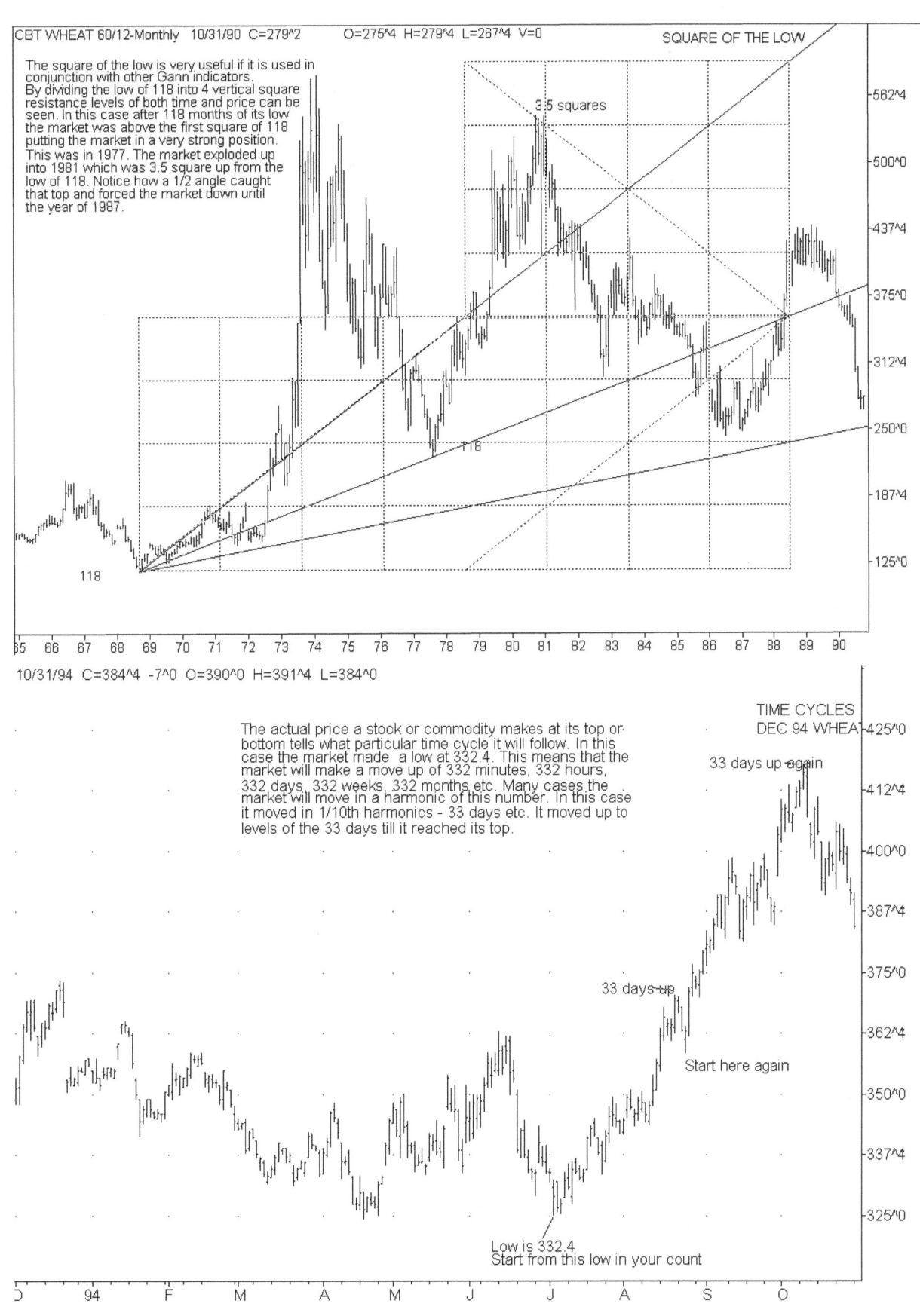

184   *Gann Masters*

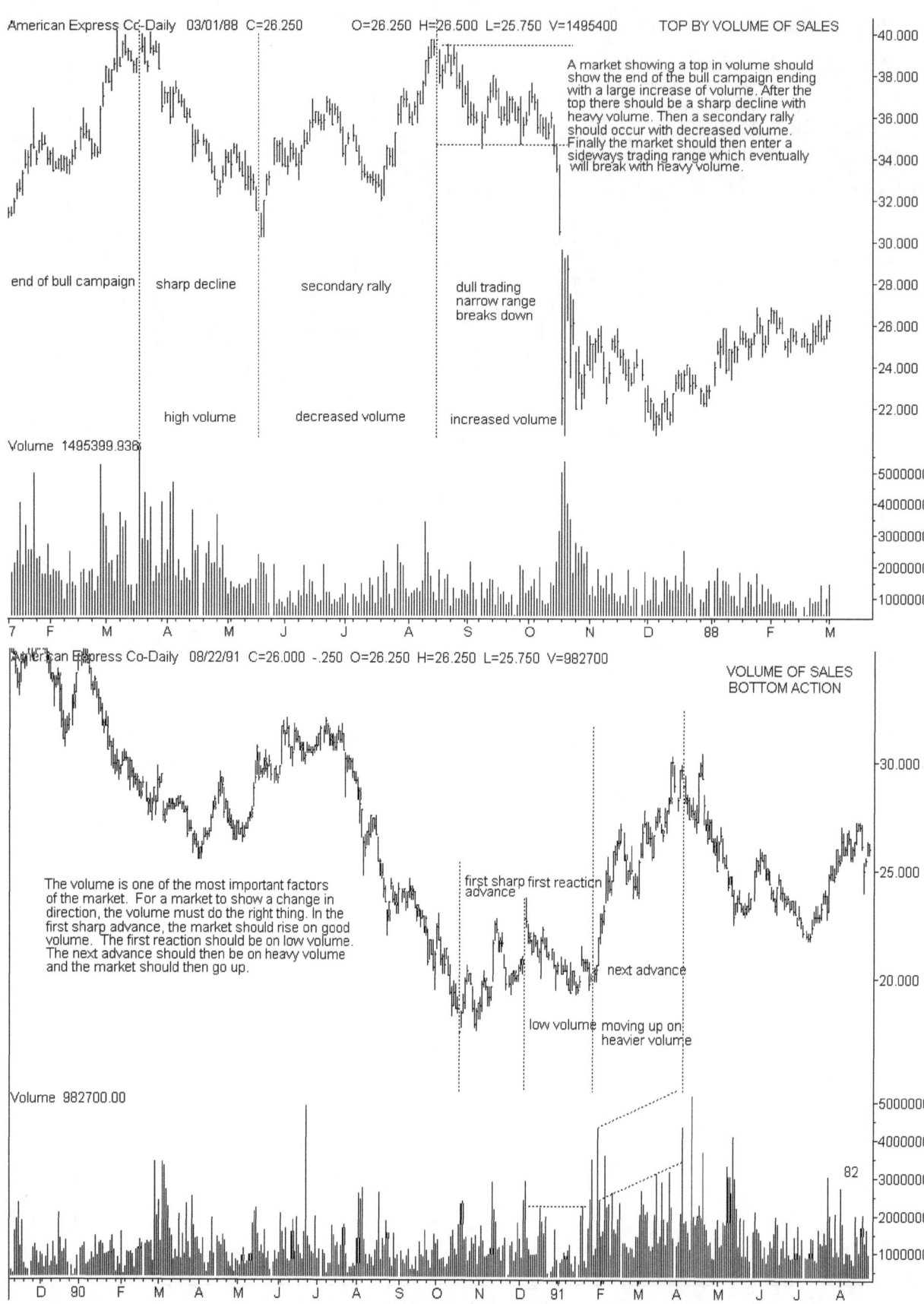

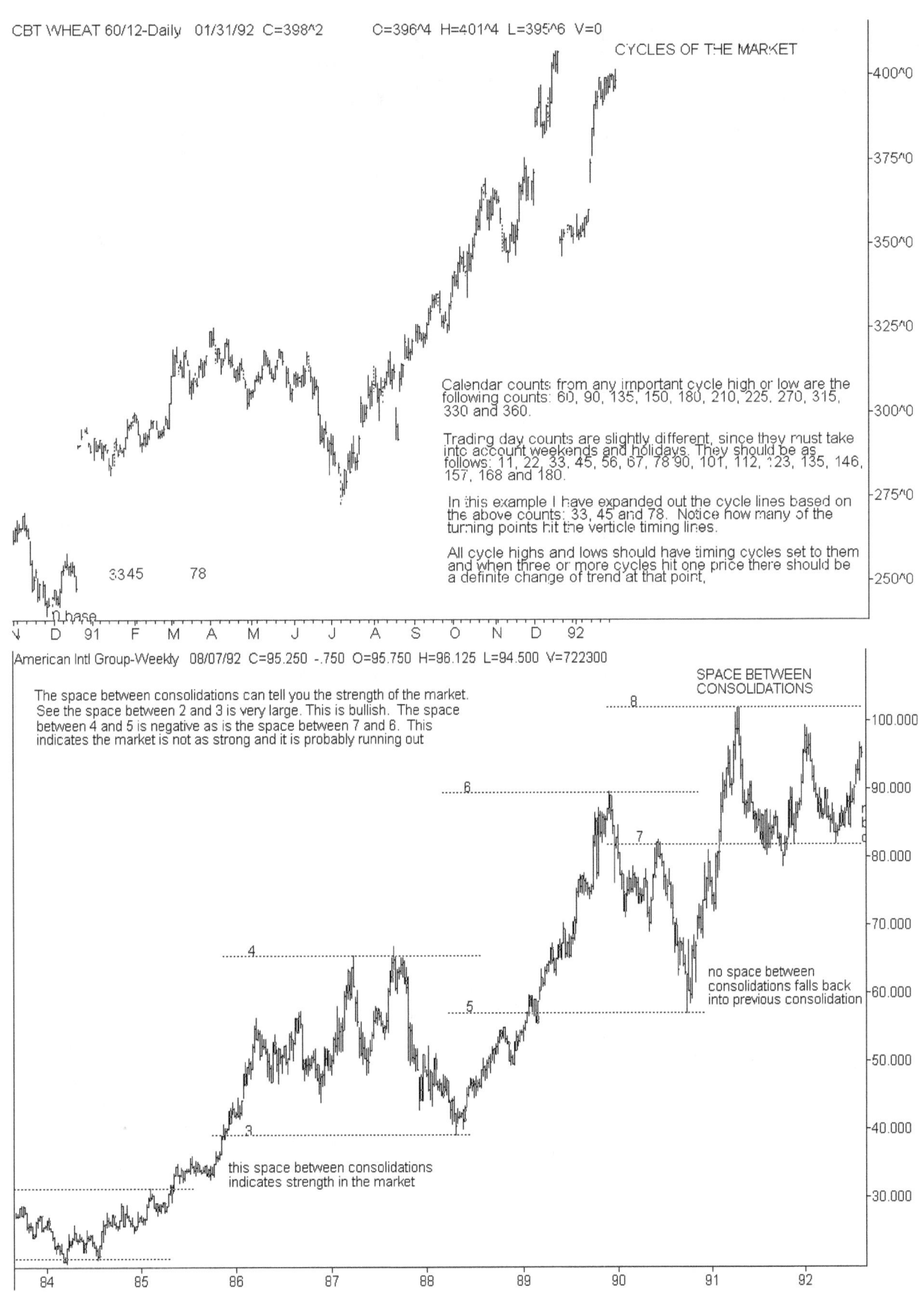

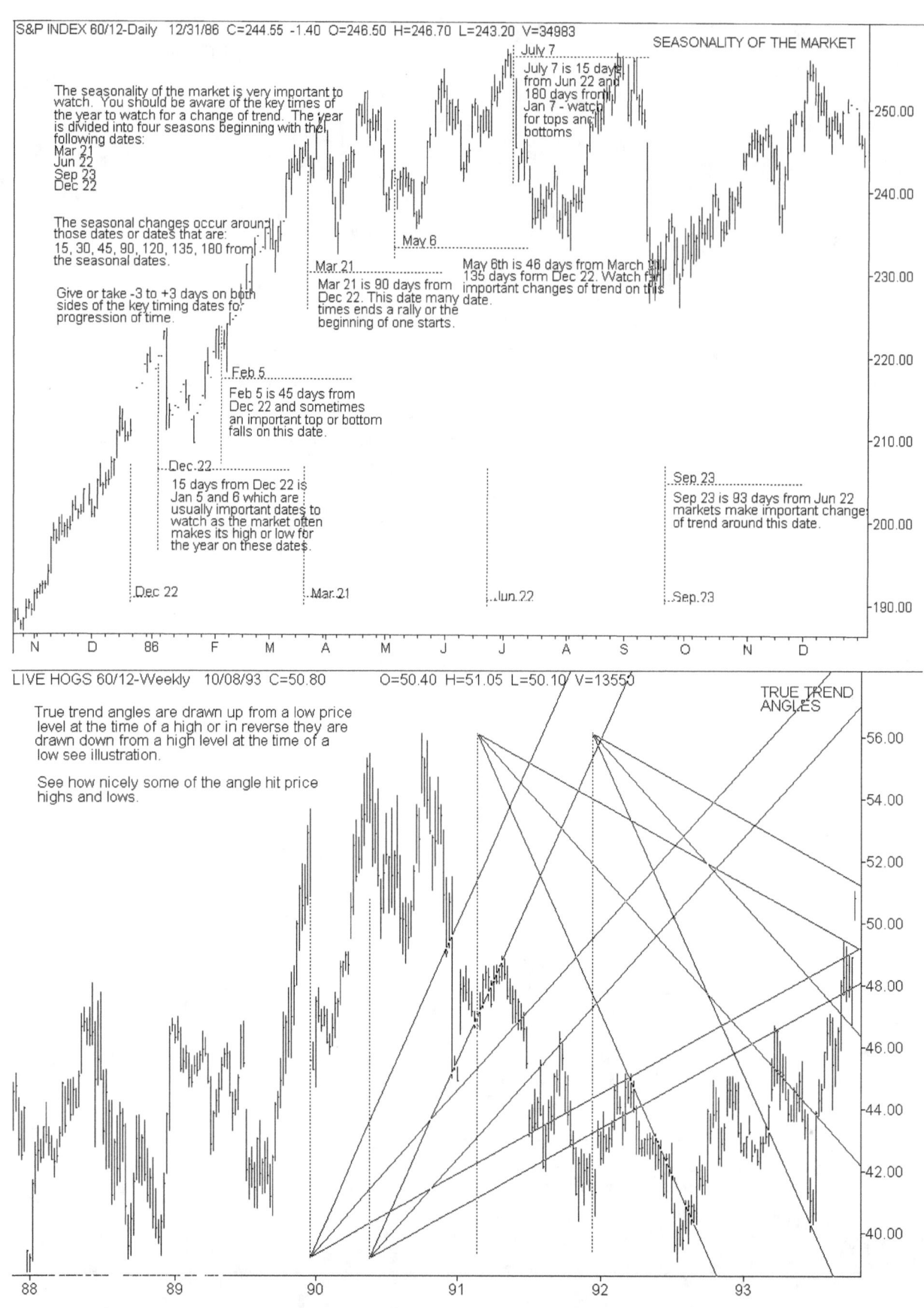

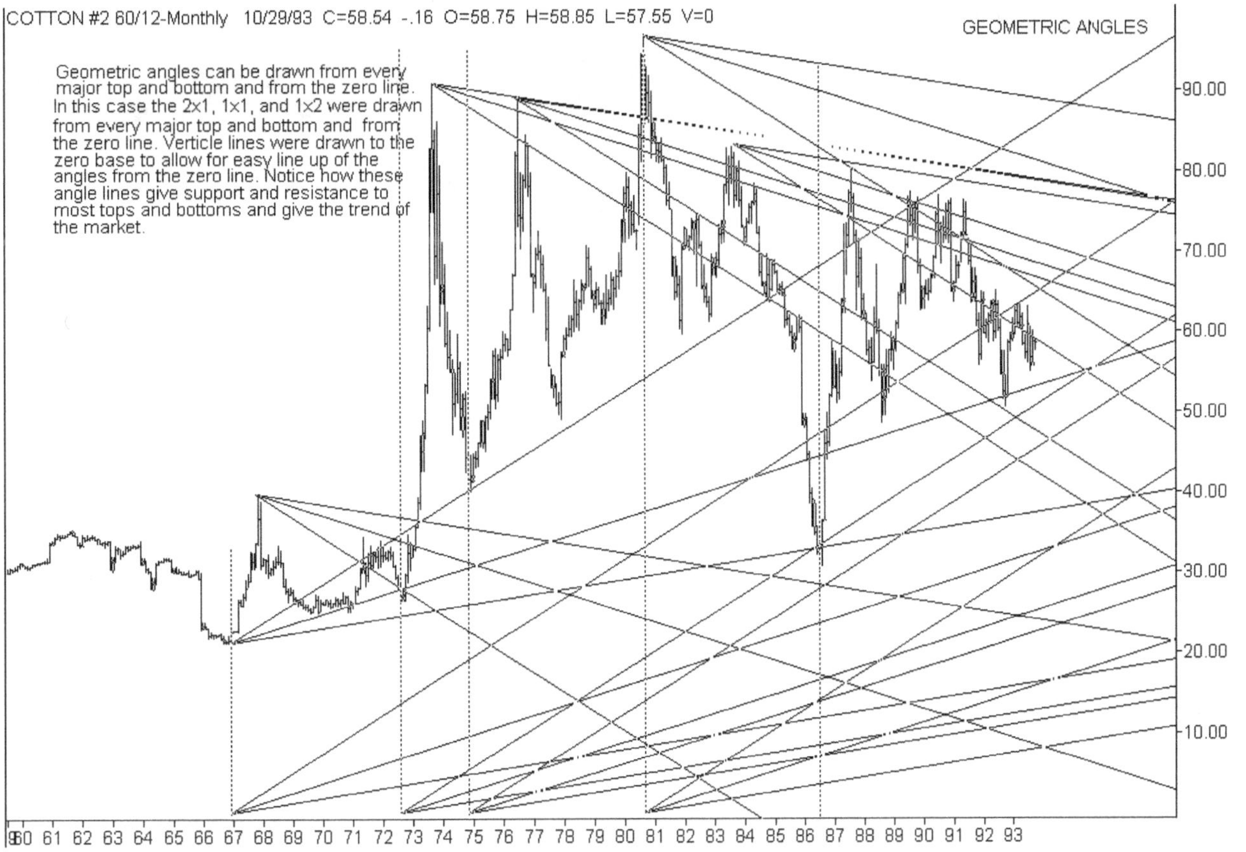
COTTON #2 60/12-Monthly 10/29/93 C=58.54 -.16 O=58.75 H=58.85 L=57.55 V=0
GEOMETRIC ANGLES
Geometric angles can be drawn from every major top and bottom and from the zero line. In this case the 2x1, 1x1, and 1x2 were drawn from every major top and bottom and from the zero line. Verticle lines were drawn to the zero base to allow for easy line up of the angles from the zero line. Notice how these angle lines give support and resistance to most tops and bottoms and give the trend of the market.
90.00
80.00
70.00
60.00
50.00
40.00
30.00
20.00
10.00
60 61 62 63 64 65 66 67 68 69 70 71 72 73 74 75 76 77 78 79 80 81 82 83 84 85 86 87 88 89 90 91 92 93

COTTON #2 60/12-Weekly 10/08/93 C=58.54 O=57.70 H=58.65 L=57.70 V=0
TOP TO BOTTOM
BOTTOM TO TOP
Always check the distance from top to bottom and bottom to top. In many cases it will be the same number.
75.00
70.00
65.00
60.00
55.00
50.00
85 86 87 88 89 90 91 92 93

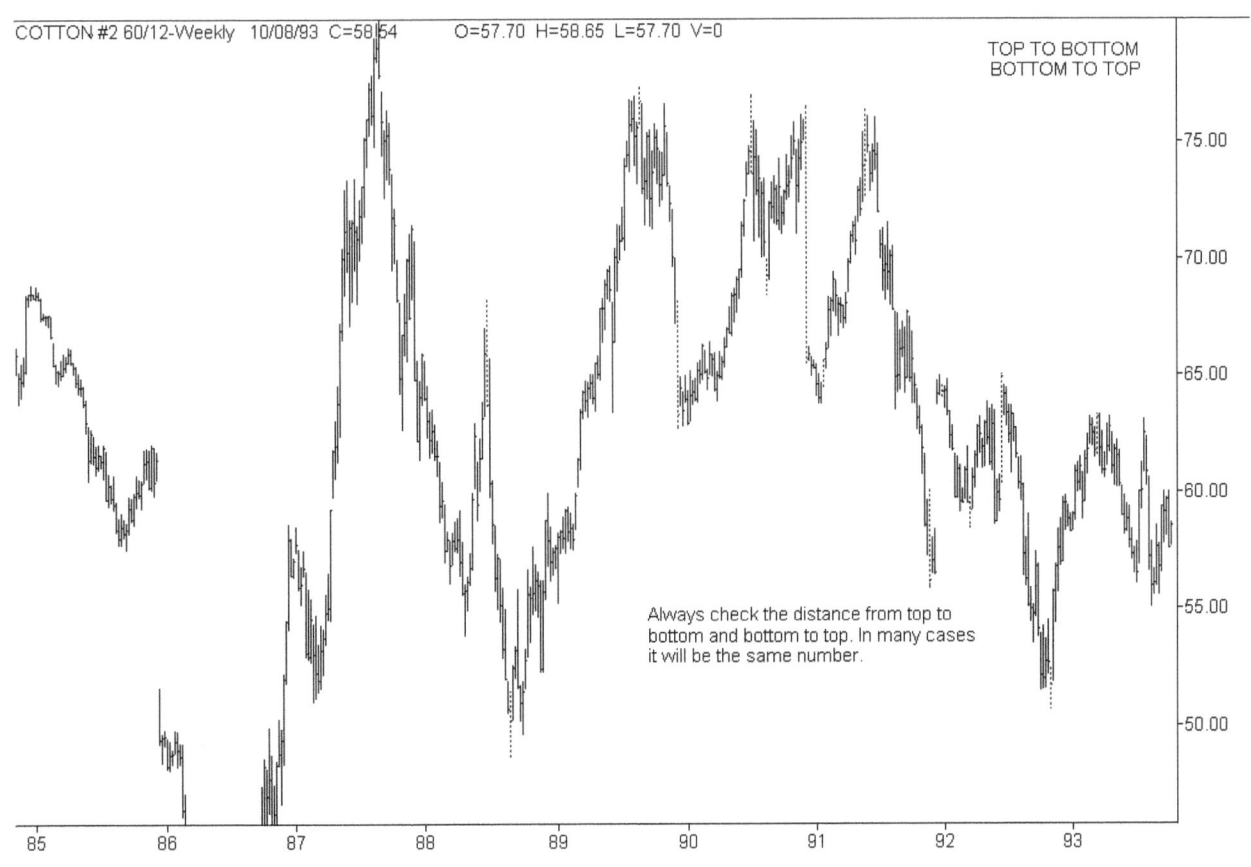

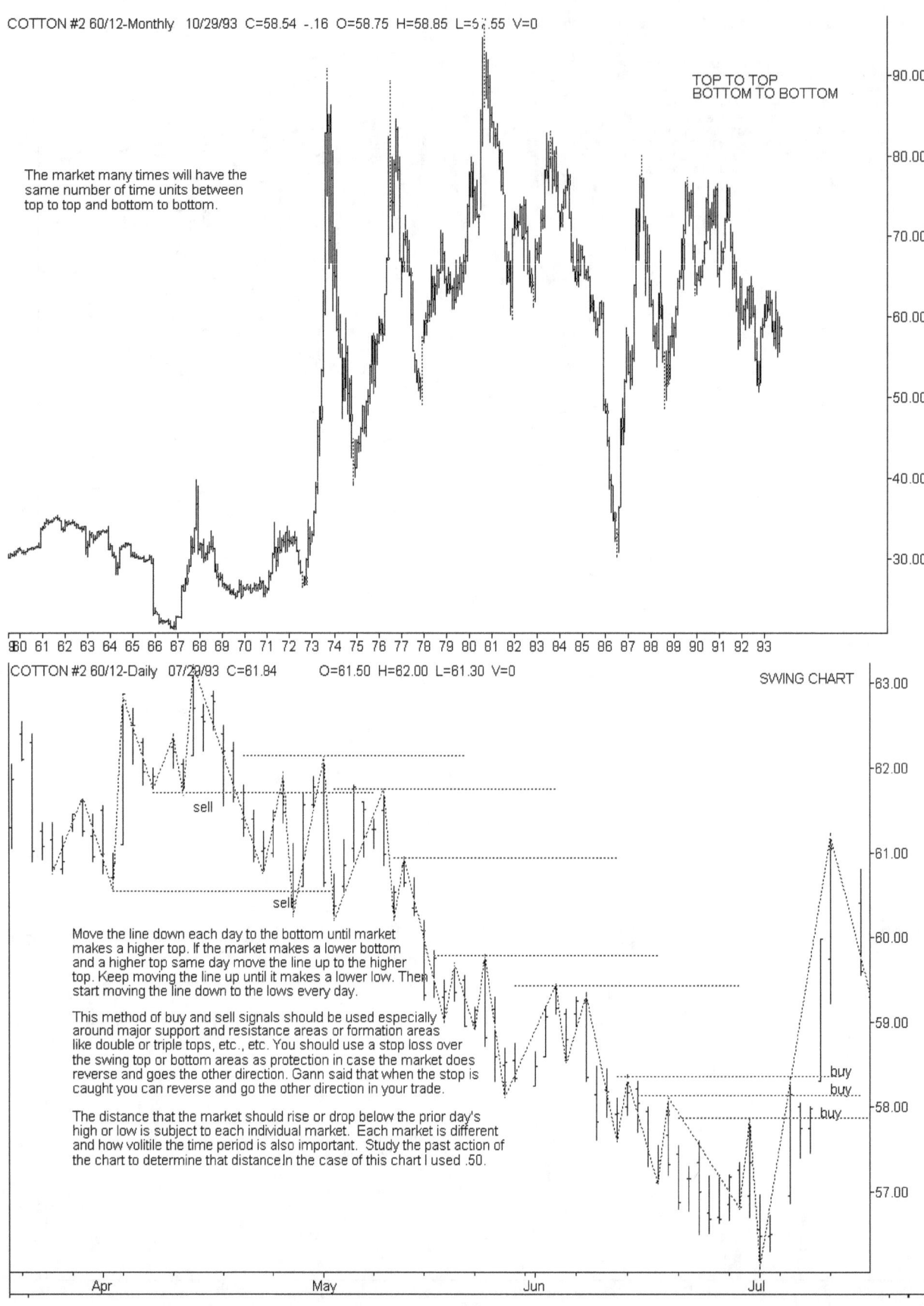

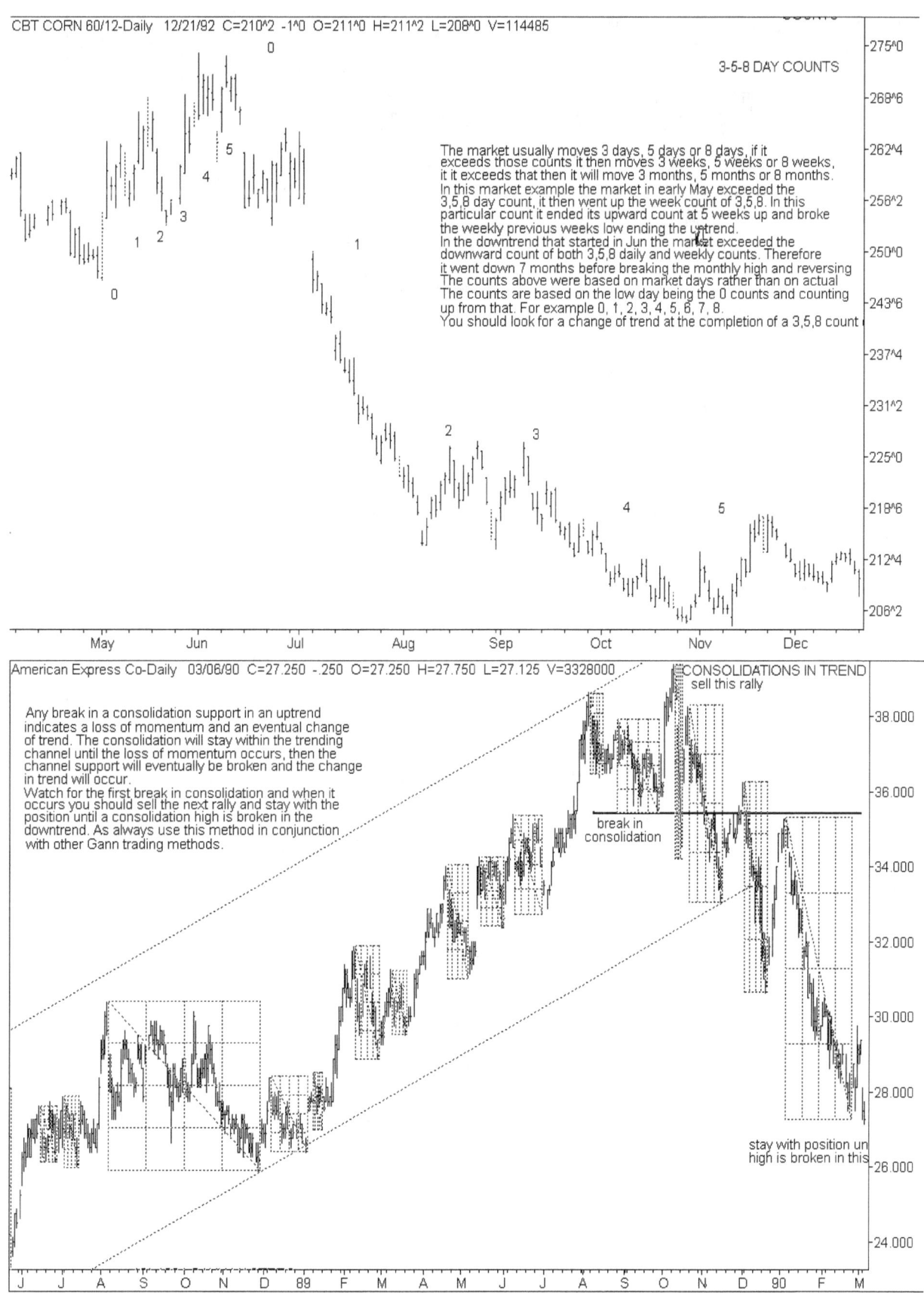

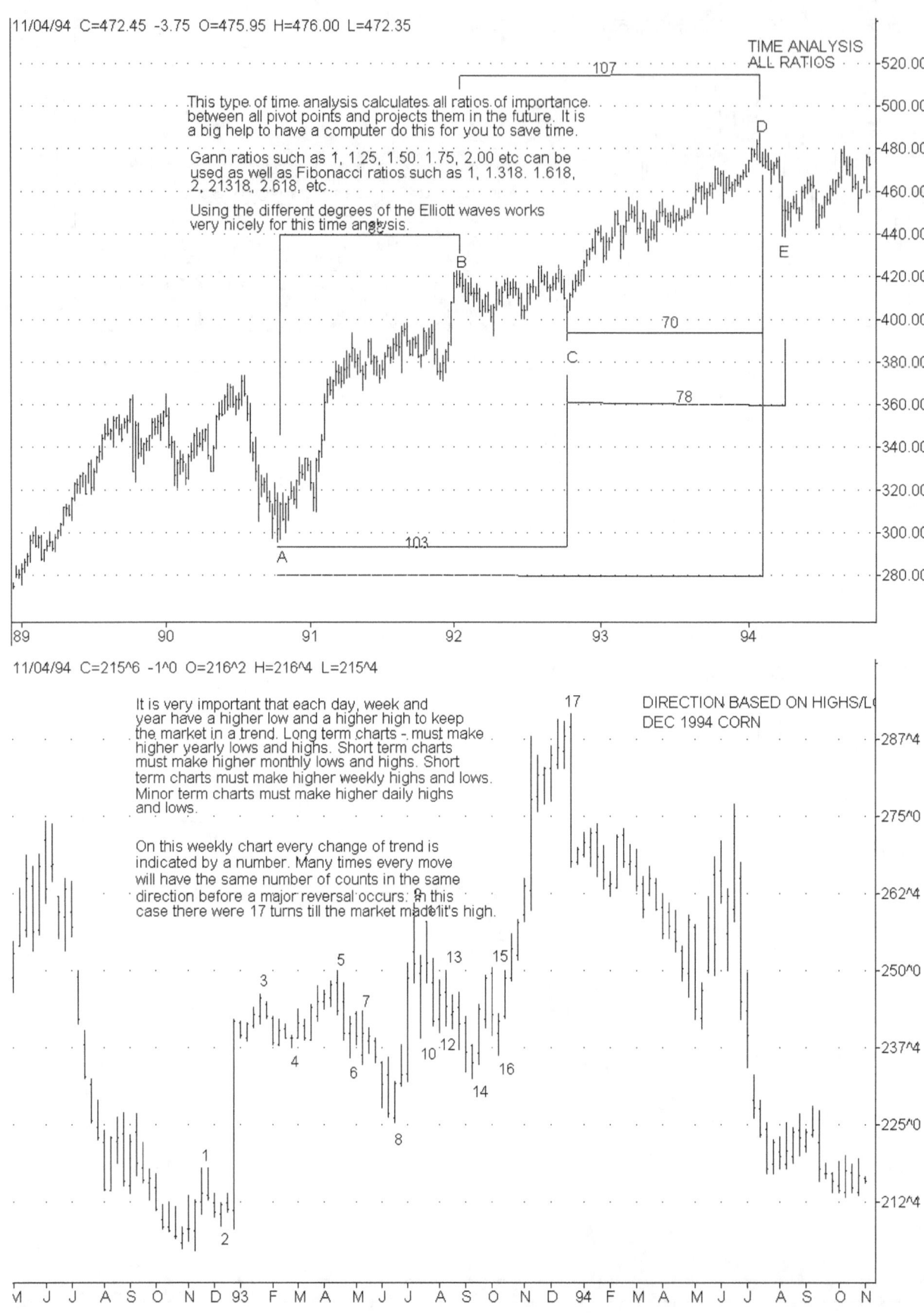

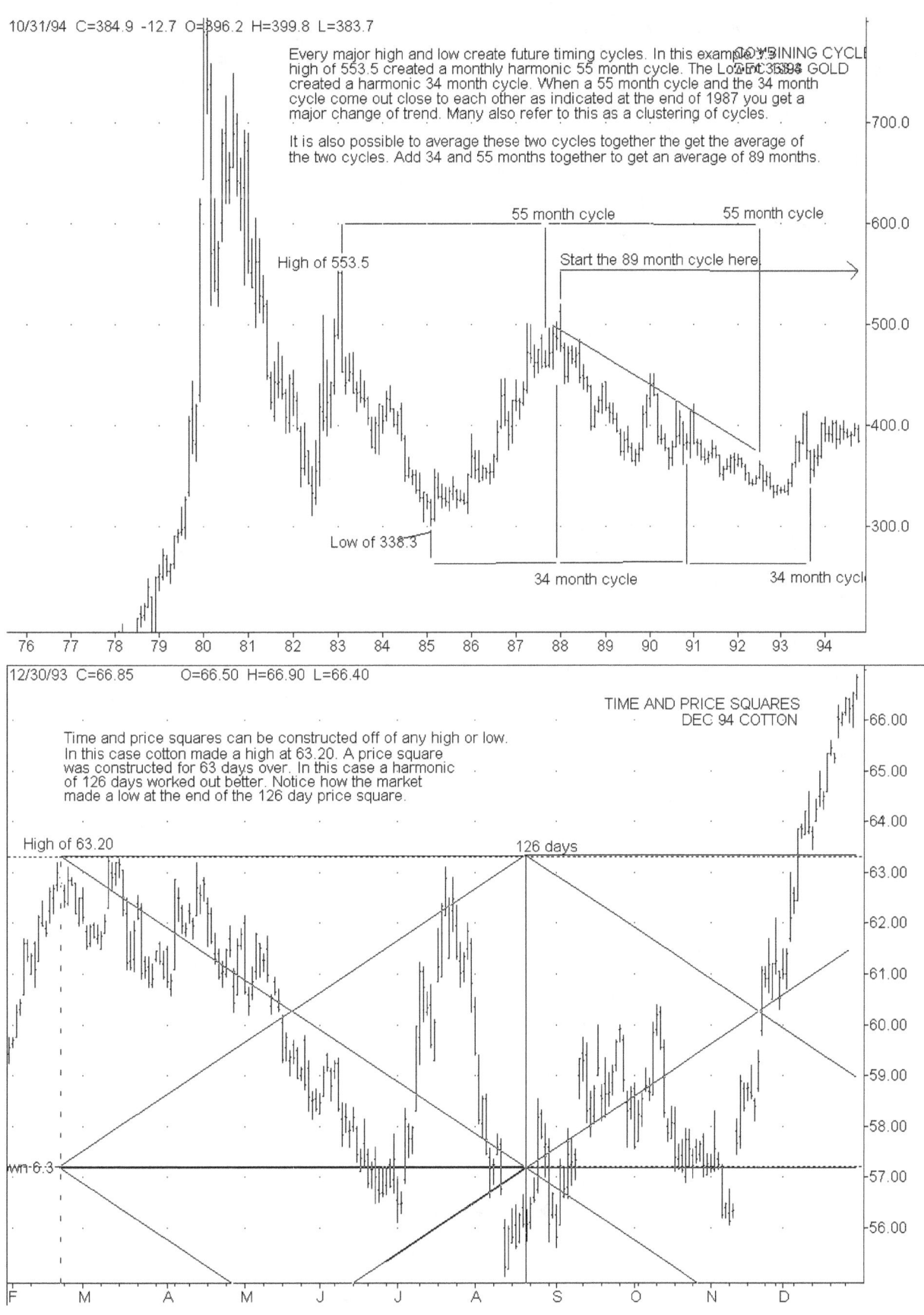

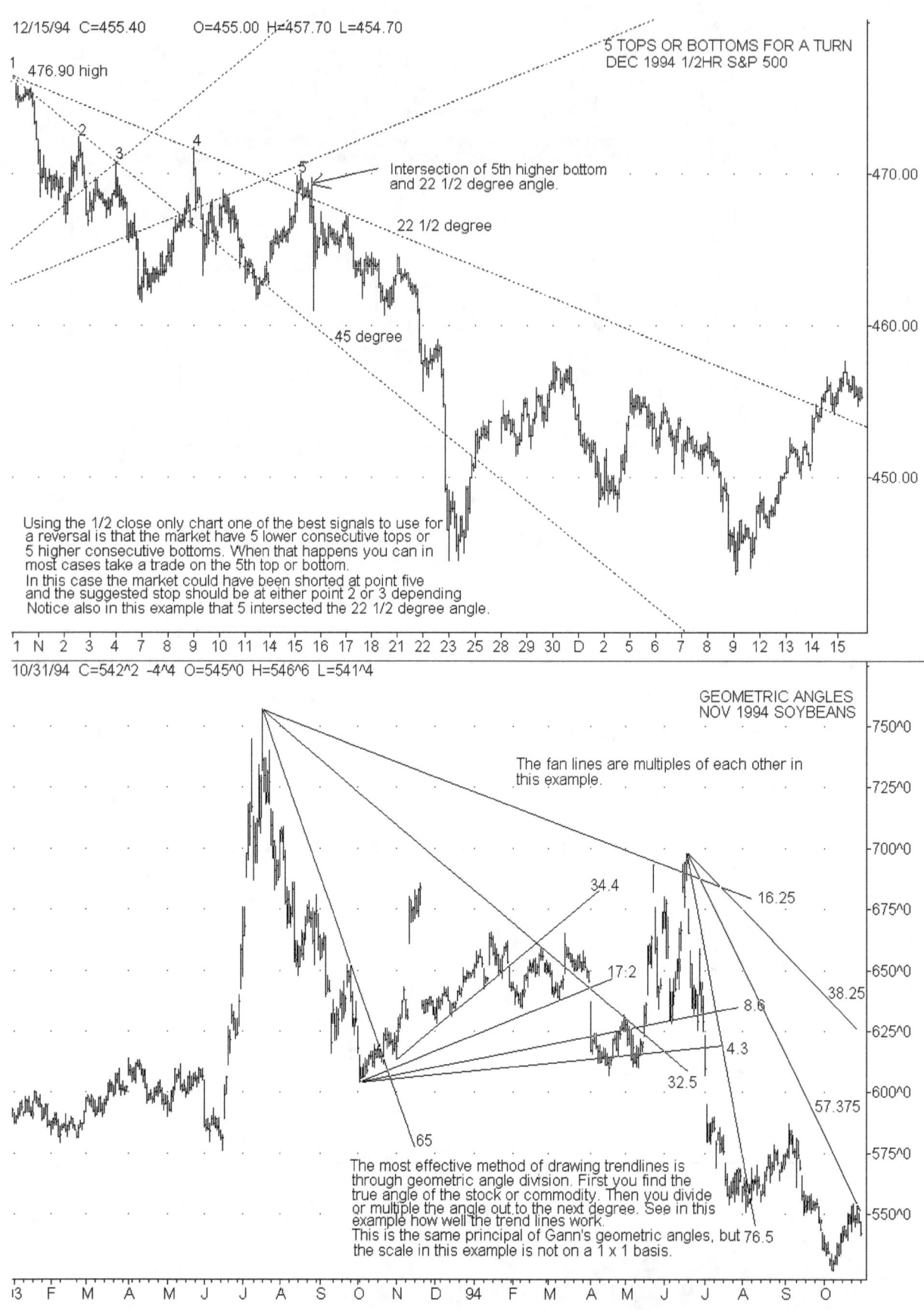

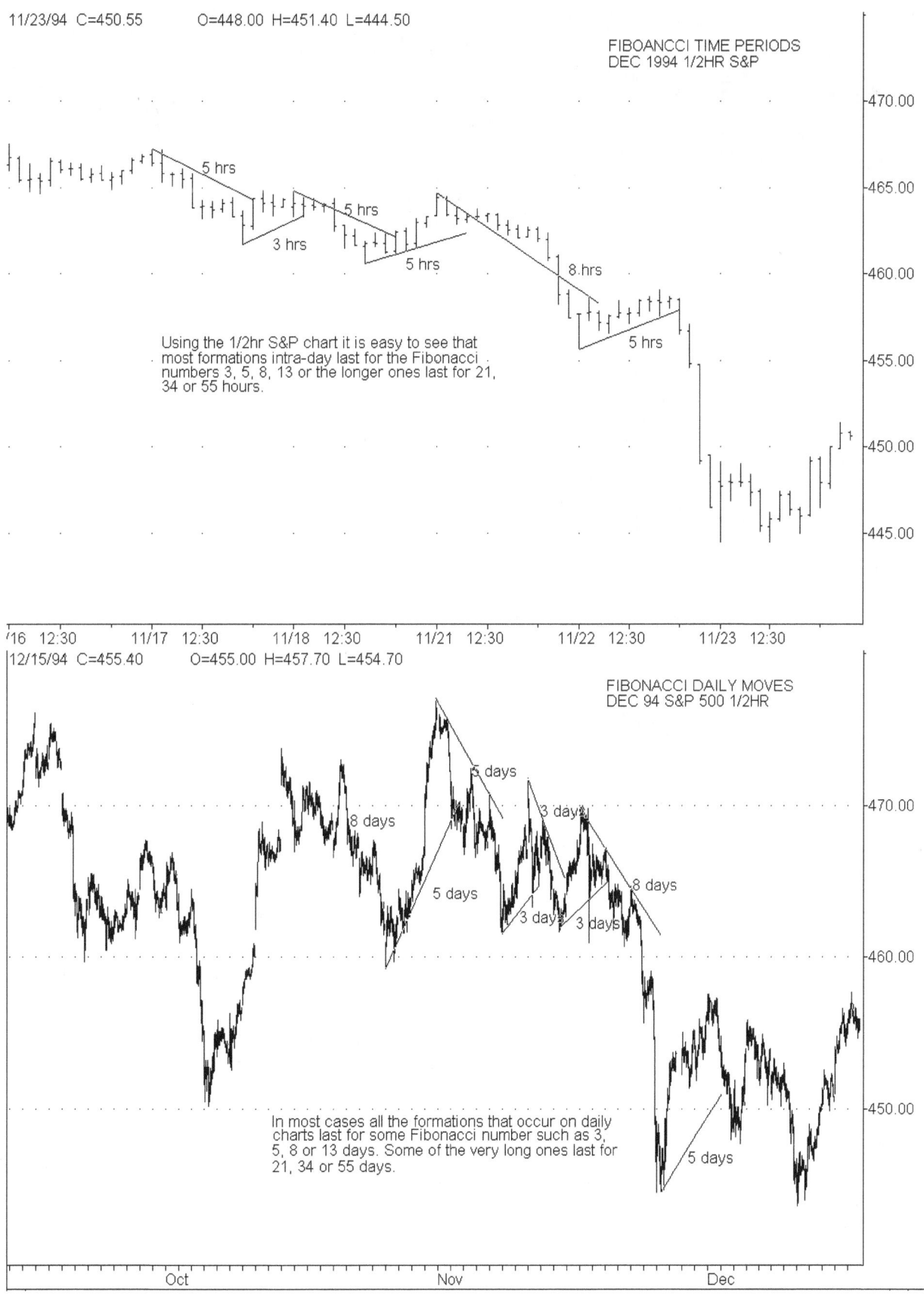

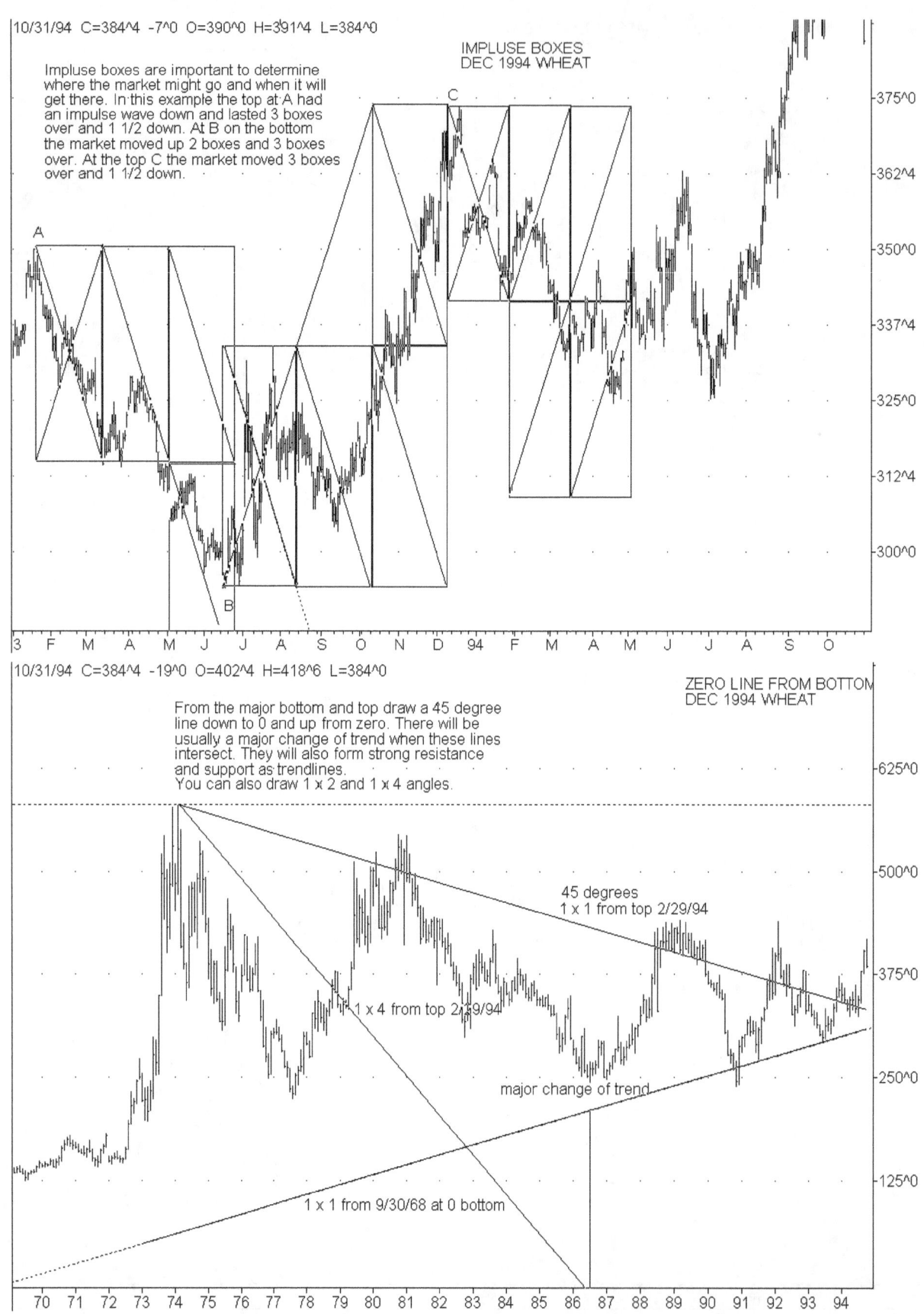

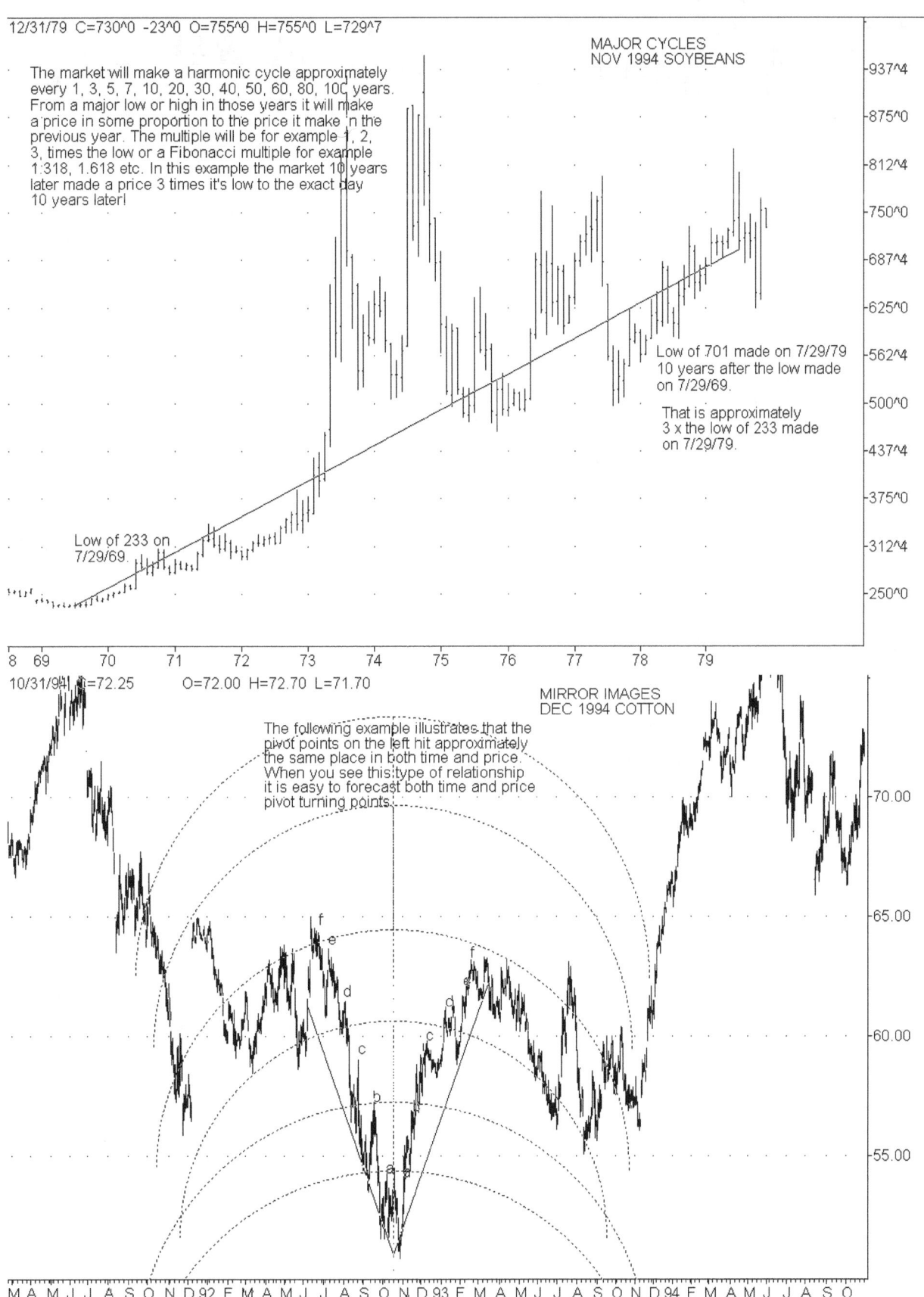

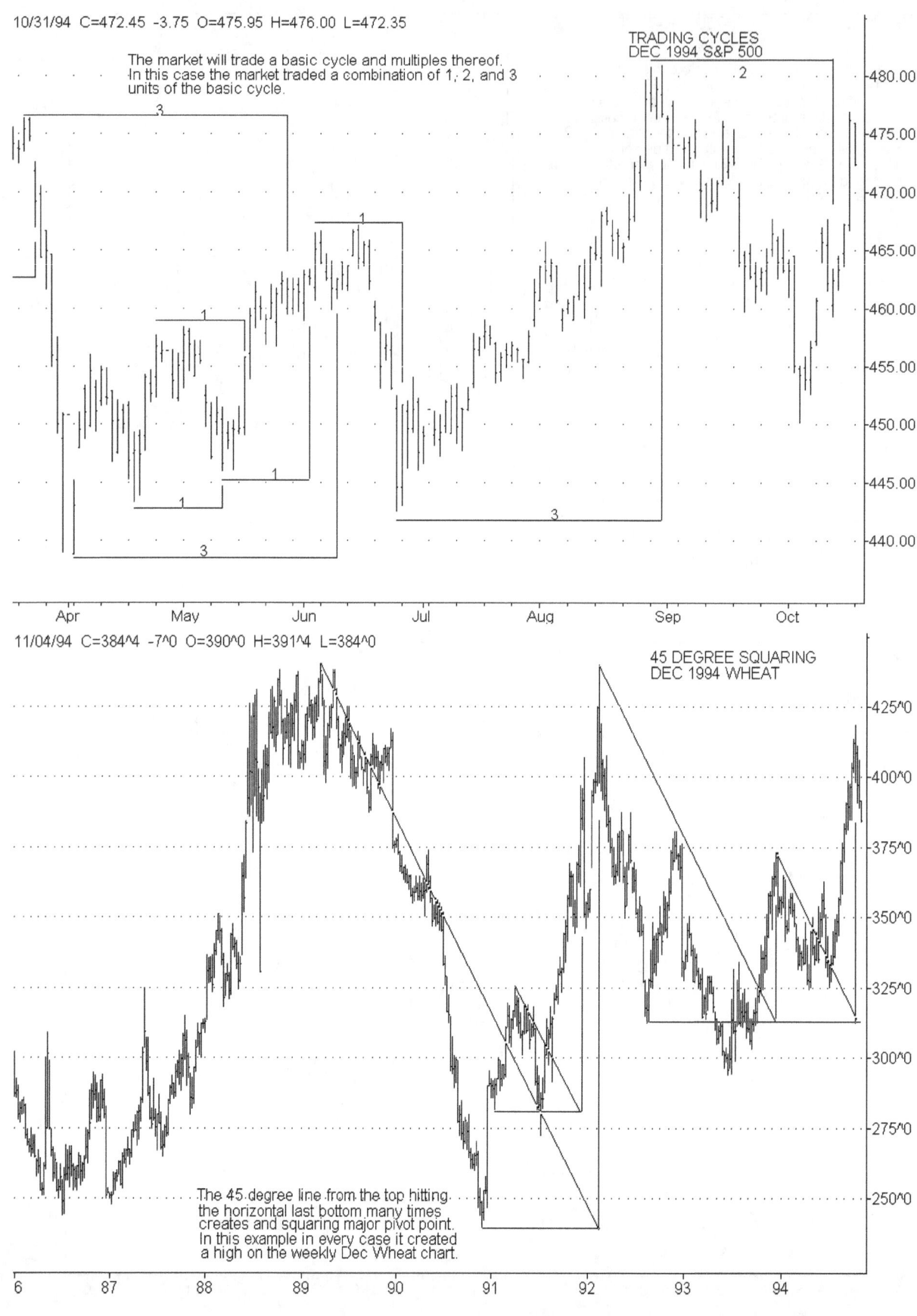

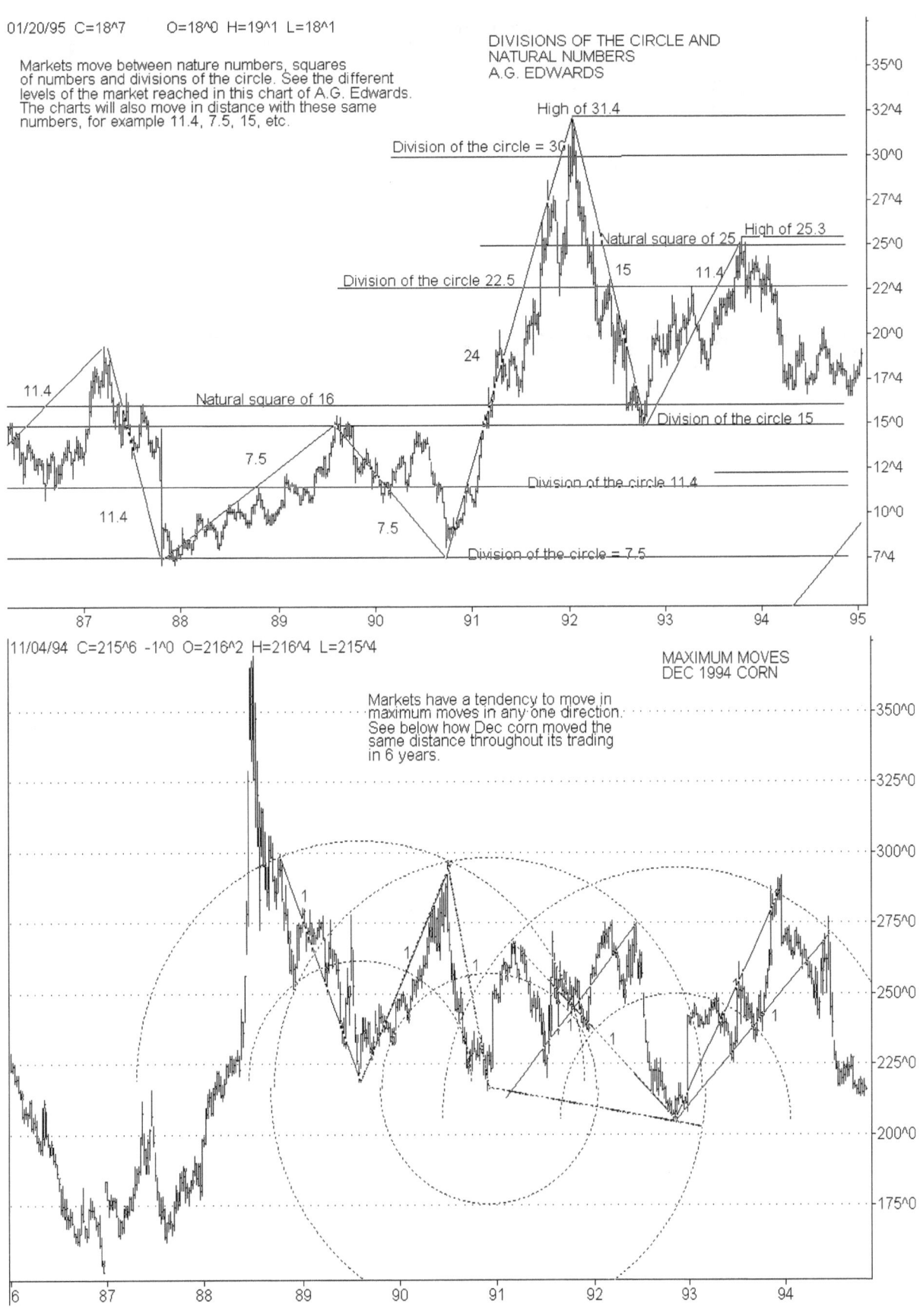

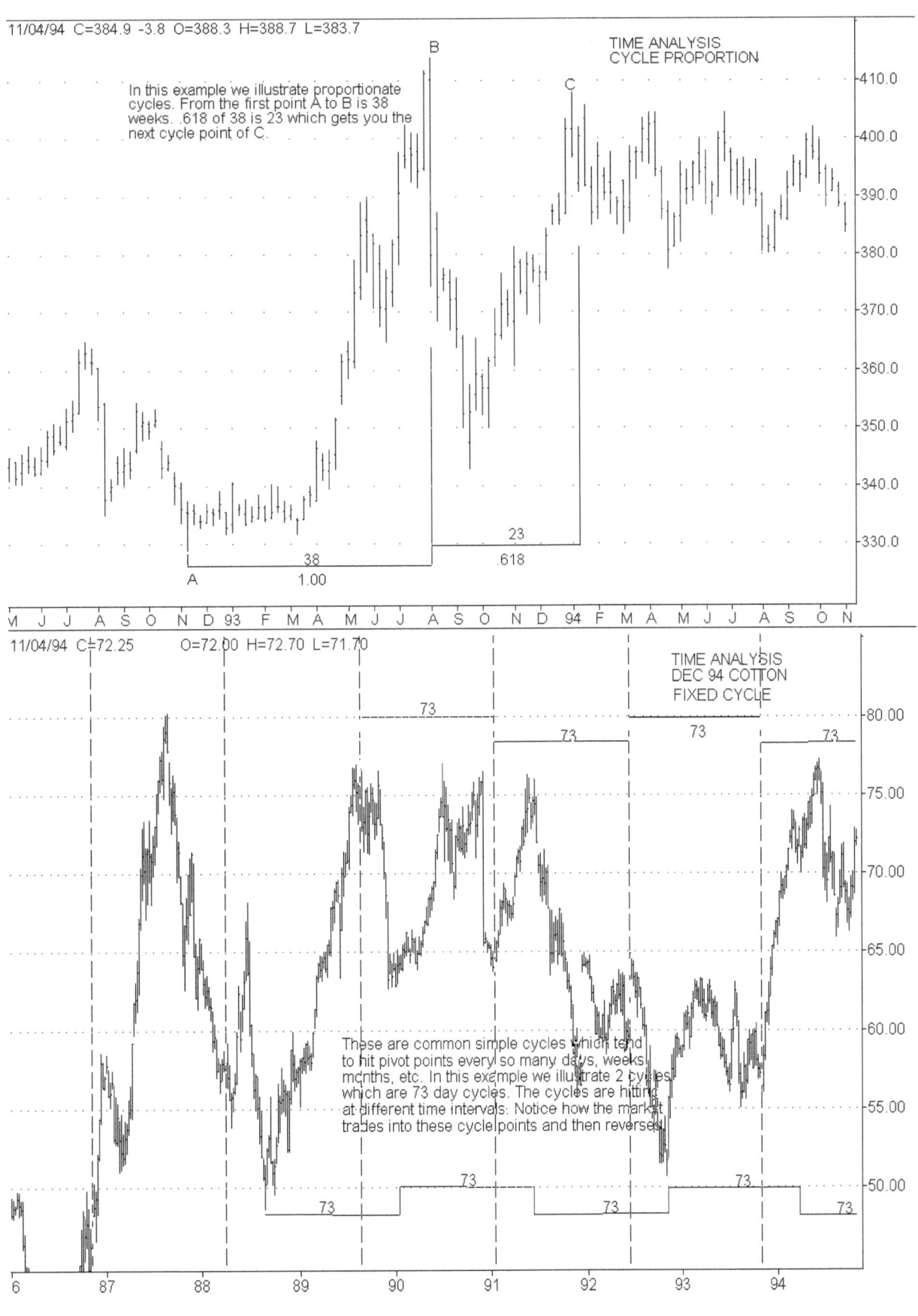

www.ingramcontent.com/pod-product-compliance
Lightning Source LLC
Chambersburg PA
CBHW080243180526
45167CB00006B/2397